THE COMMUNITY IN URBAN SOCIETY

THE COMMUNITY IN URBAN SOCIETY

Larry Lyon
Baylor University

WAVELAND
PRESS, INC.
Long Grove, Illinois

For information about this book, contact:
Waveland Press, Inc.
4180 IL Route 83, Suite 101
Long Grove, IL 60047-9580
(847) 634-0081
info@waveland.com
www.waveland.com

To Carol Townsend Lyon

Foreword

I remember years ago talking to a colleague about a proposed study that I intended to make across a number of communities. My colleague, a scrupulous researcher, asked me what definition of the community I was using for purposes of this study. I pointed out to him the enormous difficulties in trying to delineate the geographic boundaries of various communities with any theoretical precision. "How can you do research," he asked, "if you cannot clearly define your unit of investigation?"

How, indeed? Although I was eventually confident that I had overcome the difficulty my friend had pointed out, the episode impressed forcefully on my mind the multiplicity of aspects, characteristics, and approaches to the study of community—even if one confined oneself to the geographic locality and was willing to forgo such extended usages as "the medical community," "the General Motors community," and "the community of saints!"

Eventually, I found it helpful to look for the local web of relationships, especially around what came to be called the locality-relevant functions. It appeared to me that most people and organizations of all types in the locality are related to each other in various sorts of networks, or "webs," whether formal or informal, and at the same time they are similarly related to other people and organizations outside the locality. Hence, a key issue in studying communities is to understand the interplay of these two different sorts of webs.

The approach was useful, especially in helping overcome a weakness that had plagued many community studies up to that time: the tendency to seek to explain communities solely in terms of internally generated phenomena, as though the rest of society "out there" had little impact on the lives of local people.

While many of my colleagues acknowledged that the approach I took had some merit, it was to me a source of constant enrichment to see them taking quite different approaches. I found it not only difficult, but—more important—irrelevant, to question which of the many different approaches was superior: *the* definitive approach. They all illuminated aspects of the community, helping in the understanding of some aspects better than others, but none of them was the ultimate, all-inclusive resolution of community variability.

For this reason, I find especially appealing the approach taken by Larry Lyon in *The Community in Urban Society*. In this book, he has given extensive attention to what many might agree are three of the most fruitful and systematically pursued approaches to the study of communities: the approaches from typology, from ecology, and from systems theory. He also treats the more recent application of conflict theory to the study of communities. He gives the reader the sound advice to recognize the strengths and weaknesses of each approach, and to make use of the approach that best fits the question under investigation. He suggests that it is best to employ what he calls a pragmatic eclecticism, an austere term that nevertheless "hits the nail on the head." He examines the kinds of questions that each approach to the community is most useful in understanding, as well as those with which a given approach is not particularly helpful.

As one who has been engaged for some decades trying to absorb what others have found and doing research and theorizing of my own, I am impressed by a number of other aspects of this book.

Perhaps in no subject other than community studies is it more difficult—and indeed fruitless—to try to understand the meaning of the knowledge we now have accumulated without at the same time being aware of the theoretical context within which that knowledge has been gained. In a sense, the history of community theory is an unfolding of a sort of Hegelian dialectic, with each theoretical formulation and attendant body of research findings having within itself the seeds of its own destruction—to change the allusion from Hegel to Marx. I mean this not in the sense that the old must be scrapped, but that, as Thomas Kuhn has pointed out in reference to such paradigms, as each vein is pursued and elaborated, it begins to go beyond the contribution it has made and, when pressed still further, starts to show its own limitations, its own anomalies. Lyon has succeeded in capturing much of this process as he deliberately gives the reader an account of the development of various lines of inquiry, their history as well as their fruits.

Much the same can be said in respect to research methodology. More than most texts, this book explains the manner in which different modes of research were employed in the development of various sets of findings. The reader is presented with knowledge, not floating in a vacuum, but bounded to earth in terms of the research approach with which it was gained.

The book also emphasizes the importance of relating what we

know about communities to the prospect for improving them. Thus, attention is given to the "loss of community" and the attempt to regain it; the quality of life studies; community development; planned communities; and the characteristics that many people seek in community improvement efforts. In this connection, special emphasis is given to what has been learned about the structure and exercise of power to influence decisions within communities, a topic which itself well illustrates the importance of a historical approach to understanding current knowledge and theory, as well as the need to understand the research methodologies through which such knowledge was obtained.

To accomplish the above tasks requires a courageous effort. To attempt it at all is praiseworthy; to do it well is especially felicitous.

Though an "old hand" in this field and understandably familiar with much of what is described in this volume, I have been gratified again and again at suddenly coming upon a statement that pulls together different bits and pieces from the vast kaleidoscope of American urban communities and makes them more understandable to us all.

Roland L. Warren
Professor Emeritus
Brandeis University

Preface

The community is one of the most important and interesting fields in social science, yet in some ways it is a field that doesn't exist. It is difficult to say exactly where community research and theory merge into urban sociology, local politics, rural development, regional studies, formal organizations, or any number of other related fields of inquiry. It's even difficult to say precisely what a community is. Yet no field was more instrumental than community studies in influencing the early development of sociology. When Robert Park and his colleagues at the University of Chicago established the academic legitimacy of sociology, the community was their primary unit of analysis. Accordingly, few fields cover more important philosophical, epistemological, or practical concerns than community sociology. The community is that special place where theory and the "real" world come together. And further, I believe that no field holds greater promise for those with a reformist bent. You can't save the world, but you can improve a community! I try to communicate these exceptional aspects of community sociology in this book.

One of the best books on community sociology since Ferdinand Tönnies' *Gemeinschaft und Gesselschaft* is Roland Warren's *The American Community*. In fact, Warren's decision not to produce a fourth edition of his classic theoretical text played a significant role in my decision to write this book. *The American Community* had considerable influence on my views, but my *The Community in Urban Society* is probably more akin to Warren's earlier and less well-known *Studying Your Community*. My book is more of a text than *The American Community*. It includes several methodological chapters absent from *The American Community* and other community texts. These methodological chapters have produced considerable differences of opinion among the initial reviewers of this manuscript. Some felt that methodological issues should be reserved for research books, while others believed as I do that community research is sufficiently different from other research areas to deserve special and separate treatment. And until a book devoted to community research methods is published, I believe these methodological chapters are necessary because my best opportunities to do something practical as a "professional sociologist" have always come from my community research skills. The community is more than an abstract object of theoretical inquiry; it is also a place where my family and I live and a place that I can study and improve. That is what this text is about.

This book also reflects my belief that knowledge should not be presented apart from the events that produced it. There is a lot of "sociology of sociology" in *The Community in Urban Society*. Local conditions change. New research techniques emerge. "Knowledge" about the community is inherently transitory. In the 1960s, I was taught that we had all lost our feelings of the psychological community. In the 1970s, I learned that the conflict built into capitalist societies was ripping apart what little territorial community remained. And now, in the 1980s, we "know" that the psychological feelings of community still exist and that the conflict was a "temporary" phenomenon doing little to diminish the continuance of the territorial community. An understanding of why we approach the community as we do and how new conditions require new approaches is necessary in studying a phenomenon as dynamic and "slippery" as the community.

This book represents a "stage" and hopefully an "achievement" for me as a sociologist, and I want to thank some of those who played major roles in my reaching this stage. Charles Tolbert, my first sociology professor at Baylor, introduced me to the power of the "sociological imagination." Mike Grimes at the University of Houston, and then Charles Bonjean at the University of Texas at Austin, focused that imagination on the community. The Baylor University Research and Faculty Development Committees provided continued assistance. And most recently, Roland Warren provided the insight and encouragement necessary to complete this project. More personally and more importantly, no one played roles as significant in my reaching this stage than my parents. Most people thank their parents at times like this, but I cannot imagine most people receiving the long-term, total support and love that J. L. and Joan have provided me.

The Community in Urban Society also benefited from the assistance of many other people: Al Hunter, Sylvia Fava, Allen Martin, Tom Hanks's writing group, and scores more. My sincerest thanks to all of you. Had I listened more closely to your suggestions, this book would probably have been better. It is clearly better for the times I did follow your suggestions. More than anyone else, though, the book benefited from the personal support and assistance of my wife, and it is to her this book is dedicated. Thank you, Carol.

LARRY LYON

Contents

List of Figures

List of Tables

BASIC APPROACHES TO THE COMMUNITY

In spite of, and perhaps even because of, the primacy of the "city" and the "community" as focal points for social science theory and research, considerable disagreement still exists over answers to such basic questions as: What is a community? How does a community differ from a city? How have communities changed, and why? What are the best ways to conceptualize and study communities? In the first six chapters, we will examine the most prominent answers to these questions and, in the process, be exposed to some of the seminal thinkers of the last two centuries: Ferdinand Tönnies, Karl Marx, Max Weber, Emile Durkheim, Georg Simmel, Robert Park, and Talcott Parsons.

The community, more than the city, has long been an intellectual will-o'-the-wisp, always intriguing but often just beyond our conceptual grasp. As we will see in the first chapter, the community, with its lack of formal organization and absence of political boundaries, presents special problems for analysis and even for definition. In these initial chapters the community is defined in a number of ways, with different definitions leading to different approaches which in turn result in different views of the community. Of course, conceptual disagreements are hardly unique to the study of community; they are common throughout the social sciences. In these sciences a direct and positive relationship exists between a phenomenon's importance and the level of controversy over how it is to be defined and studied. Thus, the fact that the first chapter of this text considers many definitions of community and the next four chapters outline four different approaches to the community is a testament to the importance this concept has had in the intellectual development of the social sciences generally and sociology specifically.

The final chapter in this section reconsiders the four major approaches and develops a theme that is followed throughout the book—a pragmatic eclecticism arguing that since no single approach to community works best in all situations, use the one that works best for the situation at hand. In addition to reflecting my own bias in this area, it allows new students of community to be exposed to all the predominate approaches in the field.

Chapter One

The Concept of Community

This chapter introduces community sociology by first examining the various definitions of community, explaining why community has been such an important but nebulous concept, and adopting a general definition of community for use throughout the book. Then, it outlines the origins of community theory and research and, finally charts community sociology's rise, decline, and revival. We shall consider in this chapter only the most important developments in community sociology and even those only briefly. However, this summary sets an agenda for the entire book, so that the concepts mentioned briefly here appear in more detail in subsequent chapters.

DEFINITIONS OF COMMUNITY

Community is a word with many, some say too many, meanings. For example, one early review of community definitions found ninety-four separate uses of the term (Hillery 1955), and even if most of these definitions are related somehow to a set of common concepts, such variations can be exasperating. If a course title includes this term (e.g., Community Sociology, The American Community, Community Studies), what can be expected in the subject matter? Would a course in community politics be different from one in urban politics? Is a community a city? Is it a lifestyle? Do you live in a community? Would you want to?

Most of us probably think of a small to medium-size town when conjuring up a mental image of community—a town with white picket fences and white smiling faces (from television reruns, Andy Griffith's

Mayberry will do nicely). As we will soon see, such an image fits well with many definitions of community. The term often does imply a small-town nostalgia in which neighborly, homogeneous people care about and help one another. Sometimes, however, a community is defined in a way that includes a modern-day ethnic neighborhood in a large city (Suttles 1972), a large corporation (Minar and Greer 1969), an informal professional group such as the "scientific community" (Kuhn 1962), or even a philosophical and psychological commitment to communal lifestyles (Nisbet 1953).

Why So Many Definitions?

Whenever a word has several meanings, it seems unscientific, perhaps better suited for the subtleties of philosophy than for the rigorous precision required of scientific terms. Yet, in the social sciences the most important concepts are often among the most imprecise. In economics, inflation can be defined in a number of ways, with the most popular measure—the Consumer Price Index—under continual attack. Psychologists disagree on the definition of basic concepts such as personality, neurosis, and psychosis. Even though a concept such as intelligence can be measured precisely through a myriad of standardized tests, its meaning is still elusive; witness the "Intelligence is what intelligence tests measure!" approach. Similarly, in sociology, considerable controversy exists as to the meaning of a term such as social class. Sometimes it is used as an inclusive concept, referring to an aggregate social position that includes education, occupation, and family background. At other times it refers only to economic ranking. Still, there are probably no concepts in the social sciences more basic, more important, or more useful than the ones we have mentioned.

In fact, in the social sciences, there seems to be an inverse relationship between the importance of a concept and the precision with which it is defined. Because basic concepts such as those mentioned above are important to almost all social scientists and because scientists vary in their personal and professional viewpoints, basic concepts are interpreted differently. For example, a liberal economist will be as concerned with supply and demand as a conservative economist, but he or she may make very different assumptions about the meaning and relationship of those concepts. Similar examples include Freudian and Skinnerian psychologists and their conceptions of neurosis or Marxist and structural-functional sociologists and their definitions of social class. Thus, the competing and sometimes contradictory definitions of community indicate the degree to which the concept is important to a large number of sociologists representing diverse approaches and areas of interest. Bearing this in mind, we turn now to the task of defining community.

Defining Community

One of the first American sociologists to define community was Robert Park. As we shall see later in this chapter, Park and his colleagues in the Sociology Department at the University of Chicago were instrumental in establishing community as a central concept in American sociology, but for now it is sufficient simply to examine his early attempt to define community:

> The essential characteristics of a community, so conceived, are those of:
> (1) a population territorially organized, (2) more or less completely rooted
> in the soil it occupies, (3) its individual units living in a relationship of
> mutual interdependence . . . (Park 1936, p. 3).

This initial attempt at defining community was not the only definition to appear. In fact, the number of various definitions that developed after Park is astounding, even for a concept as central to early American sociology as community.

Building on Park's definition. Less than twenty years after Park's attempt, George Hillery, Jr. (1955) found no fewer than ninety-four separate definitions of community in the sociological literature. Hillery encountered definitions of community as a group, a process, a social system, a geographic place, a consciousness of kind, a totality of attitudes, a common lifestyle, the possession of common ends, local self-sufficiency, and on and on. The only area of complete agreement was the rather obvious point that communities are made up of people. Such variation is an extreme example of the conceptual imprecision discussed at the beginning of this chapter. Fortunately, however, there were some areas of partial agreement. Hillery found that sixty-nine of his ninety-four community definitions contained the common elements of area, common ties, and social interaction.[1] From these three elements, then, it should be possible to construct a definition that reflects the most common uses of the term.

If we defined a community as people living within a specific area, sharing common ties, and interacting with one another, we would have a definition that largely agrees with most of the definitions Hillery analyzed. Interestingly, we would also have a definition very much like Robert Park's initial concept. The large number of competing definitions Hillery found indicates the central importance of community to

---

[1] An update shows that while community definitions have changed in the twenty years following Hillery's analysis, a majority of the definitions still include area, common ties, and social interaction. An important change is that "in spite of the considerable ambiguity and fuzziness which still characterizes community conceptualization, some advance in specificity and precision has been made" (Sutton, Jr., and Munson 1976, p. 19).

American sociology during the 1930s and 1940s, and the fact that most definitions included area, common ties, and social interaction suggests that Park's early definition had considerable influence on subsequent community analysis.

The implications of imprecision. Even if we settle on a definition of community as being a territorially organized population with common ties and social interaction, considerable imprecision remains. The type and degree of these three elements remain nebulous. The area of the community might be a politically defined municipal boundary, an economically defined zone of metropolitan dominance, or a psychologically defined neighborhood. Likewise, the basis of the common ties or bonds (family, ethnicity, propinquity, social class, religion), as well as the amount and quality of social interaction, can vary. So, we are still left with a definition broad enough to include a sprawling, multicounty metropolis, an ethnic neighborhood, or a largely rural village.[2] In short, a community can encompass many different kinds of human organizations.

This flexibility gives community sociology a breadth not found in either urban or rural sociology in that the study of community is not quite so compartmentalized as these neighboring subfields. Additionally, the focus on common bonds and social interaction provides a continuing concern for the quality of life, a concern that is not as apparent in other fields.

Although some sociologists view the broad and sometimes competing definitions of community as a problem that requires more specific definitions (e.g., Hillery 1963; Freilich 1963; Rossi 1972),[3] another, and perhaps more accurate, view is that the multiple definitions of community indicate the importance of the term to sociology. As Albert Hunter (1975, p. 538) eloquently noted, "the very looseness of the concept [community] is valuable in providing a common whetstone on which to sharpen the cutting edge of competing ideas." And the presence of such competition is more a sign of a dynamic, significant sociological concept rather than a problem requiring a narrower, "scientific" definition.

---

[2] Although the community remains a broad concept, certain uses of the term are eliminated by this definition. For example, a scientific community could not exist under these conditions. Scientists may interact on occasion and they may share certain values, but there is no specified territory, no place. Scientists may be analyzed more specifically and probably more effectively as a subculture rather than as a community. Similarly, a corporation is not a population *living* in a specific area and is better described as a formal organization.

[3] As examples, see Hillery's (1968) use of "vill" as a more specific term and Bernard's (1973) distinction between "community" as a psychological concept and "the community" as a geographic entity.

In sum, to study community is to study people living in and identifying with a particular place and to give special attention to the type, quality, and bases of their interaction. Such a broad definition includes much of the subject matter of sociology, so it is not surprising that community theory and research have played a major role in the development of American sociology.

THE ORIGINS OF COMMUNITY THEORY; TÖNNIES'S *GEMEINSCHAFT* AND *GESELLSCHAFT*

If it is possible to mark the beginning of community sociology, it is probably 1887, with the publication of Ferdinand Tönnies's book, *Gemeinschaft und Gesellschaft* (usually translated as *Community and Society*). Tönnies contrasted the types of human relationships appearing typically in extended families or rural villages (*Gemeinschaft*) with those found in modern, capitalist states (*Gesellschaft*). *Gemeinschaft*-like relationships are based on a natural will (*wesenwille*) that includes sentiment, tradition, and common bonds as governing forces. The basis for this natural will is in either the family or the "soil" (i.e., living and working in a common place). *Gemeinschaft* is characterized by a strong identification with the community, emotionalism, traditionalism, and holistic conceptions of other members of the community (i.e., viewing another as a total person rather than only as a segment of his status or viewing a person as significant in her own right rather than as a means to an end).

In contrast, *Gesellschaft*-like relationships are based on a rational will (*kurwille*) that includes, of course, rationality, as well as individualism and emotional disengagement as key elements. The basis for this rational will is urban, industrial capitalism. *Gesellschaft* is characterized by little or no identification with the community, affective neutrality, legalism, and segmental conceptions of other members of the community. In short, *Gesellschaft* is the opposite of *Gemeinschaft.*

According to Tönnies, *Gemeinschaft* and *Gesellschaft* are both ideal types. That is, there is no place one can find totally *Gemeinschaft*- or *Gesellschaft*-dominated relations. Rather, they are hypothetical, extreme constructs, existing for the purpose of comparison with the real world. A community in which all authority is traditional, where all interactions are completely holistic and emotion rules totally over logic, has never existed. A society in which all authority is based on law, where people are always only a means to an end and logic has completely displaced emotion, also does not exist. Instead, all human organizations are somewhere between the two extremes. Tönnies, in his comparison of *wesenwille* and *kurwille*, explains that

> between these two extremes all real volition takes place. The consideration that most volition and action resembles or is inclined toward either

one or the other makes it possible to establish the concepts of natural will and rational will, which concepts are rightly applied only in this sense. I call them normal concepts. What they represent are ideal types, and they serve as standards by which reality may be recognized and described (Tönnies 1963, p. 248).

By comparing our own relationships to these two ideal types, we view ourselves more clearly and can chart movement toward one type or the other.

Tönnies, in common with many of his contemporary sociologists (e.g., Durkheim and Weber), held that European social relationships were becoming more *Gesellschaft*-like. Likewise, in America, community sociologists were particularly concerned with the type and quality of human relationships as our society seemed to become progressively more oriented toward *Gesellschaft*. In fact, concern with the loss of *Gemeinschaft*-like relationships in an increasingly *Gesellschaft*-dominated society is one of the basic and continuing themes in community sociology. It is also a principal concern in this book. As Tönnies's ideas took root in American sociology, however, numerous revisions and extensions occurred.

THE RISE OF COMMUNITY THEORY AND RESEARCH IN AMERICAN SOCIOLOGY

The concept of community was so central to early American sociology that the following outline of the development of community theory and research is in many ways an outline of American sociology as well. First, we will show how community theory (in the form of Tönnies's *Gemeinschaft/Gesellschaft* typology) was the foundation for many of the most prominent theories in American sociology. Then, the role the community played in the pioneering research and theory developed at the University of Chicago will be considered. The popularity and influence of the classic holistic community studies on both American sociology and society will be briefly analyzed, and as a final example of the early predominance of community theory and research in American sociology, the tremendous outpouring of research into community power will be examined.

Typological Theory

Although Max Weber pioneered the methodology of ideal types, Tönnies's use of contrasting, opposite ideal types became, arguably, the most common and useful analytic tool in American sociology. We can find this concept reflected in many of the most important American theoretical efforts. Early typologies, such as Cooley's primary/secondary groups, MacIvers's communal/associational relations, Odum's folk/

state distinction, Sorokin's familistic/contractual relationships, and Redfield's folk/urban continuum, are among the foremost theoretical efforts of American sociology, and each of these explanations of social change can be traced to the seminal ideas of Tönnies. More recent and equally important efforts, such as Howard Becker's sacred/secular continuum and Talcott Parsons's pattern variables, are also related to the *Gemeinschaft/Gesellschaft* typology.

We will explore many of these models in Chapter 2 and see how they build on Tönnies's ideas, but for now it is sufficient to recognize that the same theoretical concepts that marked the beginning of community sociology also provided the framework for many of the major advances in social theory.

The Chicago School

To a substantial degree, sociology became an accepted part of American academia through the efforts of Robert Park and his colleagues at the University of Chicago. Park, the chairman of the sociology department, was joined by Ernest Burgess, Louis Wirth, Roderick McKenzie, Frederick Thrasher, Nels Anderson, Harvey Zorbaugh, Paul Cressey, Clifford Shaw, and Walter Reckless in authoring the now-classic studies of the urbanization process in Chicago. The theoretical basis for their research was borrowed from the already established and accepted science of biology. Employing ecological concepts such as competition, symbiosis, evolution, and dominance that were used originally to explain the interrelationships in the plant and animal kingdoms, they demonstrated that the scientific methods developed in biology could successfully explain the structure and dynamics of American cities. As a result, they were able to establish sociology as an academically and scientifically legitimate discipline. Thus, sociology won out over many other new disciplines that were also competing for academic acceptance (Hawley 1968, p. 329; Martindale 1981, p. 94–95).

The community played a major role in the Chicago school's ecological analysis. The first introductory sociology textbook was produced at the University of Chicago (Small and Vincent 1894), and it devoted more pages to community than any other subject. At that time, the community—whether it was a Jewish ghetto, an upper-class neighborhood, or the entire city of Chicago—was the most important single object of sociological inquiry.

Tönnies's concept of increasingly *Gesellschaft*-like relationships can be seen throughout the human ecology emphasis of the Chicago school. The most famous example is in Louis Wirth's "Urbanism as a Way of Life" (1938). In this article, Wirth explains how three ecological variables—population size, density, and heterogeneity—combine to produce a more *Gesellschaft*-like lifestyle. Wirth was not the only

Chicago sociologist to deal with movement toward *Gesellschaft*-like relationships. Some of the best-known portraits of the weakened social integration and accompanying disorganization that beset Chicago during the rapid urbanization of the 1920s can be found in Anderson's *The Hobo* (1923), Thrasher's *The Gang* (1927), Zorbaugh's *Gold Coast and Slum* (1929), Wirth's *The Ghetto* (1928), Shaw's *The Jackroller, A Delinquent Boy's Own Story* (1930), and Cressey's *The Taxi Dance Hall* (1932).

Holistic Studies: The Lynds' Research in *Middletown*

While the ecological version of community sociology was flourishing at Chicago, Robert and Helen Lynd were pioneering another form of community research: holistic studies that described the various parts of the community and explained their interrelationships. Originally, the Lynds did not set out to study an entire community. Rather, their goal was to study only the religious beliefs and practices in a medium-size American city, Muncie, Indiana. However, it soon became clear that religion did not stand in isolation from other local institutions. To understand religion, they found it necessary to uncover the relationships between local religious beliefs and practices and other social phenomena in the community. Thus, the Lynds' book describing and explaining life in *Middletown* (Muncie, Indiana) includes not only a chapter on "Engaging in Religious Practices" but chapters entitled "Getting a Living," "Making a Home," and "Using Leisure" as well.

Middletown, published in 1929, was both a literary and sociological phenomenon. It became a bestseller with a wide general audience (a rare event for a sociology book). For sociologists, it became a classic community study. Colin Bell and Howard Newby (1972, p. 82) describe *Middletown* quite accurately as "a magnificent and imaginative leap forward" that "provided a model for sociological advances." It is, in short, the best-known, the most widely cited, and probably the most influential community study ever published.

A primary reason for its significance and acceptance lay in the rich, relatively objective description of small-town (approximately thirty-five thousand residents) life. Muncie is described in very much the same way as an anthropologist would detail the activities of a preindustrial village. The research methods were decidedly eclectic, including participant observation, content analysis of historical records, and closed-ended and open-ended questionnaires. *Middletown* describes the various activities and beliefs of Muncie residents in copious detail (e.g., the time different groups arise in the morning, the amount of time spent on household chores, sex roles, the parents' aspirations for their children, political and religious values); but, of equal importance, the Lynds also attempted to explain *why* Muncie is the way it is. For example, they explained how religious and political values supported business interests and why residents could claim that there were no class differences in Muncie when their own research revealed class difference so pervasive as to affect virtually every aspect of life.

The publication of *Middletown* began a long series of holistic community studies, not the least of which was the Lynds' sequel, *Middletown in Transition* (1937). In their return to Muncie, the Lynds analyzed the local effects of the national depression. They found that the Depression had allowed one family, the X family, to monopolize the economic means of production, which enabled them to control the entire community. In an often cited interview, a Muncie resident reports that

> if I'm out of work I go to the X plant; if I need money I go to the X Bank, and if they don't like me I don't get it; my children go to the X college; when I get sick I go to the X hospital; I buy a building lot or house in an X subdivision; my wife goes down town to buy clothes at the X department store; if my dog strays away he is put in the X pound; I buy X milk; I drink X beer, vote for X political parties, and get help from X charities; my boy goes to the X YMCA and my girl to their YWCA; I listen to the word of God in X subsidized churches; if I'm a Mason, I go to the X Masonic Temple; I read the news from the X morning newspaper; and, if I am rich enough, I travel via the X airport (Lynd and Lynd 1937, p. 4).

The Lynds' description of unequally distributed local power and influence was in some ways the forerunner of another type of community research—one that in terms of sheer quantity ranks about as high as any set of research efforts in sociology: community power research.

Community Power

The exposé of the X family notwithstanding, serious, extended study of community power began with the publication of Floyd Hunter's *Community Power Structure* in 1953. Hunter was originally involved in community planning and development in Atlanta. However, he became frustrated with the inability of his Community Planning Council as well as other local entities to produce meaningful social change. Consequently, he attempted to learn how power was distributed in Atlanta and to discover the "real" leaders. If these leaders could be identified, he reasoned, then appropriate communication with or pressure on these leaders might be able to produce significant local change.

Using a variety of methods, most of which were based on face-to-face interviews with strategically placed people in Atlanta, Hunter uncovered a group of forty community influentials. Most of them were businessmen with no official position in local government (only four were government personnel), yet they met with one another frequently to determine the future of Atlanta. In short, Hunter concluded, democracy was not operating as it should. The elected officials of the community had relatively little influence on important, supposedly public, decisions.

Naturally, Hunter's findings were controversial. Political scientists were especially skeptical, not only of Hunter's findings, but of his research methods as well. Robert Dahl's *Who Governs?* (1961), a study of decision making in New Haven, set the tone for the polemic that followed. Dahl avoided the interview techniques used by Hunter that asked for the names of powerful people. Rather, he focused on actual decisions that had been made in the community, identified conflicting positions and their supporters, and determined whose views prevailed. Equally significant to the differences in research methods, the findings of *Who Governs?* were in many ways the exact opposite of *Community Power Structure*. Dahl found a pluralistic democracy in New Haven with an elected official, the mayor, playing the pivotal role in most major community decisions.

The quantity of research and debate that followed these two books on community power was remarkable. Hundreds of articles and books describing the power distribution of one community or another and voluminous exchanges between pluralists and elitists were published. And now, as a result of that research and debate, it is possible to measure, at least to a degree, the distribution of power in a community and thereby determine who does and does not govern.

THE DECLINE OF COMMUNITY AND THE RISE OF THE MASS SOCIETY

The preceding discussions indicate just how prominent a place the community has held as a subject of inquiry in American sociology. Yet, despite the heuristic value of Tönnies's seminal ideas on subsequent social theory, despite the dominance of community in the most prominent sociology department, despite the appeal of holistic studies to both social scientists and the general public, and despite the tremendous outpouring of scientific research following the first community power studies, these community-based activities all but came to a halt in the 1950s and 1960s.

The Decline of Community Theory and Research

By 1970, Tönnies's ideas had become less relevant for community analysis. Bell and Newby began their book *Community Studies* (1972) with the only partially whimsical question "Who reads Ferdinand Tönnies today?" The answer, at least in the late 1960s and early 1970s, was hardly anyone. The most influential application of Tönnies's ideas was provided by the pattern variables of Talcott Parsons (Parsons and Shils 1951), but Parsons's analysis was seldom directed toward the territorial community; it focused rather on the entire society.[4]

Similarly, the significance of the community as a research site began to fade. Ecological models of urban or community growth (e.g., Burgess' early concentric zone model and the subsequent modifications discussed in Chapter 2) were criticized when urban ecologists encountered city after city that were exceptions to the rules. Additionally, considerable ecological research began to be directed at census tracts and other units more precisely defined than the community. Many ecologists even suggested dropping the nebulous, philosophical term "community" and substituting more neutral or specific concepts such as place, neighborhood, region, tract, or metropolitan area.

Holistic studies of the *Middletown* genre became rare, with Arthur Vidich and Joseph Bensman's *Small Town in Mass Society* (1958) being one of the last widely cited research efforts. Holistic approaches were not well-suited to large cities, and the relevance of small-town research became questionable. Vidich and Bensman even concluded that events in the larger, mass society that lay beyond the local community were more important in their effects on Springdale (the small town they studied) than events in Springdale itself!

Community power research suffered a similar demise. By the 1970s, very few communities were being studied in order to uncover the distribution of power. Although most of the methodological debate had subsided with a general agreement that combinational techniques featuring multiple approaches to measuring power were best, many began to question whether it was necessary to measure the distribution of local power. The chief problem was that knowledge of community power seemed to be largely irrelevant in explaining and predicting community events (e.g., Aiken 1970; Lyon 1977). Again, the most common explanation of this lack of relevance was that events beyond the local community had more influence on local phenomena than the distribution of local power.

On all fronts, then, the tides of community theory and research began to subside in the 1950s and 1960s. After 1957, the American Sociological Association no longer included community sections in its annual meetings. The community fell from the highest pinnacles of sociological concern to the low levels reserved for historical curiosities,

---

[4] And given the radical attack on the potential conservatism of Parsons's ideas, as well as his remarkably obtuse writing style, one might also ask "Who reads Talcott Parsons today?"

such as regional studies, rural sociology, or the sociology of religion.[5] When we occasionally referred to or read community theory and research, it was to see only where sociology had been. The community appeared to have very limited relevance to contemporary sociology.

There are numerous reasons for the decline of interest in various types of community theory and research. Some are unique to their own areas and unrelated to the causes of the decline in other types of community analysis. However, one major trend in American society in general and American sociology in particular can be seen as a substantial contributor to the decline of community sociology in *all* areas: the analysis of America as a mass society.

The Rise of the Mass Society

A mass society is a standardized, homogeneous, society devoid of major ethnic and class divisions and, most importantly for the community, devoid of substantial regional and local variation. Because of mass media, standardized public education, and residential mobility, the intercommunity variation in norms, values, and behavior has been reduced to a remarkable degree. The territorial community, then, is of little scientific importance in a mass society. Residents of New York, New Haven, New Orleans, and New Deal, Texas (population 637) will be much more alike than they are different. They watch the same TV shows and movies, read the same magazines and syndicated columnists, study the same textbooks in the same grades, and travel from one city to the next with ease. Under such circumstances, the logical site of scientific inquiry is the national society, not the local community.[6]

In the late 1950s and 1960s, theories about the structure and dynamics of *societies* became common. Similar theories about *communities* were no longer in vogue. Research based on national samples replaced studies of single communities. Decisions reached in corporate headquarters and state and national capitals far beyond the local commu-

---

[5] Just as with the community, the fields mentioned here have experienced a measure of renewal after an extended period of decline. The sociology of religion probably resembles the community most closely in both the high level of initial importance and the strength of its recovery.

[6] Just as with the concept of community, as the idea of America as a mass society gained prominence, the definitions of mass society became more numerous. William Kornhauser (1959), and Edward Shils (1972) played pioneering roles in its development. Maurice Stein (1960) initially explained the effect of the mass society on the community (see Chapter 7 of this volume) while Robert Nisbet (1953) and David Riesman (1953) analyzed its effects on individuals.

nity precluded the relevance of community power. In short, the rise of interest in the mass society was matched by the concomitant decline in analysis of the community.

THE REVIVAL OF COMMUNITY AS A TOPIC OF SOCIOLOGICAL INQUIRY

At this point, students reading this book as a text may well conclude that they made a serious mistake by registering for a course in a dead or, at best, dying field. Fortunately (for both the students and teacher), community sociology has experienced a revival. The community section of the American Sociological Association was reconstituted in 1972. A decade later, it had grown to over 400 members, ranking in size with other large and established sections such as "theoretical sociology" and "sex and gender." Ecologists are again developing models of community structure (Abu-Lughod 1971) and growth (Greenwood 1975). Holistic community studies appear to be making a comeback, led by a third visit to Middletown (Caplow et al. 1982). New community power studies are being conducted with new techniques (e.g., computer-aided network analysis methods, see Galaskiewicz 1979) and new practitioners (e.g., journalists, see Trounstine and Christensen 1982). If all this were not enough to document a revival of interest in the community, perhaps the surest sign is that sociologists are even reading Tönnies again! And, more important, they are finding his concepts of *Gemeinschaft* and *Gesellschaft* as keys to understanding the community in American society (Poplin 1979; Warren 1983).

The main reason for the revival of interest in community sociology lies in the development of a more circumscribed view of America as a mass society. It has become clear that significant ethnic and racial differences in values and behavior continue to exist. Perhaps more important for community sociology, we have discovered that significant differences in local politics, economics, and lifestyles exist between communities and that substantial amounts of *Gemeinschaft*-like attitudes and activities continue in the small towns and urban neighborhoods.[7] Thus the preeminence of the standardized, *Gesellschaft*-like, mass society was clearly overstated in the 1960s, and, conversely, the widely perceived decline in the relevance of the local, *Gemeinschaft*-like community has proven to be premature, at best.

In the 1980s, a more balanced view of the community in urbanized

---

[7] The literature establishing the limits of the mass society is becoming voluminous. Among the more important works are Glazer and Moynihan (1963), Bonjean (1966), Glenn (1967), Clark (1971 and 1983), Kasarda and Janowitz (1974), Hunter (1975), Wellman and Leighton (1979), and Guest et al. (1982), and Ahlbrandt (1984).

American society is being developed. The community is obviously no longer a self-contained, self-sufficient, homogeneous village, but neither has it become an impotent group of unrelated, alienated, anonymous residents with little or no local ties. The modern American community is linked with the larger society in so many ways that to study it without acknowledgment and analysis of these links is fruitless, but the practice of ignoring the local community because of these abundant links is equally sterile. Today, community sociology is attempting to discover, describe, and understand the interaction between the mass society and the local community. As a theoretical base for exploring this interaction, the most common approaches to conceptualizing the community in urban society are considered, beginning with the typological approach in Chapter 2.

Chapter Two

The Typological Approach: Community on a Rural/Urban Continuum

The typological approach is the most fundamental of all approaches to the community. It is also one of the most important in all of sociology. Robert Nisbet makes the case for the importance of the typological approach in *The Sociological Tradition* (1966, p. 71):

> Nowhere has sociology's contribution to modern social thought been more fertile, more often borrowed from by other social sciences, especially with reference to the contemporary study of undeveloped nations, than in the typological use of the idea of community. Through this typology, the momentous historical transition of nineteenth-century society from its largely communal and medieval character to its modern industrialized and politicized form has been taken from the single context of European history in which it arose and made into a more general framework of analysis applicable to analogous transitions in other ages and other areas of the world.

Not only will we be examining some of the major contributions to community sociology, this typological section includes many of the seminal ideas in social science as well.

CLASSIC TYPOLOGIES

As we examine some of the key concepts in social science, we will be reviewing the contributions of the pioneers in social science as well:

Weber, Durkheim, Simmel, Redfield, Wirth, and, especially, Ferdinand Tönnies.

Ferdinand Tönnies (1855–1936): *Gemeinschaft und Gesellschaft*

At the relatively young age of thirty-two, German philosopher and sociologist Ferdinand Tönnies published *Gemeinschaft und Gesellschaft* (1887) and provided the foundation for virtually all the subsequent developments in the typological approach. His theory of movement from a *Gemeinschaft* lifestyle based on *wesenwille* to a *Gesellschaft* lifestyle based on *kurwille* is outlined in the preceding chapter, allowing us to focus on the implications of his work here.

Certainly much of the significance of Tönnies's typological approach lies in the use of contrasting ideal types on opposite ends of a continuum. Yet, Pitirim Sorokin (1963) correctly points out that using polar extremes hardly originated with Tönnies. Earlier polar types can be found in the analyses of Confucius, Plato, Aristotle, St. Augustine, and Ibn Khaldun. Similarly, Max Weber is usually credited with fully developing the ideal type as a useful theoretical and empirical construct. Why, then, is Tönnies seen as the founder of the typological approach?

Tönnies, unlike predecessors such as Confucius or Khaldun, was able to observe and analyze the *Gesellschaft*-producing effects of the industrial revolution on the *Gemeinschaft*-like, medieval nations of Europe. Thus, he was able to construct a model of social change with implications for industrializing or industrialized societies that is of continued relevance. Further, Tönnies, more than Weber, explicitly demonstrated the utility of *polar* ideal types for comparison with real-world phenomena. It is Tönnies, then, who almost immediately influenced the subsequent typological approaches of Weber, Durkheim, and Simmel, and, indirectly, later influenced the analysis of Louis Wirth, Robert Redfield, Howard P. Becker, and Talcott Parsons.

Max Weber (1864–1920): Rationalization

Weber's contributions to sociology, political science, and economics are manifold, but for our purposes, we are concerned primarily with his contributions to the typological approach, and here we find remarkable similarities with the earlier analysis of Tönnies. In Weber's classics *The Protestant Ethic and the Spirit of Capitalism* (originally published in 1904–5), *Economy and Society* (originally published in 1921, but written between 1910 and 1914) and *Sociology of Religion* (originally published in 1920–21), we find Tönnies's theme of a communal, medieval Europe being transformed into an individualistic, capitalistic Europe. Weber refers to the transformation as the result of increasing "rationalization," but the phenomena being described are virtually identical to moving from *Gemeinschaft* to *Gesellschaft*. For example, Weber's distinctions between rational actions based on "efficiency" and the "amount of return" (*zweckrational*) and the more *Gemeinschaft* actions based on values (*wertrational*), emotion (*affektuell*), or tradition (*traditionell*) are similar to Tönnies's original typology.

These four types of action are ideal types that Weber compared to actual occurrences of behavior, and he concluded, much like Tönnies, that Europe was becoming increasingly *zweckrational*. For example, his study of religion focused on the growing rationalization of religious life from magic into "book religion." In law, he found the personalized justice of traditional or charismatic leaders replaced by rationally enacted, codified laws from objective, legal-rational rulers. In music, he contrasted the spontaneous music of Asia and Africa with the standardized music of a European symphony. In sum, Weber's cross-cultural and historical analysis led him to conclude that the trend of world history was toward increasing rationalism, or in Tönnies's terms, toward increasing *Gesellschaft*.

Emile Durkheim (1858–1917): Mechanical and Organic Solidarity

Much like Weber, the French sociologist Emile Durkheim influenced the social sciences in ways far beyond his writing on community typologies. Still, one of his most enduring contributions is to be found in his distinction between *Gemeinschaft*-like "mechanical" solidarity and *Gesellschaft*-like "organic" solidarity.

In *The Division of Labor in Society* (1893), Durkheim described the dissolution of medieval social ties based on similarity. Medieval Europe was a homogeneous society. Values concerning politics, economics, family, and religion were almost universally accepted. Likewise, lifestyles showed little variation from village to village and from generation to generation. Society, Durkheim explained, was held together by a "mechanical" solidarity in which everyone was alike. However, an industrial revolution in England and political revolution in France destroyed the basis for mechanical solidarity. Violently different ideas about politics, economics, and religion developed, and different lifestyles (based on an infinitely more complex division of labor) became common. What, Durkheim asked, is the "glue" for the new *Gesellschaft*-like Europe? What is the new basis for social solidarity? His answer was an "organic" solidarity based on mutual interdependence. That is, individuals work together for the common good because they must. Self-sufficiency is no longer possible in a *Gesellschaft*-like society.

Although Durkheim reasoned that "organic" solidarity is now

necessary at the societal level, he believed it to be psychologically inadequate at the individual level. The theme of his classic work *Suicide* (1897) was the need for associational memberships to offset the loss of the communal, group identifications common to mechanical solidarity. In *Suicide*, we find not only an analysis of problems associated with movement from *Gemeinschaft* to *Gesellschaft* but a proposed solution to the "quest for community" problem so central to community sociology. Durkheim demonstrates that close, personal group relationships in families or religious worship can provide some of the psychological integration (i.e., *Gemeinschaft*-like community) necessary in a society based on "organic" solidarity.

Georg Simmel (1858–1918): "The Metropolis and Mental Life"

The German philosopher and sociologist Georg Simmel is responsible for some of the richest, most insightful analysis of urban life ever written. In an often-reprinted lecture delivered in the winter of 1902–3, he describes "The Metropolis and Mental Life," exploring the relationship between the urban environment and the psychic experience of the inhabitants by focusing on their uniquely urban experiences, attitudes, and behaviors. In so doing, he practices a social psychology that shows how a multitude of characteristics (e.g., intellectuality, emphasis on a precise time schedule, a belief in causality, individuality, and most notably, a blasé attitude) are part of an urban or *Gesellschaft* lifestyle. For Simmel, a key to understanding the *Gesellschaft* psychology predominate in the great metropolises of Europe was to consider the role of a money economy:

> The metropolis has always been the seat of the money economy. Here the multiplicity and concentration of economic exchange gives an importance to the means of exchange which the scantiness of rural commerce would not have allowed. Money economy and the dominance of the intellect are intrinsically connected. They share a matter-of-fact attitude in dealing with men and with things; and, in this attitude, a formal justice is often coupled with an inconsiderate hardness. . . . By being the equivalent to all the manifold things in one and the same way, money becomes the most frightful leveler. For money expresses all qualitative differences of things in terms of "how much?" Money, with all its colorlessness and indifference, becomes the common denominator of all values; irreparably it hollows out the core of things, their individuality, their specific value, and their incomparability. All things float with equal specific gravity in the constantly moving stream of money (Simmel 1902-3, "The Metropolis and Mental Life," quoted from Wolff 1978, p. 411).

A plumber, then, who charges $20 per hour to repair your faucet is twice as valuable as a teacher who receives $10 per hour for instructing your child, but that plumber is only one tenth as valuable as a surgeon who repairs your heart at $200 per hour. A Picasso painting that sells for $1 million is ten times better than a Rembrandt that may go for $100,000, and so on. Simmel's imagery in this lecture for describing the urban, *Gesellschaft* lifestyle is unsurpassed. The same can be said for his dispassionate analysis. For example, he explains that while

> metropolitan man is "free" in a spiritualized and refined sense, in contrast to the pettiness and prejudices which hem in the small-town man . . . [i]t is obviously only the obverse of this freedom if, under certain circumstances, one nowhere feels as lonely and lost as in the metropolitan crowd (Simmel 1902-3, "The Metropolis and Mental Life," quoted from Wolff 1978, p. 418).

Although Simmel's European contemporaries were the founding fathers of modern sociology, even Tönnies's, Weber's, and Durkheim's descriptions do not match his rich imagery. Further, their primary focus was more at the societal level than on local phenomena. It is, rather, in the American sociologist, Louis Wirth, that we find typological analysis in the tradition of Georg Simmel.

Louis Wirth: "Urbanism as a Way of Life"

Wirth was a student of urban ecologist Robert Park (who had been a student of Simmel's) in the sociology department of the University of Chicago. Although the ecological approach to community is treated separately in this book, Wirth's classic article "Urbanism as a Way of Life" is considered here because it remains American sociology's definitive statement of *Gesellschaft*. Wirth notes many of the same characteristics as Simmel—the blasé attitude, time schedules, individuality—but differs considerably from his European predecessor in accounting for their origin. While Simmel focused mainly on a money economy and only to a lesser extent on population size, Wirth (1938) maintained that three population characteristics cause the distinctive urban lifestyle and that "on the basis of three variables, number, density of settlement, the degree of heterogeneity of the urban population, it appears possible to explain the characteristics of urban life and to account for the differences between cities of various sizes and types." If his proposition were wholly true, this book could be considerably shorter, and community life much easier to understand. Still, his article was the impetus for an outpouring of research evaluating the causes of *Gesellschaft*, and we shall consider that research later in this chapter. For now it is sufficient to summarize what is possibly the most-cited, most influential article ever written in American sociology (Bell and Newby 1972; Saunders 1981).

Wirth reasoned that large population *size* would necessarily result in *Gesellschaft* characteristics such as a more specialized division of labor and more impersonal, segmented relations. He explained how the increased population *density* of the city requires a greater tolerance of individual differences but nevertheless results in more "competition," "exploitation," and "disorder." That, in turn, leads to more "formal controls" on behavior. Finally, the higher levels of urban *heterogeneity* were seen as producing a more complex stratification system, a money economy, more stereotyping, and categorical thinking. In other words, Wirth employed the spatial-population variables predominant in the ecological analysis of the Chicago school to account for the differences between *Gemeinschaft* and *Gesellschaft* described in the classic European works of Tönnies, Weber, Durkheim, and Simmel. And although later tests of his theory often found it wanting, the initial field research of the anthropologist Robert Redfield provided strong support for Wirth's ideas.

Robert Redfield: "The Folk Society"

Also a student of Robert Park at the University of Chicago, Robert Redfield published his now-famous study of four Mexican communities only three years after Wirth's "Urbanism as a Way of Life" article appeared in the *American Journal of Sociology*. In *The Folk Culture of Yucatan* (1941), Redfield found that the smaller, the more isolated, the more homogeneous the community, the more *Gemeinschaft*-like the lifestyle. Based on his research in the Yucatan peninsula and other studies, Redfield later published the *AJS's Gemeinschaft* companion piece to the *Gesellschaft* "Urbanism as a Way of Life." Redfield's article, "The Folk Society," described the ideal *Gemeinschaft* type: "small, isolated, nonliterate and homogeneous with a strong sense of group solidarity" (Redfield 1947, p. 293). It has only a minimal division of labor, based largely on sex role differentiation and a shared means of production. He describes the ideal folk community as economically self-contained, with no dependence on the larger surrounding society. Culturally, it is traditional and uncritical and is based on religion and kinship.

When Redfield's "The Folk Society" is combined with Wirth's "Urbanism as a Way of Life," we have a rural/urban continuum with the polar types defined in considerable detail. Any actual community or society can be placed at some point between the two opposite types and then compared with other actual cases to determine existing levels of *Gemeinschaft* or *Gesellschaft*. By the 1950s, then, the rural/urban continuum was in place as a major approach to community theory and research. There have, however, been some recent innovations in this approach that transformed it into something quite different from the original *Gemeinschaft/Gesellschaft* perspective.

RECENT INNOVATIONS IN THE TYPOLOGICAL APPROACH

In the 1950s, Howard P. Becker and Talcott Parsons used the typological approach to establish themselves as major (and in Parsons's case, *the* major) social theorists of postwar American sociology. While their work is clearly in the *Gemeinschaft/Gesellschaft* tradition, both made several key modifications in the Tönnies et al. approach.

Howard P. Becker: Sacred/Secular

Howard Becker's sacred/secular continuum is clearly built upon the works of Tonnies and Weber (Becker, 1957), but there are some notable differences. Unlike Tönnies, Becker sometimes discusses movement away from the *Gesellschaft*-secular end of the continuum and toward greater sacredness.[1] Also, unlike Weber, Becker refers to his polar types as constructed types rather than ideal types. Partially, this change was due to his belief that "ideal" is too value-laden and therefore too susceptible to misleading connotations. More important, however, was his insistence that the characteristics of the type be based on an actual "culture case study" rather than a purely mental construct.[2] For Becker, an example of a constructed type would be Redfield's folk society—an extreme case for comparison with real world phenomena, but with characteristics derived from his empirical field work in the Yucatan peninsula.

Becker's key distinction between the sacred and secular is the reluctance to (sacred) or readiness for (secular) change. In an extremely sacred society, for example, martyrdom to preserve religious values would be a common response to an attempted change in orthodoxy. Conversely, in a highly secular society, one might find a scientist risking life or limb in pursuit of new knowledge. In fact, these kinds of sacrificial activities would be empirical references for his constructed types.

---

[1] In Becker's *Man in Reciprocity* (1956, p. 171) he refers to "Germans 'turning back the clock' from the Weimar secularity to Nazi sacredness." While this is an uncommon occurrence, it is a continuing phenomenon (e.g., the revival of sacred authority in Iran) related in no small part to the "quest for community" thesis discussed throughout this book.

[2] For some, the distinction between "ideal" and "constructed" types is of considerable importance (Becker 1940; Sjoberg 1960; McKinney 1966) because the constructed type is derived from empirical data and possibly superior to the more abstract ideal types. This distinction is, however, technical and somewhat ambiguous. For most purposes, the terms can be treated as interchangeable.

Becker maintained that all societies were within the extremes, possessing sacred and secular values. Further, he moved away from the evolutionary view of growing *Gesellschaft*-like secularization. He argued that skipping stages and reversing movement were possible and that when a society reached extreme secularization, charismatic leadership can often lead to a sudden reversal to extreme sacralization. Becker refined typological theory in a way that made it more compatible with historical events, but at the same time, he reduced its predictive and explanatory power. No longer could simple predictions be made about an increasingly *Gesellschaft*-like society, and no longer could social change be explained by an evolutionary model.

Talcott Parsons: Pattern Variables

Without serious qualification, it can be argued that the zenith of the typological approach was reached in 1951 with the publication of Talcott Parsons and Edward Shils' *Toward a General Theory of Action*. Building on Tönnies's *Gemeinschaft/Gesellschaft* types, they developed what became, perhaps, the most widely cited aspect of Parsons's influential structural-functional theory—the four pattern variables of social action:

1. affectivity/affective neutrality—referring to whether gratification is immediate or deferred.
2. diffuseness/specificity—referring to whether relationships are holistic and cover a large number of situations (e.g., mother-child) or narrow and constrained to only a single basis for interaction (e.g., bureaucrat-client).
3. particularism/universalism—referring to whether special standards are applied to special groups (e.g., neighbors, kin, strangers) or whether the same standards are applied to all (e.g., citizens).
4. quality/performance (originally designated as ascription/achievement)—referring to whether an object is based on what it is (e.g., an antique clock), or what it does (i.e., tells time with less precision than a low-priced Timex).

Parsons believed that although a social structure (e.g., a society, a community, or an interpersonal relationship) may seem to be typically *Gemeinschaft* or *Gesellschaft*, closer inspection would reveal a mixture that varied along the four polar types of the pattern variables. For example, Parsons argued that while a modern physician's relations to patients would be *Gesellschaft* when compared to the more affective, particularistic treatment of a tribal medicine man, "by virtue of the canon that 'the welfare of the patient' should come ahead of the self-interest of the doctor, this was clearly one of *Gemeinschaft*" (Parsons and Smelser 1956, p. 34). Thus, the pattern variables can be viewed as a multidimensional refinement of Tönnies's original polar types.

As we shall see later in this chapter, the pattern variables can be used to estimate the magnitude of the "loss of community" phenomenon. However, Parsons was not particularly interested in the local community. Rather, he felt his pattern variables applied to all forms of social actions and usually adopted a micro-interpersonal unit of analysis or a macro focus on entire societies that in either case bypassed the community.

The Third Type: Post-*Gesellschaft* Societies

There is a still emerging theoretical position stating that modern industrial societies have moved beyond the elements of *Gesellschaft* and are entering an entirely new basis for social relationships. Various names for this new stage have been offered: "The Global Village" (McLuhan 1965), "The Postindustrial Society" (Bell 1973), "The Third Wave" (Toffler 1980), and "The Information Society" (Naisbitt 1982). The claims of distinctiveness for this new type are often quite extensive. Alvin Toffler (1980, p. 10) sees us entering

> a genuinely new way of life based on diversified, renewable energy sources; on methods of production that make most factory assembly lines obsolete; on new, non-nuclear families; on a novel institution that might be called the "electronic cottage"; and on radically changed schools and corporations of the future. The emergent civilization writes a new code of behavior for us and carries us beyond standardization, synchronization, and centralization, beyond the concentration of energy, money, and power.

Still, the most pertinent question for those who argue for a post-*Gesellschaft* typology is precisely what Toffler takes as given: Are we already entering into a new social order based on relationships *fundamentally* different from the *Gesellschaft* condition described by Tönnies less than one hundred years ago? Perhaps the best way to explore this question is to compare the three "polar" (if it is possible to have *three* poles) types. Anthony Richmond (1969) has contrasted the three types in order to show the distinctiveness of the new type. The degree to which each of Richmond's post-*Gesellschaft* characteristics has or will become predominate is debatable, but for students of community at least, the key debate centers on interaction. If electronic communication via computer-linked terminals replaces the written word, that would not, in itself, constitute a new "wave," "stage," or "type." Rather, we would want to know if this new form of communication significantly changed social interactions. Will a computer-linked social network replace the associations that replaced informal neighboring? Will people begin to view one another, their communities, or their societies in substantially different ways? Between *Gemeinschaft* and *Gesellschaft*, the answer is reasonably clear and affirmative. Between *Gesellschaft* and post-*Gesellschaft*, it remains too early for a clear consensus opinion.

	Gemeinschaft	Gesellschaft	*Post*-Gesellschaft
Typical way of interaction	Communities	Associations	Social networks
Principal mode of production	Agricultural	Mechanical	Automated
System of stratification	Quasi-feudal	Class	Meritocracy
Main means of communication	Oral	Written	Electronic
Main means of transport	Horse and sail	Rural-urban	Interurban

For now, we would do well to remember that much *Gemeinschaft*-like community remains even in our industrialized mass society. Thus, even if a third "wave" is upon us, we would expect considerable *Gesellschaft* to remain in a post-*Gesellschaft* society. The transformation into this third type may not be as sweeping as its proponents claim.

WHY IS THERE MOVEMENT TOWARD *GESELLSCHAFT*?

Although there is near unanimity concerning both the distinctiveness of *Gesellschaft* from *Gemeinschaft* and the general trend toward a more *Gesellschaft*-like society, there is little agreement on why *Gesellschaft* is distinctive and why there is movement toward the *Gesellschaft* end of the continuum. We will begin by investigating the popular causal variable of the classic typologists—capitalism.

Capitalism: A Marxist Explanation

If capitalism is the key causal variable, then the presence of capitalism as a new economic system would be the major cause of the distinctive *Gesellschaft* lifestyle. Simmel's focus on the role of a money economy comes to mind here.[3] Similarly, the spread of capitalism and its advancement into successive stages of economic development would account for the movement toward more *Gesellschaft*-like societies. In this regard, the explanation is within the province of a Marxist approach to the community. In *The German Ideology* Marx and Engels (1846) show how capitalism propels the industrial revolution through the develop-

---

[3] It should be remembered that Tönnies also associated capitalism with the highest forms of *Gesellschaft*.

ment of new factory-based towns. This begins the breakdown of the medieval-*Gemeinschaft* lifestyle and its replacement with the alienation of *Gesellschaft:*

> Within the capitalist system all methods for raising the social productiveness of labor are brought about at the cost of the individual laborer; all means for the development of production transform themselves into means of domination over, and exploitation of, the producers; they mutilate the laborer into a fragment of a man, degrade him to the level of an appendage of a machine, destroy every remnant of charm in his work, and turn it into a hated toil; they estrange him from the intellectual potentialities of the labor process in the same proportion as science is incorporated in it as an independent power; they distort the conditions under which he works, subject him during the labor process to a despotism the more hateful for its meanness, they drag his wife and child beneath the wheels of the juggernaut of capital (Marx 1867, *Capital*, quoted from Nisbet 1966, p. 291).

Thus, capitalism "sows the seeds of its own destruction" by clustering together the alienated workers in these new urban centers.

Although capitalism has yet to destroy itself, we find today a major approach to the problems of urban, *Gesellschaft*-like societies based on the proposition that capitalism is the key causal variable. The conflict approach will be considered shortly, but for now it is sufficient to note that when it overlaps with the typological approach, it does so by offering capitalism as the driving force behind the movement to *Gesellschaft*.

Population Characteristics: An Ecological Explanation

Just as the conflict approach overlaps community typologies on the question of why there is movement toward *Gesellschaft*, the ecological approach overlaps here also. Although Simmel provided the initial ecological arguments for an increasing population size leading to *Gesellschaft* relations, it is in Wirth's "Urbanism as a Way of Life" that population characteristics are most clearly linked to lifestyle.

The research testing Wirth's propositions about population size, density, and heterogeneity is now legion. And as is often the case when there is a large body of research, the results are somewhat contradictory. Still, most of the empirical evidence is at odds with Wirth's theory. *Gemeinschaft* patterns have been found in large centers of dense, heterogeneous populations such as London (Young and Willmott, 1957), Cairo (Abu-Lughod 1961) and Boston (Gans 1962). And, conversely, rural areas possessing small, diffuse, homogeneous populations have shown distinctively *Gesellschaft* characteristics. For example, Oscar Lewis (1951) studied the same Mexican village of Tepoztlan originally referred to by Redfield as extremely *Gemeinschaft*. He found not *Gemeinschaft*-like harmony and consensus, but rather a "pervading quality of fear, envy and distrust in interpersonal relations" (Lewis 1951, p. 429). In short, studies of the effect of population size (Srole 1972; Fischer 1973; Freedman 1978), density (Feldman and Tilly 1960; Roscow 1961; Gans 1962; Palen 1981), and heterogeneity (Sjoberg 1960; Glazer and Moynihan 1963; Suttles 1968) have failed to find the causal relationships with lifestyles posited in Wirth's "Urbanism as a Way of Life."

Industrialization: A Technological Explanation

One of the most thorough refutations of Wirth's theory also supplied some of the most compelling evidence for industrialization as the key causal variable in movement toward *Gesellschaft*. Gideon Sjoberg's *The Preindustrial City* (1960) analyzed the ecological and social conditions in preindustrial cities of medieval Europe and other parts of the world. He reported two major findings:

1. Urban centers existing prior to an industrial revolution exhibit certain common characteristics such as nonrational economics, an ascriptive class system, extended families, and restricted formal education.
2. Modern industrial cities differ significantly from preindustrial cities in that industrialization requires rational, centralized, extracommunity economics; a class system based on achievement; a small, flexible family; and mass education.

Sjoberg, then, has found that while preindustrial cities may have had relatively large, dense and heterogeneous populations, they were decidely *Gemeinschaft*-like. It is only after an industrial revolution that more *Gesellschaft*-like characteristics appear. His technological explanation of movement toward *Gesellschaft* is opposed to Wirth's ecological explanation, and subsequent cross-cultural survey research has substantiated Sjoberg's thesis. Alex Inkeles and David H. Smith (1974) administered surveys in Argentina, Chile, India, Israel, Nigeria, and Bangladesh and found a wide range of *Gesellschaft* characteristics associated with working in factories. Seventy-six percent of the factory workers in these nations exhibited *Gesellschaft* personality traits, compared to only 2 percent of the respondents with no factory or other formal organization experience. Cross-cultural research in "moral development" (Kohlberg 1980; White, Bushnell, and Regnemer 1978) shows similar results: namely, that children living in industrialized societies progress more rapidly and develop a more complex attitude toward morality than children in nonindustrial societies.

$\longrightarrow$ Still, it would be incorrect to infer from this research that industrialization alone can explain the emergence of *Gesellschaft* characteristics.

The moral development research, for example, also shows rural/urban differences beyond levels of societal industrialization (White, Bushnell, and Regnemer 1978) and even Sjoberg (1960) rejects a wholly technological explanation of society.

More Recent Research: The Validity of the Typological Approach and Multiple, Interrelated Causation

A considerable body of empirical research has been inspired by the typological approach to community. Some of it is directed toward assessing the validity of the typological approach.

Are there really community or society types? Do communities or societies actually vary along the dimensions suggested by the typological theorists? What little research that exists on this question suggests an affirmative answer. Joseph McKinney and Charles Loomis (1958) tested Parsons's typological approach in two communities in Costa Rica. They found that social patterns in these two communities could be accounted for with a typological continuum and that "Tonnies' analysis of *Gemeinschaft* and *Gesellschaft* and the related work of other theorists attacking similar problems is still relevant" (McKinney and Loomis 1958, p. 574). A much larger sample from the Human Relations Area File provided similar conclusions. Linton Freeman and Robert Winch (1957) applied Guttman scalogram analysis to eight *Gemeinschaft/Gesellschaft* type variables (e.g., barter and exchange versus a money economy) in forty-eight societies and found that six of the variables did indeed vary in a systematic unidimensional pattern similar to that posited by the typological approach.

Multiple causes for movement. Still, most of the typological research has been directed at accounting for the movement from *Gemeinschaft* to *Gesellschaft*. Some has been field research similar to Redfield's, but usually more indirect, survey-type methods have been applied. An influential example of this type of research is James Kasarda and Morris Janowitz's (1974) survey of over two thousand residents in one hundred communities throughout England. They found that the social class of the residents, their age, and especially the length of residence in the community have more of an influence on the presence of *Gemeinschaft* characteristics (such as having numerous friends and relatives in the community) than population size and density. A conclusion from their survey is that the degree to which *Gemeinschaft* or *Gesellschaft* characteristics exist is due to a number of different variables, some ecological, some cultural. Other publications (Suttles, 1972; Fischer 1975; Berry and Kasarda 1977; Christenson 1979) have made similar cases for the complexity of accounting for movement toward

Gesellschaft, but now there is some question concerning whether this complexity is worth unraveling.

EVALUATING THE TYPOLOGICAL APPROACH: IS THAT ALL THERE IS?

When Tönnies, Weber, Simmel, and Durkheim described the distinctions between *Gemeinschaft* and *Gesellschaft*, a giant step was taken for sociological analysis generally and community analysis particularly. But since then, how far has the typological approach progressed? Roland Warren (1983, p. 78) notes with some distress that "we content ourselves with referring, often with malice, to the alleged old *Gemeinschaft*-like community, and tell each other ponderously that modern industrial communities are more *Gesellschaft*-like. Is this the last word? I hope not!" We would all hope not because if this is the last word, then it is a word uttered initially by Tönnies; and we would have added nothing of substance to it since 1887! And with all due respect to the modifications and specifications made by luminaries such as Becker and Parsons, what is there to the typological approach beyond the now obvious movement from *Gemeinschaft* to *Gesellschaft?* One disappointing, but common response to the query: That is indeed all there is to the typological approach.

That's All There Is

This stance was initially and forcefully taken by Richard Dewey (1960) in his influential article "The Rural-Urban Continuum: Real but Relatively Unimportant." Dewey maintains that the large number of descriptive characteristics is "surely excessive" (he finds forty in the typological literature) and "the lack of consensus is remarkable." Further, he finds numerous cases of *Gesellschaft* in rural areas and *Gemeinschaft* in urban areas. Dewey does admit that some urban/rural characteristics do seem to fit the typological approach, but he concludes that "it is of minor importance for sociology." His point seems to be that sociologists now know about all there is to know from this approach and that it is now time to study "society in the large."[4] Jesse Bernard (1973) makes similar criticisms of the typological approach and then argues that its minimal explanatory value is related to the changes brought by urbanization and industrialization. Thus, she maintains that the paradigm is useless to account for patterns of social interaction in postindustrial America.

Has the typological "vein" been mined to exhaustion? Dewey and

---

[4] This is related to the rise of the "mass society" perspective discussed in Chapter 1.

others (e.g., Pahl 1968; Saunders 1981) maintain that it has in terms of a cultural distinction based on how "urban" a particular *place* is. Bernard and others (e.g., Castells 1977) maintain that it is also exhausted when referring to the modernization of *entire societies*. Thus, whether *Gemeinschaft/Gesellschaft* is seen as a typological approach to a geographic form of community (a specific urban place à la Wirth) or a social interaction form of community (a lifestyle for an entire society à la Tönnies), a strong case has been made for its abandonment.

Perhaps Not

Yet the typological approach endures. Partly, it endures because it stirs a nostalgia for a more static, simple, and personal time (Williams 1973). Partly, it endures because it describes real differences in social behavior (Freeman and Winch 1957; McKinney and Loomis 1958; even Dewey 1960; Key 1968; Guterman 1969). And mostly it endures because, as Horace Miner (1952) noted over thirty years ago, "the continuum stands as an insistence that social science has something to explain here." That statement is relevant today. So is his insight about the "bottom-line" question for evaluating this approach: "The real query is, do we have a better initial answer than the folk-urban continuum to the general question of how to account for the similarities and differences observable among societies?" Do we? Is the conflict approach more powerful? Systems theory? The ecological approach? Perhaps, but before those questions can be answered, these other approaches to community must be considered.

Chapter Three

The Ecological Approach: Community as a Spatial Phenomenon

The ecological approach to community is more specialized than the typological approach. The typologists are a diverse group including "grand" theorists from Europe and America, field anthropologists, and even popular "futurists," but the ecologists are smaller in number and more specific in approach (focusing almost exclusively on the spatial patterns of the urban environment). Still, the ecological approach is not so narrow that it cannot be subdivided. There are four main divisions within the ecological approach (Theodorson 1961) that reflect its temporal development: classical, sociocultural, neo-orthodox, and social area analysis–factorial ecology.

THE CHICAGO SCHOOL: CLASSICAL ECOLOGY

Just as we can trace the origins of community typologies to Tönnies, the classical ecological approach can be traced to the sociology department of the University of Chicago and its chairman, Robert Park. At a time when sociology was competing for academic acceptance, Park was able to establish its scientific credentials by borrowing evolutionary principles from biology. And, to a degree, the current legitimacy of sociology as a discipline in the curricula of American universities is a reflection of the ecological approach pioneered by Robert Park.

Community and Society: The Human Ecology of Robert Park

For Park, human organization is a dichotomy. One part, community, is an expression of human nature that is revealed in Darwinian competition for supremacy. The other, society, is a collective phenomenon revealed in the consensus and common purpose of social groups. Society is the cultural, consensual part of human existence. Community is its biotic, competitive counterpart, and community was the area of study for the urban ecologists at the University of Chicago.

The distinction between community and society is both crucial and obscure. "Ecology," Park (1952, p. 251) wrote, "is concerned with communities rather than societies, though it is not easy to distinguish between them." Indeed it is not. In fact, we shall see how this obscure and probably artificial distinction became a major criticism of Park's urban ecology, but first it is necessary to examine the major concepts of the ecological approach to community.

Competition. Borrowing from Darwin's web of life, Park emphasized the interrelationship between the various parts of the environment. Competition is the master process that determines the spatial form and ecological functions of the interrelated web. For example, in a city, competition arises for the most desirable land. Because commercial interests can use the land most efficiently (i.e., profitably), they will prevail in the competition and dominate the city's spatial and functional development. In Park's (1952, pp. 151–52) terms, "the struggle of industries and commercial institutions for a strategic location determines in the long run the main outlines of the urban community . . . the principle of dominance . . . tends to determine the general ecological pattern of the city and the functional relation of each of the different areas of the city to all the others." Once competition has determined the spatial patterning of the city, a "symbiotic" relationship develops based on the interdependence of the various groups. For example, competition is tempered by the need of business for supplies from areas of industrial land use and customers from residential areas; industry needs retail outlets from business, and workers from residences, and so on.

Competition exists at the community level, and similarly the symbiotic relationships that develop after the competition are community based. Further, this symbiosis is the basis for normative consensus of society. Thus, community is the basis for society.

Natural areas. Natural areas are the product of competition. As early as 1926, Harvey Zorbaugh (p. 190) explained that "in this competition for position the population is segregated over the natural areas of the city. Land values, characterizing the various natural areas, tend to sift and sort the population." Park and his fellow ecologists believed that the land in any city possessed certain characteristics that would make it more efficient for one particular function. For example, land in the center of the city might be especially useful for retail business or office development. Land near a port or rail line would hold special advantages for industry. The downtown business district, the slum, the ghetto, the warehouse district, the suburb, the red light district, and the immigrant colony are all natural areas. They are culturally distinct land-use patterns determined not by society-based urban planners, but by community-based competition.

Natural areas were the most basic unit of analysis for urban ecologists. And since they were the product of *natural* competitive forces, it should be possible to generalize from the findings of their study. "Natural areas," Park (1952, p. 198) writes, "not only tell us what the facts are in regard to conditions in any given region, but insofar as they characterize an area that is natural and typical, they establish a working hypothesis in regard to other areas of the same kind." However, the generalization from studies of natural areas never reached the levels Park predicted.

Under Park's direction, his students and colleagues studied Chicago's natural areas. Zorbaugh's *The Gold Coast and Slum* (1929) and Wirth's *The Ghetto* (1928) are two of the finest examples of such studies, but even the best studies of natural areas are largely descriptive. That is, the primary goal is to define the geographic boundaries of the natural area and then describe the lifestyles and land use within it. Hence, the classic Chicago studies of this period—*The Hobo* (Anderson 1923), *The Gang* (Thrasher 1927), *The Ghetto, The Gold Coast and Slum, The Jackroller* (Shaw 1930), and *The Taxi Dance Hall* (Cressey 1932)—are classic *descriptions* of urban life, not classic *theories* of urban phenomena. It may be that the unit of analysis (the natural area) was so small that rich description of individual detail was easy while general propositions about urban phenomena were difficult. In fact, we shall encounter a similar example of atheoretical description in the descendants of the natural area approach: social area analysis and factorial ecology. In any event, it was not until the focus was directed toward the entire city that the major theoretical contributions of urban ecology were developed.

Urban Growth

When urban ecology borrowed its major principles from biology, a special view of urban growth resulted. Just as a more dominant species succeeds another in nature, the human community will have changes in land-use patterns as areas are "invaded" by dominant competitors that can use the land more efficiently. If the business area of a city grows, it may invade a residential area, and since it can use the land more efficiently (i.e., profitably), it can pay more for the land than a homeowner. Succession occurs as the land values increase, the residents move out, and the land use is transformed to meet the needs of the dominant competitor. Then, a new equilibrium is established, and the successional sequence comes to an end.

The land uses of a city, then, reflect the dominance of various users. Since dominance is established by competition and since the competition is won by those who can use the land most efficiently, the city reflects a natural, evolutionary efficiency. Thus, the scorn with which urban ecologists viewed municipal administrators' attempts to plan the land use of cities is understandable.[1]

Burgess' concentric zones. Perhaps the crowning achievement of the ecological approach was Ernest Burgess' (1925) use of dominance, invasion, and succession to account for urban structure and growth. He explained that the city could be conceptualized ideally as five concentric zones (see Figure 3–1). The land use in each zone reflects the dominance of the user. For example, Zone 1, the Central Business District (CBD), contains "quite naturally, almost inevitably, the economic, cultural, and political centers" (p. 50) because it is the most desirable, valuable property in the city. Beyond the CBD

> there is normally an area of transition, which is being invaded by business and light manufacture (II). A third area (III) is inhabited by the workers in industries who have escaped from the area of deterioration (II) but who desire to live within easy access of their work. Beyond this zone is the "residential area" (IV) of high-class apartment buildings or of exclusive "restricted" districts of single family dwellings. Still farther, out beyond the city limits, is the commuters' zone—suburban areas, or satellite cities—within a thirty-to-sixty-minute ride of the central business district.

Each zone is inhabited by those who can use it most efficiently. Skyscrapers in the CBD can build above the congestion and noise, workers living in Zone III are close enough to the factories to walk or use public transportation, and suburbanites in Zone V have the private transportation necessary for living so far from the city. Each zone reflects the dominance of the user.

---

[1] For example, see Zorbaugh's (1926) analysis of the "futile" attempts of the Chicago Zoning Commission to influence land values and growth patterns. However, recent analysis of zoning in Chicago by Shlay and Rossi (1981) concludes that urban growth is significantly influenced by zoning regulations.

FIGURE 3–1   The Burgess concentric-zone model of urban structure

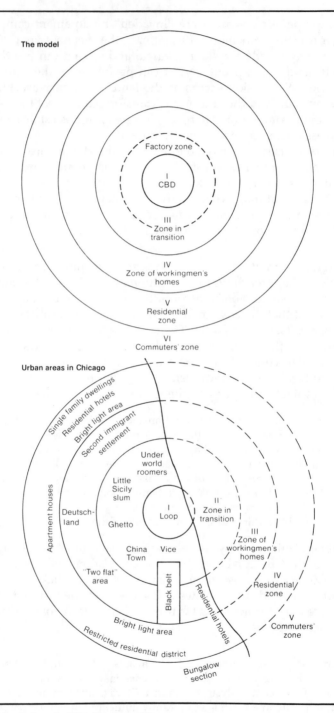

The model

Factory zone

I
CBD

III
Zone in
transition

IV
Zone of workingmen's
homes

V
Residential
zone

VI
Commuters' zone

Urban areas in Chicago

Single family dwellings
Residential hotels
Bright light area
Second immigrant
settlement

Apartment houses

Deutsch-
land

Little
Sicily
slum

Under
world
roomers

Ghetto

I
Loop

II
Zone in
transition

China
Town

Vice

III
Zone of
workingmen's
homes

"Two flat"
area

Black belt

IV
Residential
zone

Residential hotels

V
Commuters'
zone

Bright light area

Restricted residential district

Bungalow
section

Source: After Park et al., 1925, Charts I and II.

The growth of the city is largely the result of one zone invading the next outer zone. The CBD will invade (expand into) the zone of transition, which invades the workingmen's zone, and so on until a new and efficient equilibrium is established.

Hoyt's urban sectors. While Burgess' concentric zone theory is the most widely cited ecological approach to urban structure and growth, there are two subsequent theories of note. One is Homer Hoyt's (1939) sector theory (Figure 3–2). While employing land-use principles similar to Burgess', Hoyt maintained that cities grow not by expanding con-

FIGURE 3–2 Hoyt's sector theory

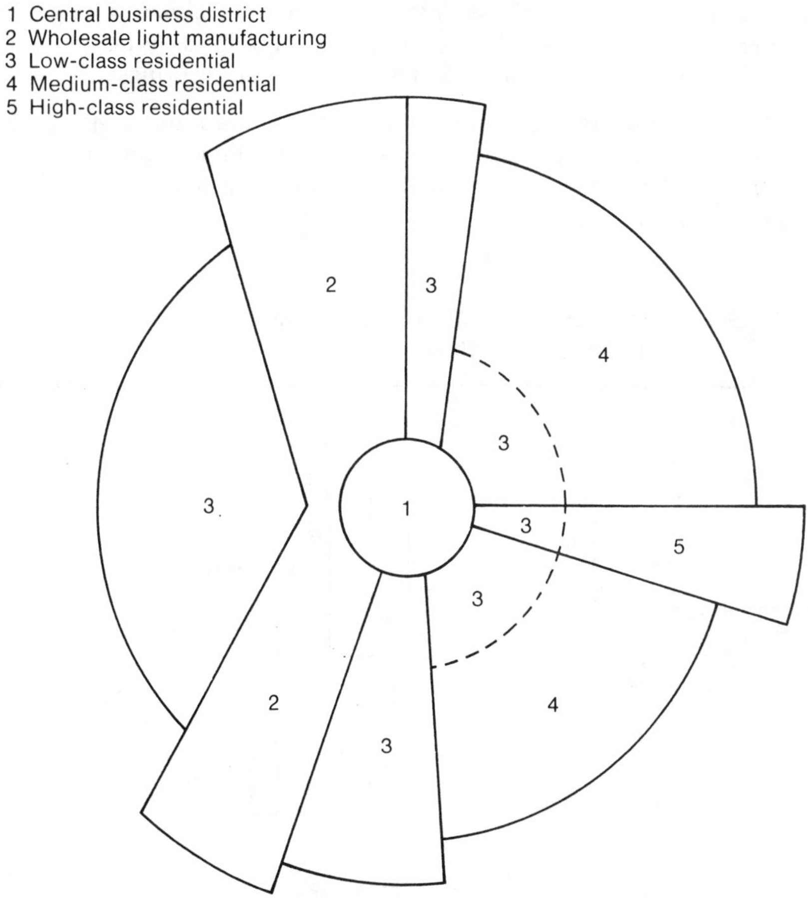
1 Central business district
2 Wholesale light manufacturing
3 Low-class residential
4 Medium-class residential
5 High-class residential
2
3
4
3
3
1
3
5
3
2
4
3

Source: Chauncey D. Harris and Edward L. Ullman. 1945. "The Nature of Cities," *The Annals of the American Association of Political and Social Science,* 242:7–17. Adapted.

centric rings, but, rather, along major transportation lines that radiate from the CBD. Heavy industry and warehouses will locate along waterways, railroad lines, and major highways. Wealthy residents consume the best remaining land, typically high ground along a major transportation artery. Poor residents occupy whatever is left over, the least desirable land. As the CBD expands and industry grows, the wealthy move farther out to avoid the accompanying noise, crime, traffic, and pollution. Some of their former homes are leveled for business growth, and others are subdivided and rented by the poor.

Harris and Ullman's multiple nuclei. Chauncey Harris and Edward Ullman (1945) developed a multiple nuclei theory of urban structure and growth (Figure 3–3). It combined elements of Burgess' and Hoyt's models but was not strictly in the ecological tradition of competition determining efficient land use. Instead, Harris and Ullman were geographers who explained the complex, decentralized structure and growth of a city through four rather common sensical rules:

1. Certain land uses demand specialized facilities and concentrate where such facilities are available. Industry, for example, requires transportation facilities and will locate along rail lines, a waterway, or major highway.

FIGURE 3–3   The Harris and Ullman multiple-nuclei model of urban structure

1 Central business district
2 Wholesale light manufacturing
3 Low-class residential
4 Medium-class residential
5 High-class residential
6 Heavy manufacturing
7 Outlying business district
8 Residential suburb
9 Industrial suburb

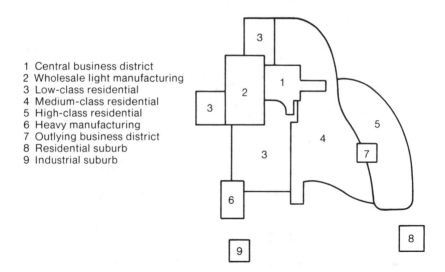

Source: Harris and Ullman, 1945, Fig. 5.

2. Similar uses of land often benefit from being close to each other. Retailers may locate in the same part of the city so that they can bring a larger number of potential customers to their area.
3. Some dissimilar land uses are typically separated. For example, residential and industrial uses will find it mutually beneficial to remain far apart.
4. Finally, the inability to pay for the desired land brings some uses together. Warehousing or grocery wholesaling would benefit from a location in the CBD but require such a large amount of land that the cost is prohibitive. Thus, such uses will cluster together in areas where land is cheaper.

Such rules are similar to what one would learn in a real estate course and are far removed from elegant ecological underpinning developed by Park, Burgess, et al. Still, Harris and Ullman's multiple nuclei theory shares with Hoyt's sector theory and Burgess' concentric zone theory the proposition that urban structure and growth is not random; rather, it is systematic and predictable. Later in this section, we look at the factorial ecologists' attempts to test the validity of that proposition and the reliability of predictions based on these three theories.

The Demise of Classical Urban Ecology

The demise of the classical ecological approach was a gradual one, brought about by cumulative criticisms that began with Milla Alihan. Alihan examined Anderson's *The Hobo* and Zorbaugh's *Gold Coast* to conclude that the supposedly crucial distinction between the biotic community and the cultural society levels is, in practice, nonexistent. She noted that Anderson and Zorbaugh did "not discriminate between certain activities carried on within a society as those of 'society' and others which are those of 'community' " (Alihan 1938, p. 82). Walter Firey (1945, 1947) continued the attack on the ecological position with his study of land use in Boston. He showed how the idea of efficient land use through economic competition could not account for the spatial patterning of Boston. Firey argued that such events as the refusal of Beacon Hill's residents to sell homes in their traditional high-status neighborhood to commercial interests and the retention of the Boston Commons Park in the middle of the CBD could be explained only through reference to sentiment and symbolism.

W. S. Robinson's (1950) illustration of the "ecological fallacy" was a different but important criticism of the ecological approach. Robinson demonstrated that the common practice of using ecological correlations (correlations between aggregates, such as the proportion of blacks in a state and the state's rate of illiteracy) to explain individual behavior (in this case, that some states had illiteracy levels because they had high levels of black population) was statistically invalid. And while it was true that ecologists theoretically focused on aggregates, their descriptions and explanations were often highly individualistic.[2]

When Robinson's criticism of ecological statistics was combined with Firey's contention that more than economic efficiency was needed to explain land use and Alihan's observation that even the ecologists could not separate the biotic community from the cultural society, the classical ecologists were in serious trouble. In fact, "by 1950, the ecological approach as developed by Park, his colleagues and students at the University of Chicago was virtually dead" (Berry and Kasarda 1977). Dead perhaps, but not quite buried and forgotten. The ghosts of Robert Park and the classical ecologists can still be found in the sociocultural, neo-orthodox, and social area analysis–factorial ecology approaches to community.

SOCIOCULTURAL ECOLOGY

Firey's study of land use in Boston did more than provide a critique of classical urban ecology. His demonstration of the importance of cultural variables such as sentiment and symbolism on spatial patterns set a new direction for many ecologists. Sociocultural ecologists maintained that urban structure and growth can be understood only if culture and values are made central to ecological theory. Besides Firey, Albert Seeman's (1938) study of how religion influenced the patterns of Salt Lake City and other Utah cities is the most notable early example of this approach. Seeman explained how the Salt Lake Basin had been revealed to Mormon leaders as the place where the Savior and his faithful would gather in the last days. Toward this end, the "City of Zion" was designed to be a utopia where farmers could live within the city and bring their surplus to the centrally located Bishop's storehouse. Salt Lake City developed a distinctive pattern of wide streets running exactly north-south and east-west, large common city blocks at the center for schools and churches, and smaller blocks at the periphery for stables and barns. More recently, August Heckscher (1977) has argued that the spatial patterns of American cities clearly reflect American values of freedom, individualism, growth, and business success. He shows, for example, how the American grid pattern of streets allows people to look down the entire street, even out to the countryside and envision urban expansion. The regularity and predictability of

---

[2] The problems associated with interpreting ecological correlations is a continuing one. Note, for example, Lineberry's (1971) discussion of the difference between ecological explanations of urban race riots that are based on communities and explanations based on individual rioters. See also Donald and Elizabeth Bogue's (1976) discussion of proper uses of ecological correlations.

the grid is seen as implying a sense of control over destiny that is absent from the curved streets of medieval Europe.

As the socioculturalists began to emphasize the role of cultural variables, they began to lose the distinctiveness of the ecological approach. The merger with mainstream sociology has become so complete, in fact, that with only a few exceptions such as Heckscher (1977), it is difficult today to distinguish the socioculturalists as a special approach to the urban community. Current analysts tend to: (1) ignore this approach (Berry and Kasarda 1977); (2) describe it historically with reference to only Firey and Seeman's research (Poplin 1979); or (3) merge it with urban ethnographies such as Herbert Gans (*The Urban Villagers: Group and Class in the Life of Italian Americans*, 1962); Elliot Liebow (*Tally's Corner: A Study of Negro Streetcorner Men*, 1967); James Spradley (*You Owe Yourself a Drunk: An Ethnography of Urban Nomads*, 1970); and Carol Stack (*All Our Kin: Strategies for Survival in a Black Community*, 1974).[3]

Perhaps the clearest remaining vestige of sociocultural ecology is in the application of symbolic interactionism to communities. Anselm Strauss' *Images of the American City* (1961) details the transformation of rural America into urban America and, in so doing, shows how our images of what a city is and should be have influenced and been influenced by urban development. Gerald Suttles's widely cited and influential *The Social Construction of Communities* (1972) builds on this tradition by presenting a sophisticated collection of articles relating the images of communities to their ecological structure. And, most recently, Albert Hunter's continuing work (e.g., *Symbolic Communities*, 1974) on symbols and sentiments in Chicago neighborhoods illustrates the blend of cultural symbolism and spatial patterning characteristic of sociocultural ecology. But such works are not common, at least in comparison to the neo-orthodox efforts we shall examine next.

Regardless of what has actually happened to the sociocultural version of urban ecology, it is now becoming increasingly difficult to identify it as a distinct approach to community.[4] Further, we can conclude that it lost much of its distinctiveness when it lost its primary emphasis on ecological variables. Apparently, it was easier to criticize the classical ecologists than to develop a distinctive blend of cultural and

---

[3] Examples of this third approach (combining the sociocultural works with urban ethnographies) include recent books by Peter Saunders (1981) and William Schwab (1982).

[4] See Firey and Sjoberg (1982) for a different view, one that sees sociocultural ecology as alive and well with vigorous ongoing research. However, much of the research they cite as examples of the sociocultural approach seem more appropriately placed within the category of the urban ethnographies mentioned above and further discussed in Chapter 14 of this text.

ecological emphases. Thus, it is to the version that maintained its primary emphasis on ecological structure and process that we now turn.

NEO-ORTHODOX ECOLOGY

The origin of neo-orthodox ecology can be marked by the publication of Amos Hawley's *Human Ecology: A Theory of Community Structure* in 1950. By this time, classic human ecology had died at the hands of its sociocultural critics, but they, in turn, had trouble developing a distinctive ecological approach of their own. Hawley, however, resurrected the ecological approach in a way that insulated it from some of its previous problems.

Amos Hawley: The Resurrection of Human Ecology

"Hawley reformulated the ecological approach and initiated its present revival within the field of sociology" (Berry and Kasarda 1977, p. 3). He did so by moving the focus of the approach away from spatial distributions (which he felt was more a geographical perspective rather than an ecological one) and on to the adaptation of human populations by means of functional differentiation. Technology, culture, and social organizations are his key types of adaptive mechanisms. Hawley also dismissed Park's distinction between the biotic and the cultural. He argued that since culture is a mechanism of environmental adaptation, it is within the study of ecology.

Hawley's view of community differed from Park's classic definition. For Hawley, the community is the one unit of analysis where all the key elements of society are present in a relatively small, easily studied place. In the community, an ecological system of interdependence develops between various groups and organizations as the local population adapts to its environment. Thus, the major ecological principle that governs the community is local "interdependence." While Park emphasized the role of conflict and his students chronicled the social disorganization of Chicago, we find in Hawley's approach a community in organized equilibrium, at least until disturbed by outside influences, and even then adjusting back into cooperative balance.

For Hawley, the ecological approach to community is a decidedly macro approach. There is little room for individual psychology. Hawley (1950, p. 179) reasoned that since the focus of ecology is on "collective" adaptations, "the irrelevance of the psychological properties of individuals is self-evident."[5]

---

[5] As an example of Hawley's macro, nonindividual approach to community, see his ecological measure of community power discussed in Chapter 13 of this text.

Hawley's redefinition of human ecology set a course for neo-orthodox ecologists that is still being followed today. And, today, one of the most influential neo-orthodox ecologists is Otis Dudley Duncan.

O. D. Duncan: The Ecological Complex

Otis Dudley Duncan (1959) has added to the neo-orthodox approach his "ecological complex" of four basic, interrelated, reference variables: population, organization, environment, and technology (or POET). These variables (see Figure 3–4) include the standard population measures (size, heterogeneity), organization types (developed as adaptation for survival), environmental phenomena (including all variables external to the community), and technological developments (skills or tools to aid adaptation). The POET framework allows examination of a wide range of phenomena and insures that all crucial variables within the ecological perspective are included. In fact, most current ecological research efforts are directed at explicating the interrelationships with the POET complex (Berry and Kasarda 1977).

Duncan, perhaps even more than Hawley, has led the way in developing statistical measures of ecological phenomena. His measures of community dominance (Duncan et al. 1960; Duncan and Lieberson 1970), and residential segregation (Duncan and Duncan 1955, 1957) raised the quantitative sophistication of community analysis to levels not equaled until the factorial ecologists began to develop their craft in the 1960s.

SOCIAL AREA ANALYSIS AND FACTORIAL ECOLOGY

The degree to which social area analysis (SAA) and factorial ecology are conceptually distinct from the neo-orthodox approach is questionable, but traditionally they are categorized separately (Theodorson 1961). It is also questionable whether social area analysis will continue as a methodological tool in light of the growing emphasis on factorial ecology, but again SAA is traditionally given more coverage in community and urban texts than is factorial ecology (e.g., Poplin 1979; Schwab 1982). We will briefly review both techniques and assess their relationship to one another and to neo-orthodox urban ecology.

Social Area Analysis

SAA is the census-born descendant of classical ecology's natural areas. The natural areas were the indivisible building blocks of the larger city. Each possessed unique environmental characteristics that set it apart from other parts of the city. While the city as a whole might seem an unwieldy, disorganized, unadministrable unit, the classical ecologists believed that urban planning based on the smaller natural areas was more likely to be successful (Zorbaugh 1926; Green 1931).

The natural area's reign as urban ecology's basic unit of spatial analysis was short-lived. In 1940, the U.S. Bureau of Census began publishing data for most large American cities by census tract. Census tracts are similar to natural areas, but much smaller, averaging only four thousand residents per tract. A large city would contain several hundred tracts, and for the first time, urban ecologists were faced with more statistical data than they could assimilate. SAA was developed in order to group together similar census tracts into larger categories that fulfilled the same functions as the earlier concept of natural areas.

The three indexes. SAA was pioneered by Eshref Shevky and Marilyn Williams (1949) when they measured and described the differences between Los Angeles' 568 census tracts on three indexes: *social status* (as measured by occupational prestige and education), *family status* (fertility ratio, number of women in the labor force, and number of single family dwellings), and *ethnic status* (percent foreign-born or black).[6] The index scores allowed Shevky and Williams to group the tracts into more homogeneous social areas and to examine complex census data with just a few summary scores.

Subsequent applications of SAA (Shevky and Bell 1955; Bell 1953, 1955, 1959) showed that it allowed the identification and comparison of social areas within different cities so that generalizations could be made about the spatial patterning of urban phenomena. Further, ecological change could be measured by simply comparing two or more consecutive census dates.[7]

The debate over SAA. SAA is not without its critics. Hawley and Duncan (1957) have criticized its atheoretical nature, but Shevky and Bell (1955) have developed some theoretical underpinnings for SAA, and its applicability to other ecological theories seems obvious. A more fundamental criticism regards its choice of only seven variables (combined into three indexes) to represent the community's social areas. Bell (1955) used the mathematical technique of factor analysis to establish the validity of the seven variables and three indexes of SAA. Factor

---

[6] The terminology for the three indexes has changed over time (Bell 1958), but their statistical computation and substantive interpretation have not. Thus, for simplicity, "social," "family," and "ethnic" status are used in this chapter.

[7] Further, all of this data could be gathered quickly and cleanly—never requiring field research via original surveys or personal observation. The ecological approach to community power (Hawley's MPO in Chapter 13 of this text) has similar virtues.

analysis identifies clusters of related variables (factors) by analyzing the variables, identifying their underlying similarities, and summarizing them on a single index score (or factor score). In this way, large numbers of census tract variables can be factored to uncover basic underlying characteristics. Bell's factor analysis of tract variables of Los Angeles and San Francisco showed the existence of three underlying factors that were similar in variable construction to the social, family, and ethnic status indexes of SAA. In other words, Bell's factor analysis demonstrated that in at least two cities, groupings of census tracts by the three SAA indexes was a valid summary of census information.

However, Bell's use of factor analysis to support SAA raised as many questions as it answered. For example, *if SAA is supported by factor analysis in two cities, will it be supported in, say, ten cities?* The answer: In six cities it worked; in four there were some minor problems (Van Arsdol, Camilleri, and Schmid 1958). *Why are there only three underlying dimensions? Why not four, or more?* The answer: subsequent factor analysis has identified at least two more dimensions—mobility and size—and a case could be made for up to fourteen underlying factors in American communities (Berry and Kasarda 1977). *Will there always be the same dimensions or factors in all cities?* No. For example, an ethnic or racial segregation factor often does not appear in Southern cities because race and class are so closely related in that region (Schwab 1982). And, most importantly, *if factor analysis is used to test the validity of SAA, why not use factor analysis instead of SAA?* The answer: SAA used to be easier, but with the spread of powerful computer hardware and sophisticated software, factor analysis is about as easy. So, now factor analysis probably should be used.

Berry and Kasarda (1977, p. 123) reason that instead of SAA's seven variables, "many more variables detailing the way in which census-tract populations vary according to socioeconomic characteristics should be included in any study and that factor analysis should be used to isolate the fundamental patterns of variation in the data, be they Shevky-Bell construct patterns or otherwise." In other words, SAA often does isolate the key dimension of urban areas, but now that computer technology has made factor analysis a relatively simple technique, it becomes difficult to justify the exclusive use of SAA's seven variables. Thus, factor analysis has lead to a new approach to the urban community that already complements and may replace SAA—factorial ecology.

Factorial Ecology

Factorial ecology includes a diverse set of community studies that use factor analysis as their primary research methodology. Like SAA, it is an inherently atheoretical approach in which

[a] data matrix is analyzed containing measurements on *m* variables for each of *n* units of observation (census tracts, wards . . .), with the intent of (1) identifying and summarizing the common patterns of variability of the *m* variables in a smaller number of independent dimensions, *r*, that additively reproduce this common variance; and (2) examining the patterns of scores of each of the *n* observational units on each of the *r* dimensions. The dimensions isolated are an objective outcome of the analysis. *Interpretation of the dimensions (factors) depends on the nature of the variables used in the analysis and the body of concept or theory that is brought to bear.* Theory provides the investigator with a set of expectations regarding the factor structure which can be compared to the actual set of factors produced (Berry and Kasarda 1977, p. 123).

Like SAA, factorial ecology seems clearly within the neoclassical ecological paradigm. There is an almost total reliance on aggregate population variables, and the goal is often to plot the spatial patterning of urban phenomena. The previously mentioned factor analysis tests of SAA (Bell 1955; Van Arsdol et al. 1958), for example, fit this pattern, as do most other factorial ecology studies.

Factorial ecology is a rapidly growing and complex field. It is currently moving in several directions, many of them cross-cultural, but a brief summary of some of the findings most relevant to the community follows:

1. *Approximately five factors underly the ecological structure of American communities.* The results of factor analysis depend on the statistical techniques used, the variables employed, and the unit of analysis. Still, such studies of the ecological structures of American communities have been remarkably consistent in their findings. Reviews of factorial ecology in the United States (Bonjean 1971; Rees 1971; Hamm 1982) conclude generally that American communities vary along five dimensions: (1) socioeconomic status, (2) family status, (3) ethnicity, (4) residential mobility, and (5) population and functional size. In other words, these five factors account for much of the variation or differentiation in American communities. If an analyst wishes to understand why one community or neighborhood is different from another, differences in these five factors should be prime reasons.

2. *Some of these factors are distributed in the community in systematic patterns.* Specifically, the family status dimension is distributed in the Burgess concentric zone pattern; economic status follows sectors radiating from the CBD à la Hoyt; and population growth and racial and ethnic groups tend to cluster around multiple nuclei like those described by Harris and Ullman (Anderson and Egeland 1961; Pedersen 1967; Salins 1971). If city structure and growth were determined entirely by family status, then those families with the fewest children would be near the CBD in order to be near work and the cultural advantages of the central city. Families with more children

would locate in outer zones. If economic status were the only factor, all classes would move out from the CBD in sectors. And if race were the only factor, cities would be segregated into racial and ethnic neighborhoods. Of course, all three factors operate in most cities, producing land-use patterns more complex than any of these models can describe individually (Berry and Rees 1969).

3. *Industrialization appears to account for much of the ecological structure of communities.* In much the way the typological approach stressed the role of the industrial revolution in accounting for movement toward social characteristics of *Gesellschaft,* cross-cultural factorial ecology stressed the ecological differences between cities in preindustrial and industrial cities (Abu-Lughod 1971; Moser and Scott 1961; King 1966; Fisher 1966; Berry and Rees 1969; Ahmad 1965; Mabogunge 1965; McNulty 1969).

In SAA–factorial ecology, we find a body of research that shares with the neo-orthodox ecologists a focus on aggregate, urban data. Further, the focus on spatial patterning is probably closer to the classical ecologists than the neo-orthodox position (with its emphasis on adaptation). Thus, in neo-orthodox ecology and SAA–factorial ecology, if not in sociocultural ecology, we find the classic human ecology of Robert Park still influential. It is more empirical now, less theoretical, but the ecological perspective still represents a distinctive approach to the community. The distinctiveness and applicability of the ecological approach are illustrated in the following section with an analysis of suburbanization.

SUBURBANIZATION: AN APPLICATION OF THE ECOLOGICAL APPROACH

One of the most important changes in the spatial patterns of American cities in the last half of this century has been the rapid growth of the urban fringes. Actually, suburban growth was occurring throughout the first half of this century. However, at that time, suburbanization was simply one of several growth patterns affecting the city. Burgess' classic concentric zone model, for example, gave growth in the outlying suburban zone no more attention than growth in the other zones. It was not until the 1950s that the suburbs became virtually the *only* area of substantial metropolitan growth. And, accordingly, since that time, studies of suburbanization have increasingly occupied the efforts of urban ecologists. In fact, a recent text on urban ecology argues that suburbanization "has become the dominant feature of America's changing population distribution" (Berry and Kasarda 1977). Thus, a substantial body of ecological research has developed in an effort to better understand suburbanization. In the following overview of that research, we will learn more about the causes, characteristics, and consequences of suburbanization and simultaneously be exposed to examples of modern ecological approaches to an important urban community phenomenon.[8]

Defining Suburbanization

The basic ecological definition of a *suburb* is derived from the U.S. census and includes all areas that are: (1) within either the Metropolitan Statistical Area (MSA) or the more narrowly defined urbanized area, and (2) outside the central city. If suburbs are defined by MSA, more than ninety-eight million Americans lived in suburbs in 1980; by urbanized area, there are sixty-seven million American suburbanites. The urbanized area is clearly the more precise measure of the degree of suburbanization, but the MSA is more widely employed because it can be compared over time. In either case, American suburbs possess a very large, rapidly growing population.

Suburbanization, in turn, is defined as the general process through which an urban population spreads over an increasingly wider expanse of territory, typically expanding beyond the municipal boundaries of the central city. Within the general process of suburbanization are the more specific processes of *decentralization*—the suburban ring growing faster than the central city—and *deconcentration*—declining population density in the central city. Decentralization has been a continuing process throughout this century, while deconcentration is a post-World War II phenomenon.

The Process of Suburbanization: The POET Framework

Earlier in this chapter, Duncan's ecological complex was introduced as a framework for much of the current effort in urban ecology. As an example of how the POET variables can be used to explain ecological phenomena, the interrelationship among population, organization, environment, and technology will be used to explain the rapid increase in suburbanization (especially deconcentration) in the post-World War II period.

Population underwent a massive demographic transformation with

---

[8] The ecological approach is not the only way to study suburbanization, but it has produced more research on the subject than any other approach. The typological approach (Chapter 2) can explain much of the motivation for suburban growth, i.e., a desire to recapture the *Gemeinschaft*-like lifestyle in the suburb. Similarly, the lifestyles within the suburbs have been studied with a more holistic, ethnographic approach (Chapter 14).

the arrival of the "postwar baby boom." Between 1945 and 1958 an unprecedented demand for family housing developed. And since little residential development had occurred during World War II and the preceding depression, the United States faced a critical housing shortage.

In other words, the urban *environment* of 1950 predisposed movement toward suburbanization. Central city housing was old and often lacking in the space and modern conveniences desired by the postwar families. Also, the high density levels in many central cities made new residential developments prohibitively expensive in those locations.

The housing shortage was met through a change in *organization.* While it might have been possible to have constructed new residential areas in the deteriorating central cities, urban renewal programs began to demolish urban housing and replace it with commercial and other nonresidential structures.[9] And while urban renewal was reducing the number of central city housing units, the Federal Housing Authority and Veterans' Administration were subsidizing the costs of new suburban houses. The result was America's first significant deconcentration of urban population.

Changes in *technology* also played a key role in suburbanization. The "baby boom" years witnessed an almost 400 percent increase in the number of motor vehicles registered in the United States. Without such an increase in individual transportation, the deconcentration of urban population would have been impossible (Tobin 1976). Of course, these new automobiles and new suburban homes were expensive, even if the loans were often subsidized. Without the industrial technology that led to the increased productivity and higher per capita income of the 1950s, the suburbanization process could not have been financed.

The result, then, was a fundamental restructuring of an urban environment into a *metropolitan* environment. Old urban housing was either allowed to deteriorate or was demolished, and an exodus to new, mass-produced suburbs began. Figure 3–4 illustrates the ecological relationships necessary to this transformation.

Of course, suburbanization resulted in changes that went far beyond new spatial patterns. There were also accompanying changes in population. Not everyone was equally likely to move to the suburbs.

---

[9] In fact, Domhoff (1978) argues that there was initially a national plan for urban renewal supported by a liberal-labor coalition that would have emphasized building new housing in the central city. However, it was defeated in favor of a business-backed plan aimed at increasing downtown property values. Domhoff explains this decision from a conflict perspective; ecologists would emphasize, rather, the lower property costs in the suburban fringe.

FIGURE 3–4   The ecological complex and suburbanization

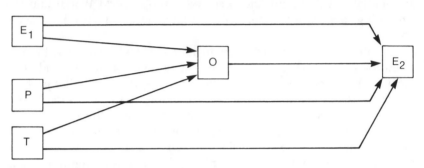

E_1-Urban <u>environment</u> (high density, inadequate housing)
P -<u>Population</u> (post-war "baby boom")
T -<u>Technology</u> (mass production of autombile,
              high industrial technology)
O -<u>Organization</u> (FHA and VA loans)
E_2-Metropolitan <u>environment</u> (decentralizing central city,
              rapid growth in suburbs)

The Characteristics of the Suburban Population

What kind of people moved to the suburbs? Where did they move from? How were they different from their central city counterparts? These questions have been the driving ones for ecological analysis of suburban populations, and their answers will allow an evaluation of the stereotypic view of suburbs being populated by homogeneous white, middle-class families who have moved from the central city in search of a more family-related lifestyle.

Much of the suburban stereotype is supported from a demographic breakdown of central city and suburban populations. Central cities, on the whole, lost white families of child-bearing age to the suburban ring. Further, the socioeconomic status of suburban residents is considerably higher than that of central city residents. However, the fact that suburban populations are different from central city populations does not necessarily mean that suburban populations are homogeneous. They are remarkably heterogeneous and becoming even more so.[10]

In fact, ecologists typically divide the suburbs themselves by type as a partial reflection of their population heterogeneity. Although the typologies can be elaborate (Boskoff 1970), the most basic distinction is between *employing* and *residential* suburbs (Schnore 1957, 1965). There

---

[10] The continuing work of John Logan and Mark Schneider (e.g., Logan and Schneider 1981, 1984; Schneider and Logan 1985) clearly illustrates the diversity of American suburbs.

are sophisticated demographic measures that allow precise description of any suburb (Schwirian 1977), but of most general interest is the finding that residential suburbs are the ones that best fit the typical suburban stereotype described above. Employing suburbs (places like Euclid, Ohio, or Pasadena, Texas) are larger, have significant amounts of industry, more racial and social class variation, and less "familism" (Long and Glick 1976). Of course, when ecologists measure "familism," they use indicators such as "percent married," "fertility ratio," "percent of population under eighteen years of age," and so on. Whether or not the suburban lifestyle actually is based on family-related values requires more direct measures. And we will return to the suburban lifestyle in Chapter 14 on holistic community research. For now, however, we will consider one final dimension of the suburbanization process—the political and economic ramifications.

Suburban/Central City Relationships: Symbiosis or Exploitation?

There are varying views on the effect a large and growing suburban population has on the public services provided by central city governments.

It may be symbiotic. There are some (although a minority) who maintain that the relationship is mutually beneficial or, in the vocabulary of human ecology, symbiotic. They believe that the central city and the suburb complement each other. J. C. Weicher (1972), for example, explains that the movement of manufacturing and industry to the suburbs helps to reduce the number of services demanded of the central city government and that sales taxes balance any initial financial advantages the suburbs might appear to enjoy.

Charles Tiebout (1972) argues that the political fragmentation that accompanies suburbanization is efficient because it provides a large number of local political entities, each with a unique set of private and public goods. Thus, citizens are free to maximize their own personal preferences through choice of residential location. Robert Dahl (1972) makes a similar argument when he maintains that the fragmentation results in a multiplicity of political areas, so that if groups fail to succeed in one area, they are able to try again in others. Further, Dahl maintains that this diffusion of local power provides checks and balances, increases individual freedom, and provides a wider option in policy choices.

It's probably parasitic. Still, a more common view is that the central city/suburb relationship is exploitive or, in more ecological jargon, parasitic. The position here is that suburban residents consume many of the central city's services but escape the costs of providing them.

Kenneth Newton (1975) argues that suburbanization allows the middle class to "shut out nonmiddle-class problems, and hence minimize the cost to the middle class taxpayer of solving these problems" Of course, the nonmiddle-class problems still exist, but the central city residents are the ones who must pay for their solution.

Two ecologists, Brian J. L. Berry and John Kasarda (1977), expand on this idea by showing that not only do suburban residents "exploit central cities . . . by not bearing their fair share of the welfare costs," suburbanites also increase the demand for central city services such as libraries, parks, zoos, museums, and other public facilities:

> As metropolitan areas continue to expand, an increasing number of suburban residents make routine use of central-city services and facilities. The additional activity in the central city created by suburban residents has also been reflected in the operating expenditures of central-city governments. Hence, *per capita expenditures for central-city services have been found to be at least as sensitive to the size of the suburban population as the size of the central-city population itself* (Berry and Kasarda 1977, p. 225).

The data analyses Berry and Kasarda marshall in support of a case for suburbanites exploiting central-city dwellers are impressive, and most students of metropolitan development would agree that certain elements of the suburban/central city relationship are inherently exploitive. This does not mean, however, that any major restructuring of this relationship is forthcoming. In fact, a recent extension of Berry and Kasarda's work by Jeffrey Slovak (1985) concludes that the exploitation of the central cities by the suburbs is greater now than when Berry and Kasarda's data were gathered.

Regardless, it's not going to change. The most widely advocated solution to this problem is metropolitan consolidation, i.e., combining the politically autonomous suburban units with the central city and forming a metropolitan-wide government. While this is certainly an equitable solution, it is also an impractical one. Too many vested interests support suburban fragmentation. Suburban residents will naturally want to maintain this system, and central city residents (especially black residents, who for the first time are assuming numerous positions of municipal power) feel they might lose their influence in a metropolitan government. There are other barriers to consolidation. Oliver Williams, Harold Herman, Charles Liebman, and Thomas Dye (1965) explain that what initially appears to be a step toward consolidation—single-purpose metropolitan agencies—is in reality the creation of another force against consolidation. The single-purpose districts, by providing those services most easily consolidated and integrated (water supply, mass transit), reduce the need to completely recombine the city and suburbs for other services. The point being that except for a handful of American communities (most notably Miami and Nashville, which have consolidated metropolitan governments), the complexity and inequality of multiple governments within a single urban area will continue. And the reasons for the continuation will lie at least as much with cultural values about family, race relations, and politics as with efficient land use.

Chapter Four

The Community as a Social System

The third major approach to the community employs a systems theory perspective. Since systems theory, unlike the typological and ecological approaches, is not usually associated with community analysis, it is necessary to provide an overview of general systems theory before making specific reference to community applications.

GENERAL SYSTEMS THEORY

The term *social system* is extremely broad, and general systems theory can take many forms, depending on the predisposition of the systems theorist. Nevertheless, it is possible to sketch an outline of systems theory by referring to some of its basic concepts. It must be remembered, however, that these concepts will have somewhat different meanings for different theorists.

The Social System

The concept of a social system is based on the idea of a structured, socially significant set of relationships between two or more units. Talcott Parsons (1951, pp. 5–6), the foremost system theorist in American sociology, defines the social system as a "plurality of individual actors interacting with each other in a situation which has at least a physical or environmental aspect, actors who are motivated in terms of a tendency to the 'optimization of gratification' and whose relation to their situations, including each other, is defined and mediated in terms of a system of culturally structured and shared symbols." Thus, a social system could be a family, a football team, a multinational corporation, a university, or even a community. Parsons, however, devel-

oped his systems theory with applications to small groups, large organizations and entire societies; the community was notably absent.
Even Charles Loomis, whose community research was discussed in
Chapter 2, ignored community applications in his book *Social Systems*
(1960). One reason for the exclusion of the community was that systems theory developed during the same time period that the idea of
America as a mass society was rising to ascendency, but as we examine
some of the major dimensions of systems theory, another reason will
become evident: The community is a unique social phenomenon with
characteristics particularly problematic for systems analysis.

Interaction and Systemic Linkage

A second look at Parsons's definition will show that social systems are
essentially networks of interaction. In systems theory, there is interaction both within and among social systems. Individuals may interact
within their family system, and in turn the family, as a system, may
interact with a religious system by worshiping at church. Analysis of
the types, bases, and structures of systems interactions constitutes
most of the applications of systems theory.

The concept of interaction is difficult to apply at the community
level. The individuals in a community system do not interact with all
the other individuals in the community. There are too many individuals for that much face-to-face interaction. Rather, the idea of "systemic linkage" is typically used to explain community interaction. In
the formal language of systems theory, *systemic linkage* refers to "a
process whereby one or more elements of at least two social systems is
articulated in such a manner that the two systems in some ways and on
some occasions may be viewed as a single unit" (Loomis 1960, p. 32).
In the case of the community, then, we have a system linked both to
microsystems such as individuals, families, and institutions and to
macrosystems, usually the larger national society.

Boundary Maintenance

Although social systems are interrelated, each system is also distinct. A
system can endure only as long as it can encourage cohesiveness and
loyalty among its member units. Loomis (1960, p. 31) defines *boundary
maintenance* as "the process whereby the identity of the social system is
preserved and the characteristic interaction pattern maintained."
Loomis (1960, p. 32) provides several examples of boundary maintenance:

> They may be primarily physical, as political boundaries, prison walls,
> zoning restrictions, or prescribed use or nonuse of facilities; or they may

be primarily social, as are the life styles of social classes or the preference for endogamy. They may be spontaneously or unconsciously applied, as in the family display of company manners; or they may be planned and rationally applied, as in the travel restrictions imposed extensively by totalitarian states and less extensively by democratic societies. They may be expressed in group contraction as in casting out deviants; or they may be reflected in group expansion, as in the uniting of parallel labor unions, as similar groups find boundary maintenance facilitated by joint effort.

Notice that none of these examples specifically includes the community. Such an exclusion is understandable because the boundaries are difficult to define. Roland Warren (1978, p. 156) refers to St. Augustine's definition of God when trying to establish the boundaries of community: "an infinite circle whose center is everywhere and whose periphery is nowhere." Communities do have boundaries, sometimes geographic, sometimes psychological, sometimes social, but the imprecise nature of these boundaries makes systems theory difficult to apply. Nevertheless, systems theory can be applied to the community, despite the inherent difficulties.

APPLICATIONS OF SYSTEMS THEORY TO THE COMMUNITY

Typically, systems theory is described as having a great potential as an approach to the community, but to date, systems theory has provided only three significant contributions to our understanding of the community: (1) the interactional field, (2) macrosystem dominance, and (3) horizontal and vertical patterns.

Community as an Interactional Field

The concept of the community as an interactional field within which various forms of interaction take place emphasizes the social rather than physical elements of community. Harold Kaufman has pioneered this approach. "The interactional field," writes Kaufman (1959, p. 10), "probably has several dimensions, the limits and interrelations of which need to be determined. The community field is not a Mother Hubbard which contains a number of other fields, but rather is to be seen as only one of several interactional units in a local society." The community, then, is not a geographic place where all local interactions occur. It is a more narrow concept that refers only to community-related actions.

Community-related actions. What constitutes community-related actions? The answer is not clear, but according to Willis Sutton, Jr., and Jiri Kolaja (1960), it depends on the relative amount of "communityness" they possess. Communityness depends on the degree to which: (1) an activity is locality related; (2) the actors are identified with a locality; and (3) local people participate in an activity. For example, a local bond election or fluoridation decision would rank high on communityness, but an increase of postal rates at the local U. S. Postal Service office would rank much lower. With this perspective of community, then, the focus is exclusively on those interactive fields "through which actions expressing a broad range of local activities are coordinated" (Wilkinson 1972, p. 44).

The interactive field approach has proven to be particularly effective in applying a more social-psychological, individualistic view of the community. In contrast to the aggregates of the ecological approach, individual values, motivations, and actions are important to the field theorists. Note, as an example, Norton Long's (1958, p. 254) reference to individuals in his analysis of community game playing:

> Individuals may play in a number of games, but, for the most part, their major preoccupation is with one, and their sense of major achievement is through success in one. Transfer from one game to another is, of course, possible, and the simultaneous playing of roles in two or more games is an important manner of linking separate games.
>
> Sharing a common territorial field and collaborating for different and particular ends in the achievement of overall social functions, the players in one game make use of the players in another and are, in turn, made use of by them. Thus the banker makes use of the newspaperman, the politician, the contractor, the ecclesiastic, the labor leader, the civic leader—all to further his success in the banking game—but, reciprocally, he is used to further the others' success in the newspaper, political, contracting, ecclesiastical, labor, and civic games. Each is a piece in the chess game of the other, sometimes a willing piece, but, to the extent that the games are different, with a different end in view.

When the community is viewed as an interactional field, there is an emphasis on *people* as individual actors that provides an important counterbalance to the aggregate, territorial analysis of the urban ecologists.

The nonterritorial community. This focus on the individual (and corresponding dismissal of territorial space) has produced a special nonterritorial view of the community. For example, Israel Rubin (1969) sees a community as those interactive links that bind the individual to the larger society. These links are typically found in religious groups, occupational roles, and ethnic identifications, and thus the locality is relatively unimportant:

> The territorial view of community is probably responsible for most of the fuzzy theorization that we have discussed above. For example, the romantic theme that modern man has "lost" his community is fed by the

common observation that the neighborhoods, towns, and cities have ceased to serve as significant foci of identification for the mobile man of industrial society. However, from our vantage point we see no reason for saddling the concept with the territorial element. Individuals may meaningfully relate to their respective societies through nonterritorial as well as through territorial substructures (Rubin 1969, p. 115).

The community, then, when it becomes an interactional field, ceases to necessarily be a place. It is, rather, the setting in which individuals link themselves to the larger mass society.

Network analysis. The interactional field's emphasis on individual interactions and the resulting conception of a nonterritorial community provide the basis for much of the current work in network analysis. Network analysis is an interactive systems "perspective which focuses on structured relationships between individuals and collectives" (Wellman and Leighton 1979). By precisely measuring and mapping the interactions between individuals (which is what network analysis does), it is possible to test Rubin's hypothesis about nonterritorial communities. If the most common and significant personal interactions occur between people within the same geographic area, then Rubin is wrong. If however, most of the interactions occur with people who do not live in the same area, then a nonterritorial community does exist.

Network analysis of residents in several urban neighborhoods has documented the existence of both territorial and nonterritorial communities (Laumann 1973; Wellman and Leighton 1979; Fischer 1982). Territorial communities are typically built around local kinship structures and/or workplace propinquity. Nonterritorial communities extend out to distant parents, friends, co-workers, and so on. Thus, personal interactions can either link a person to the local territorial community or to the larger nonterritorial society.

In addition to the systemic linkage between the individual and society, the influence of society's macrosystems is an important part of the systems theory approach to community. And this idea of the community as a locality-based subsystem nested within the larger society-wide macrosystem is explored next.

Roland L. Warren: Macrosystem Dominance and the "Great Change"

Roland L. Warren has made significant contributions to community theory, most of it within the framework of systems theory. The basis for Warren's analysis is the macrosystem dominance of community subsystems that result in what Warren calls "the great change."

The great change. The change, Warren (1978, p. 52) explains, "includes the increasing orientation of local community units toward extracommunity systems of which they are a part, with a corresponding decline in community cohesion and autonomy." In an extensive and insightful extension of Tönnies's *Gemeinschaft* and *Gesellschaft*, Warren traces the "great change" through seven developments in society-community relations: (1) the increasing division of labor and the breakdown of mechanical solidarity à la Durkheim; (2) growing differentiation of interests and associations; (3) increasing systemic relationships to the larger society via Durkheim's organic solidarity; (4) more bureaucratization and impersonalization à la Weber; (5) the transfer of functions to profit enterprise and government, functions traditionally allocated to families and local ad hoc groupings; (6) urbanization and subsequent suburbanization; and (7) changing values, such as the gradual acceptance of governmental activity in traditionally private concerns, the shift from moral to causal interpretations of human behavior, and a change in emphasis from the "Protestant Ethic" of work and production to enjoyment and consumption. The cumulative effect of these seven changes is to create a new kind of American community almost totally dependent on the larger mass society.

Macrosystem dominance. The community becomes a reflection of the larger society, or in Warren's terms, "a node of the macro system." Thus, one finds similar land use, values, and behaviors in all American communities:

> To be sure, there are differences among communities in values, norms, dominant interests, styles, and other cultural aspects. But again, if one is to watch the *public behavior* of people on a busy street corner, or at the supermarket, or in their homes, or at athletic events, one would be hard put to it to know that one is in Pittsburgh rather than St. Louis, in Bridgeport rather than in Rockland, in Atlanta rather than in Denver. Surely, the thought systems, the ideational and behavioral patterns indigenous to the locality are important, but an observer from Mars would be struck by their overwhelming similarity as one moves across the country, indicating once more that they may best be considered local enactments or implementations of thought and behavior systems of the national culture. (Warren 1978, p. 429).

There are two inferences that can be drawn from the dominance of the macrosystem. One is that a research focus on the community is clearly misplaced. For example, Brian Taylor (1975) argues that community studies that analyze local systems typically miss the prime cause of the social problems they encounter:

> To begin with, so far as problems have been examined at all, the use of a *locality framework* has tended to restrict attention to problems within the

settlement-area, and thus either to miss some problems altogether or to ignore their true locations, which in many cases are in social systems which extend beyond the village, parish, slum, suburb or town itself, in the context of the wider society.

The causes of crime, poverty, pollution, and other community problems lie not so much with the characteristics of the local subsystem as with the society's macrosystem. The state of the national economy, for example, will be reflected in local unemployment rates. In terms similar to those used for the mass society, the macrosystem is the prime mover. Causes and cures for social problems will be found at the national, not the local, level. Thus, one implication of macrosystem dominance is that community studies are no longer justified.

Warren (1978, p. 442), however, reaches a different conclusion about macrosystem dominance and the role of community studies:

> There must be some broad area of middle ground for investigation between the incurably romantic conception of community as a focal point of virtually all meaningful social activity and the equally remote conception of a territorially undifferentiated mass society in which people's relation to the macrosystem is utterly independent of their geographic location. For in this admittedly difficult theoretical area lie numerous questions not only of theory, ideology, and social policy but also of focal issues around which people are increasingly involved. Many people want locality to be made more, not less, relevant to the administration of the police, to the operation of the schools, to the ownership and operation of business enterprise, to the operation of the sanitation department, the health department, the social agencies, the location of highways, transit systems, and on and on through some of the most hotly contested issues of the day. Like Mark Twain's comment about the fallacious report of his own death, the death of the community has been highly exaggerated. Transformed, si'—muerto, no!
>
> The theoretical task, and also the practical one, is to determine with greater depth of analysis those areas—many of the critical issues of our time—where the local organization of social life is an integral component of the social problem.

Yes, but how is this transformed community to be studied? How does one reach the "middle ground" where the role of the community in the macrosystem can be analyzed? Warren's answer—the conceptualization of horizontal and vertical patterns—provides one of the major contributions of systems theory to community.

The horizontal and vertical pattern of systemic linkage. According to Warren (1978, p. 243), a community's vertical pattern is "the structural and functional relation of its various social units and subsystems to extracommunity systems." The great change greatly strengthened the vertical pattern. The horizontal pattern is "the structural and functional relation of the community's various social units and subsystems to each other." And after the great change, the existence of a significant community system depends upon the strength of its horizontal pattern. In other words, the local units within the community are now so closely linked (vertically) with extracommunity systems that the question of whether the community remains a significant social system depends largely upon the degree of linkage (horizontally) among the various local units.

Warren's analysis of "locality-relevant functions" can illustrate the distinction between the vertical and horizontal patterns. He specifies five functions (production-distribution-consumption, socialization, social control, social participation, and mutual support), their typical community unit, and their typical horizontal and vertical patterns.

Production-distribution-consumption will be used as an example. It is an economic function that is at least partially locality-relevant.

Major locality-relevant function	Typical community unit	Typical unit of horizontal pattern	Typical superior unit of vertical pattern
Production-distribution-consumption	Company	Chamber of Commerce	National corporation

The company in this example is linked to two systems: the extra-community national corporation and the community-based Chamber of Commerce. When production quotas are changed, workers are hired or fired, or wage scales are modified, the vertical pattern is in evidence. These events will have significant effects on the community, but their impetus is extracommunity. Typically, they are results of decisions made by the national corporation or by the local company in consultation with the national corporation. Since the great change, more local companies are controlled by corporations headquartered elsewhere.

This is far removed from the locally owned factories of the X family in Middletown that we examined in Chapter 1, and, in fact, today the X family no longer owns those factories. They are, rather, owned by a conglomerate based in Chicago. Even the local workers will now be affiliated with national unions based outside the community. Note, as an example, how Warner and Low (1947, p. 108) describe the strengthening of the vertical patterns in their classic holistic study of Yankee City:

> Two fundamental changes have been occurring concomitantly, in recent years, in the social organization of Yankee City shoe factories. The

first is the expansion of the hierarchy upward, out of Yankee City, through the expansion of individual enterprises and the establishment by them of central offices in distant large cities. The second is the expansion of the structure outward from Yankee City through the growth of manufacturers' associations and labor unions, also with headquarters outside Yankee City and with units in many other shoemaking communities in New England and elsewhere. Both . . . decrease Yankee City's control over its shoe factories by subjecting the factories, or segments of them, to more and more control exerted from outside Yankee City.

In short, the great change has significantly strengthened the vertical patterns of systemic linkage for locality-based economic functions, but what of the horizontal patterns?

The great change has not strengthened the horizontal patterns to the degree it has the vertical patterns. Still, horizontal patterns continue. In Warren's example, the company's membership in the local Chamber of Commerce would be a link between it and other units in the community. Thus, chamber-sponsored programs such as a local Better Business Bureau or a merchants-supported promotion of "Founders' Day" would be evidence of horizontal patterns within locality-based economic functions. A complete analysis of the systems related to the community economy, then, would require studying both vertical and horizontal patterns.

Figure 4–1 shows all five locality-based functions and Warren's examples of horizontal and vertical patterns. In each case, the great

FIGURE 4-1   Schematic analysis of major locality-relevant functions

Major locality-relevant function	Typical community unit	Typical unit of horizontal pattern	Typical superior unit of vertical pattern
Production-distribution-consumption	Company	Chamber of Commerce	National corporation
Socialization	Public school	Board of Education	State Department of Education
Social control	Municipal Government	City Council	State government
Social participation	Church	Council of churches	Denominational body
Mutual support	Voluntary health association	Community welfare council	National health association

Source: Warren 1978: Figure 6–1.

change has strengthened the vertical pattern of systemic linkage. And, it would appear that in some cases the vertical pattern has become considerably more important than its horizontal counterpart.

Warren's systems theory approach has emphasized the growing dominance of the macrosystem (the *Gesellschaft*-like mass society) on the local subsystems, but he has also provided a conceptual tool (the horizontal pattern) for discovering and perhaps strengthening the local subsystem (the *Gemeinschaft*-like community). Thus, it is Roland L. Warren who has made some of the most significant demonstrations of the applicability of systems theory to the community.

The Conflict Approach: Marx Finally Comes to the City

Systems theory, with its basis in inherently conservative structural functionalism, is often seen as the theoretical antithesis of conflict theory, with its basis in Marxist analysis. Yet, in one important characteristic they are similar: both are major social science paradigms with relatively limited relevance to the community. Marxists, much like system theorists, typically focus on nation-states, not the communities within them. Hence, just as with the preceding section on systems theory, we must first outline the major dimensions of the theory before turning to the local applications.

Considerable confusion can develop in discussing Marxism since the terms can refer to a political ideology, an economic system, an epistemological philosophy, or any combination of the three. And when these broad terms are often used interchangeably with neo-Marxism and the conflict approach, the lack of definitional precision expands geometrically.[1] For our purposes, however, *Marxist analysis* will refer to the classic statements of Marx and Engels. *Neo-Marxism* refers to positions developed by largely European social scientists in the 1960s and 1970s—positions built on Marx's principles of economically based class conflict. The *conflict approach* is the most inclusive, referring to Marxist and neo-Marxist approaches, as well as the non-Marxist analysis of conflict provided by American sociologists in the 1950s and 1960s. We will examine all three variations in this section, beginning with the most influential theories ever developed by social scientists.

---

[1] There are two other terms that can add to the definitional confusion here. Sometimes the approach examined in this chapter will be called either a political economy or structural approach.

CLASSIC STATEMENTS: MARX AND ENGELS

The nineteenth-century analysis of Karl Marx and Friedrich Engels set in motion debates and controversies in both academic and political spheres that continue unabated over a hundred years later. Although Marx's writings are typically (and correctly) given more consideration than those of his friend and collaborator, Engels, in terms of the community, the writings of both men are more equal. Engels, in fact, provided more examples of local analysis than Marx. Thus, we will examine Marx's writings for the theoretical underpinnings of this approach and then turn to Engels's works for the few existing local applications of classical Marxist analysis.

Karl Marx (1818–1883)

The German philosopher, economist, and sociologist Karl Marx[2] explained the movement toward *Gesellschaft* in terms of a change in the "means of production," in this case, a change from agricultural production based on the land to industrial production based on the factory. Further, this change in the means of production brought about a change in the ruling class—the owners of the means of production. Thus, while the structure of medieval Europe supported the class interests of the landed aristocracy, the emerging structure of industrial Europe would support the capitalist class, the new owners of the means of production. The industrial-based capitalists, the *bourgeoisie*, were the new ruling class. Since the bourgeoisie owned the means of production, the working class (the *proletariat*) was completely dependent upon them for jobs. Thus, the proletariat could be exploited through low wages and poor working conditions.

Marx, however, believed there were inherent, dialectical contradictions within industrial capitalism that would inevitably lead to its demise. Specifically, the desire for greater profits would lead to even greater exploitation, alienation, and degradation of the working class. At this point, a "class consciousness" would develop among the proletariat as they realized that their class interests were in opposition to the bourgeoisie. The proletariat would revolt and overthrow the bourgeoisie, which in turn would lead to a classless, workers' utopia:

> If the proletariat during its contact with the bourgeoisie is compelled by the force of circumstances to organize itself into a class; if by means of a revolution it makes itself into the ruling class and, as such, sweeps away by force the old conditions of production, then it will, along with these conditions, have swept away the conditions for the existence of class

---

[2] The most complete statement of Marx's ideas is in his classic treatise *Capital* (1867). For an outline of his views, see the *Communist Manifesto* (1848).

antagonisms and of classes generally, and will thereby have abolished its own supremacy as a class.

In place of the old bourgeois society, with its classes and class antagonisms, we shall have an association in which the free development of each is the condition for the free development of all (Marx and Engels 1848, *Manifesto of the Communist Party*, quoted from Feuer 1959).

Marx's analysis was almost exclusively on the macro level. The city was merely a place where the evils of capitalism are particularly visible (Saunders 1981). Engels also viewed the city as the site of capitalistic excesses, but, unlike Marx, he devoted much of his writings to a description and analysis of urban capitalism.

Friedrich Engels (1820–1895)

Engels, in his first major work, *The Condition of the Working Class in England in 1844* [1845], describes the *Gesellschaft*-like conditions of the city in terms that echo Simmel's "The Metropolis and Mental Life." Engels's analysis however, is much more critical. While Simmel finds increased freedom in the impersonal city, Engels finds only unnatural alienation:

> The very turmoil of the streets has something repulsive, something against which human nature rebels. The hundreds of thousands of all classes and all ranks crowding past each other, are they not all human beings with the same qualities and powers, and with the same interest in being happy? And have they not, in the end, to seek happiness in the same way, by the same means? And still they crowd by one another as though they had nothing in common, nothing to do with one another, and their only agreement is the tacit one, that each keep to his own side of the pavement, so as not to delay the opposing streams of the crowd, while it occurs to no man to honour another with so much as a glance. The brutal indifference, the unfeeling isolation of each in his private interest becomes the more repellent and offensive, the more these individuals are crowded together, within a limited space. And, however much one may be aware that this isolation of the individual, this narrow self-seeking is the fundamental principle of our society everywhere, it is nowhere so shamelessly barefaced, so self-conscious as just here in the crowding of the great city. The dissolution of mankind into monads, of which each one has a separate principle, the world of atoms, is here carried out to its utmost extremes (Engels 1958, pp. 30–31).

While capitalism creates the urban ills, it is unable to cure them. Neo-Marxists (e.g., Tabb and Sawers 1978) still refer to Engels's critique of what today would be called urban renewal, and the neo-Marxist solution to the problems of urban slums is still the same as Engels's:

The breeding places of disease, the infamous holes and cellars in which the capitalist mode of production confines our workers night after night, are not abolished; they are merely shifted elsewhere! The same economic necessity which produced them in the first place produces them in the next place also! As long as the capitalist mode of production continues to exist it is folly to hope for an isolated settlement of the housing question or of any other social question affecting the lot of the workers. The solution lies in the abolition of the capitalist mode of production (Engels 1969a, p. 75).

Still, the city represented more to Marx and Engels than simply an extreme example of capitalist exploitation. The city was to play a crucial role in bringing about the overthrow of the bourgeoisie. Marx and Engels, in the *Communist Manifesto* (1848) argued that the bourgeoisie had actually rendered a service to the proletariat by creating cities that have "rescued a considerable part of the population from the idiocy of rural life." Engels expanded on this idea in *The Condition of the Working Class* [1845]:

The great cities are the birthplaces of labour movements; in them the workers first began to reflect upon their own condition and to struggle against it; in them the opposition between proletariat and bourgeoisie first made itself manifest. . . . Without the great cities and their forcing influence upon the popular intelligence, the working class would be far less advanced than it is (Engels 1969a, p. 152).

In classical Marxism, then, there was an ambivalent view of the city. On the one hand, the city manifested the most extreme evils of capitalism; on the other hand, it provided the necessary conditions for the proletarian class consciousness that led to capitalism's destruction. In either case, however, it remained only a reflection of the larger, capitalistic society. The city is not the major focus of classic Marxist analysis.

NON-MARXIST CONFLICT APPROACHES

Until recently, conflict has not been a popular subject for American sociologists. We saw how neo-orthodox ecologists replaced competition with equilibrium. Similarly, systems theory, with its structural-functional underpinnings, tends to view conflict as an unnatural and negative phenomenon. Some of this reluctance to include conflict was due to the conservatism of the times and the linking of conflict with Marx and Marxism. Even when an elaborate theory such as Lewis Coser's *The Functions of Social Conflict* (1956), was built on conflict, it was based on Simmel rather than Marx. When examining the analysis of community conflict by American sociologists, then, it is not surprising that two major studies treat conflict as a somewhat negative phenomenon and make no reference to the works of Marx.

James S. Coleman: "Community Conflict"

James Coleman's most enduring contribution to community sociology is his analysis of local controversy. Coleman's monograph, *Community Conflict* (1957), gathers together reports of numerous local controversies and seeks out their commonalities to develop a general theory of community conflict. According to Coleman, conflict typically stems from three local sources: (1) *economic issues* such as bond elections or zoning, (2) *political disputes* such as elections or revising town charters, and (3) *value conflicts* reflected in controversies such as school integration. In some communities, disputes from these sources may rekindle dormant but deep-seated hostilities between local groups. In such cases, the disputes are more likely to produce controversy.

Although the sources of community conflict may differ, "once the controversies have begun, they resemble each other remarkably" (Coleman 1957, p. 9). The dynamics that transform an initial specific issue into a widespread community conflict do not vary by issue. Rather, as Figure 5-1 illustrates, there is a general sequence of events that pro-

FIGURE 5–1   Coleman's model of community conflict

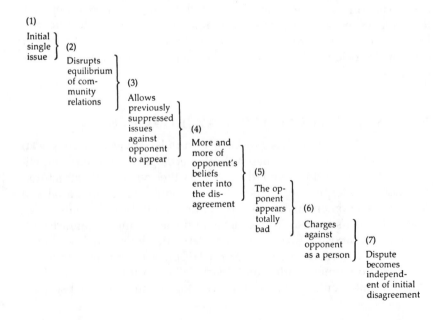

duces a dispute independent of the issue that leads to the initial disagreement.

The first step is when specific issues give way to general ones. For example, an attack on certain books in the school library might lead to a more general assault on educational policy (curricula, teaching methods). This is most likely to occur when the aforementioned latent hostilities exist in the community. At this point there is a shift from dispassionate *disagreement* to emotional *antagonism*. The hostility is characterized by personal slander and rumor.

As this antagonism develops, associations *within* the quarreling groups flourish while associations *between* the groups wither. New leaders, not governed by traditional norms of debate and compromise, emerge:

> As partisan organizations are formed and a real nucleus develops around each of the opposing centers, new leaders tend to take over the dispute; often they are men who have not been community leaders in the past, men who face none of the constraints of maintaining a previous community position, and feel none of the cross-pressures felt by members of community organizations. In addition, these leaders rarely have real identification with the community. In the literature they often emerge as marginal men who have never held a position of leadership before (Coleman 1957, quoted from Warren and Lyon 1983, p. 325).

At this point, the controversy is likely to develop into a major conflict. Various organizations and individuals begin to choose sides and word-of-mouth communication takes over:

> As the controversy proceeds, the formal media of communication—radio, television, and newspapers—become less and less able to tell people as much as they want to know about the controversy, or the kinds of things they want to know. These media are simply not flexible enough to fill the insatiable need for news which develops as people become more and more involved. At the same time, the media are restricted by normative and legal constraints against carrying the kind of rumor which abounds as controversy proceeds. Word-of-mouth communication gradually fills the gaps, both in volume and in content, left by the mass media. Street-corner discussion amplifies, elaborates, and usually distorts the news that it picks up from the papers or the radio. This interpersonal communication offers no restraints against slander and personal charges; rather, it helps make the rhetoric of controversy consistent with the intensity (Coleman 1957, quoted from Warren and Lyon 1983, p. 327).

In short, the developments described by Coleman conform to what he calls Gresham's Law of Conflict. Those who advocate community conflict win out over those who would maintain order:

> The harmful and dangerous elements drive out those which would keep the conflict within bounds. Reckless, unrestrained leaders head the attack; combat organizations arise to replace the milder, more constrained preexisting organizations; derogatory and scurrilous charges replace

dispassionate issues; antagonism replaces disagreement; and a drive to ruin the opponent takes the place of the initial will to win. In other words, all the forces put into effect by the initiation of conflict act to drive out the conciliatory elements and replace them with those better equipped for combat (Coleman 1957, quoted from Warren and Lyon 1983, p. 329).

In spite of his generally negative views of community conflict, Coleman does not offer much in the way of conflict control and resolution. He does emphasize that since the events leading to community conflict are mutually reinforcing, it is best to break the cycle early in the process. If traditional community leaders take an early and united stand against the dissident groups, the conflict can be diverted into normal, nonthreatening channels. As an example, Coleman shows how an attack on some of the public school's library books in Scarsdale, New York, was deflected when eighty-one local leaders published a statement of support for the school on the front page of the local newspaper. However, the wrong kind of initial response can intensify the conflict. Coleman believes that race riots, for example, are likely to develop when the police display an antagonistic attitude toward blacks but do not take sufficiently forceful action to quell the initial rioting.

William A. Gamson: The Causes of "Rancorous" Conflict

Most of Coleman's analysis was directed toward the dynamics of community conflict, with little concern paid to *which* communities are the most likely to experience conflict. William Gamson, however, made the likelihood of "rancorous" community conflict the focus of his research.

Gamson (1966) studied fifty-four issues in eighteen New England communities to learn why some communities would experience "rancorous conflicts" characterized by actions that are " 'dirty,' 'underhanded,' 'vicious' and so forth," while other communities experienced more "conventional conflicts" where "established means of political expression are used." Using elite interviews and available data sources, Gamson labeled each community as either one characterized by rancorous or conventional conflict.

Gamson (1966, p. 78) discovered a strong relationship between rancorous conflict and political instability, finding that "only one of the conventional towns is undergoing political change while two-thirds of the rancorous towns are undergoing such change." Further, Gamson (1966, p. 79) found that "the average degree of acquaintance among opponents is substantially lower in rancorous than in conventional towns." Thus, he concludes that: (1) shifts in political control produce a structural strain toward rancorous conflict, and (2) a lack of community integration (few opponents are acquainted with one another) can also lead to more rancorous conflicts.

Finally, in what was a rather remarkable observation for the times, Gamson (1966, p. 81) noted that rancorous towns were not all bad. In fact, the conventional towns were often boring:

> Because of the negative connotations of a term like "rancorous conflict," some final observations about the towns studied here are worth making. Many of the conventional communities are rather dull and stagnant, while some of the rancorous ones are among the most vital. Some of the conventional towns not only have an absence of rancorous conflict but a general absence of change; the rancorous towns have the strains that accompany change but some of them also have the advantages of stimulation and growth. The absence of rancorous conflict is no necessary sign of an ideal community.

This is a surprising conclusion for the conservative times in which it was made, but it is still a long and radical step to the European neo-Marxists who were beginning to turn their attention to the urban community.

NEO-MARXIST CONFLICT APPROACHES

Until recently, neo-Marxists followed in the tradition of their founder and focused almost exclusively on the nation-state. In the late 1960s, however, several Marxist perspectives on urban phenomena suddenly appeared. Why? Two American neo-Marxists, William Tabb and Larry Sawers (1978, pp. 4–5), offer this explanation:

> One may ask why suddenly in the 1960s and 1970s have so many Marxists begun studying cities and so many urbanologists turned to Marx. Indeed, why did not Marxists pay attention to urban problems before the 1960s? Marx's followers prior to the last decade or so have tended to focus on the core relations of capitalism. While cities were often considered to be the site of class struggle, the space itself hardly seemed important or worthy of special study. . . . This changed in the 1960s. The middle-class exodus from the cities and consequent loss of the tax base, the civil-rights movement, and the urban conflagrations all drew attention to the cities. Struggles over urban space intensified as community groups fought for their homes against highways and urban renewal. Many came to see these struggles over "turf" as forms of class struggle. . . . As the antiwar movement drew to its successful conclusion in the early 1970s, many radicals redirected their attention away from imperialism and to urban problems. By the mid-1970s, the left-right punch of inflation and unemployment had brought several cities to the point of fiscal disaster and pushed many others close to the brink. Marxists, therefore, could no longer ignore the urban crisis, and Marxist urbanology blossomed.

Still, the initial neo-Marxist approaches to community were almost exclusively a European phenomenon. Marxist analysis has always had a larger following in Europe than in the United States, and even today variations in Marxist theory are typically European in origin. So, it is with a Spanish sociologist that we begin our examination of neo-Marxist conflict approaches.

Manuel Castells: From "The Urban Question" to "The Grassroots"

Castells's conflict approach to the community is most fully developed in his book *The Urban Question* (originally published in 1972 and translated into English in 1977). Like most Marxists, he begins the book by characterizing all non-Marxist approaches as "ideological." By ideological, he means that they are not scientific, but rather are "giving the reassuring impression of an integrated society, united in facing up to common problems" (Castells 1977, p. 85). Hence, the typological approach and urban ecology are rejected along with community power studies and urban planning as ideological justifications of the status quo. However, Castells goes even further and dismisses other neo-Marxian approaches as ideological as well.[3] It is Castells's position, apparently, that his is the only truly scientific approach to the city.

Castells's view of the city is based on the Marxist epistemology of Louis Althusser (1969, 1971). Althusser removes the usual primacy of economics in determining a political and cultural superstructure and replaces it with a complex system based equally on economic, political, and cultural functions. Castells applies this three-level system by arguing that the function of the urban system cannot be political because local political boundaries are arbitrary and local politics is typically subservient to national politics; and it cannot be cultural since cities share their culture with the rest of society. Thus, the function of the city is economic. More specifically, the economic function of the city is consumption rather than production. It is the place where the workers consume housing, food, leisure, and other goods and services in order to replenish their capacity for labor.

Further, it is in the city that the dialectical contradiction between production and consumption appears—a conflict between the need to produce at the highest possible level of profit and the need to reproduce labor power through local consumption. Individual capitalists will find little reason to invest in the consumption commodities necessary to replenish the work force. Thus, the quality of life of the workers deteriorates. It falls, then, to the state to maintain the capitalist system

---

[3] Especially interesting is Castells's (1977, Chapter 6) rejection of the Marxist-humanist analysis of Henri Lefebvre. Lefebvre (1976) develops a more individualistic interpretation of Marx similar to the works of David Harvey that are discussed in the following section. Castells is more structural than Lefebvre, and this apparently accounts for the rejection.

by constructing low-cost housing units, subsidizing food costs, maintaining social facilities, and so on. This is why, Castells argues, consumption had become increasingly political. The state, by creating a capitalist welfare system, protects the capitalists from their own excesses:

> The state apparatus not only exercises class domination, but also strives, as far as possible, to regulate, the crises of the system, in order to preserve it.
> It is in this sense that it may, sometimes, become reformist. Although reforms are always imposed by the class struggle and, therefore, from outside the state apparatus, they are no less real for that: their aim is to preserve and extend the existing context; thus consolidating the long-term interests of the dominant classes, even if it involves infringing their privileges to some extent in a particular conjuncture (Castells 1977, p. 208).

While state support of local consumption supports the system by replenishing the work force and reducing class conflict, it nonetheless generates a new set of contradictions. Since the state pays the increasing costs of replenishing labor power while the private capitalists reap the profits created by labor power, the state goes deeper into debt:

> In fact, the fiscal crisis of the inner cities was a particularly acute expression of the overall fiscal crisis of the state, that is, of the increasing budgetary gap created in public finance in advanced capitalist countries because of the historical process of socialization of costs and privatization of profits. The crisis is even more acute for the local governments of larger inner cities because they express the contradictory expansion of the 'service sector.' On the one hand, corporate capital needs to build directional centres which require concentration of service workers and public facilities downtown. On the other hand, if social order is to be maintained, the state has to absorb the surplus population and to provide welfare and public services to the larger unemployed and underemployed population concentrated in the inner cities (Castells 1977, p. 415).

The fiscal crisis of New York City in 1974–75 and its threatened bankruptcy are symptoms of these problems (Castells 1977, pp. 415–20).[4] One would further suppose that the growing national debt is another example of this contradiction.

As the level of state debt increases, there must eventually be a reduction of labor-replenishing commodities. New York, for example, scaled back its welfare benefits and municipal wages. Similarly, the national government in recent years has been reducing support for social programs. This reduction in the workers' quality of life may lead to "urban social movements" against the capitalist state, but such a development is problematic since there must also be a "socialist

---

[4] See Friedland, Piven, and Alford (1978) and Block (1981) for somewhat similar analyses of the urban fiscal crisis.

organization" (for Castells, this would be a communist party) to organize and politicize the unrest. Without the party, "urban contradictions are expressed either in a refracted way, through other practices, or in a 'wild' way, a pure contradiction devoid of any structural horizon" (Castells 1977, pp. 271–72). Apparently, it is the absence of a viable communist party in the United States that allows the state to reduce social programs with only little organized resistance. Hence, the outlook for the American city is grim:

> So, unless the progressive forces of the U.S. are able to develop a major movement, with enough social and political support to rectify the dominant trend in the forthcoming urban policies, what could emerge from the current urban crisis is a simplified and heightened version of the exploitative metropolitan model with the addition of massive police repression and control exercised in a rapidly deteriorating economic setting. The suburbs will remain fragmented and isolated, the single-family homes closed off, the families keeping to themselves, the shopping centres more expensive, the highways less well-maintained but people forced to drive further to reach jobs and to obtain services, the central districts still crowded during the office hours but deserted and curfewed after 5 P.M., the city services increasingly crumbling, the public facilities less and less public, the surplus population more and more visible, the drug culture and individual violence necessarily expanding, gang society and high society ruling the bottom and the top in order to keep a 'top and bottom' social order intact, urban movements repressed and discouraged and the urban planners eventually attending more international conferences in the outer, safer world. What could emerge if the urban movements fail to undertake their political tasks is, perhaps, a new and sinister urban form: the Wild City (Castells 1977, pp. 426–27).

The Wild City, beset by urban riots, crime, and drug abuse, is probably a better description of American cities during the time of Castells's original writing (the turbulent late 1960s) than the more (relatively) tranquil 1980s. However, even if the Wild City has not developed fully, most of the urban ills Castells attributes to capitalism remain at disturbing levels.

More recently, however, Castells's *The City and the Grassroots* (1983) analyzes "urban social movements" in the form of neighborhood organizations building a common "community" much more than it analyzes drugs and violence of the Wild City. His new book is an apparent recognition of the decline in urban violence and focuses more on political contests such as the struggles of homosexuals to build their own community in San Francisco.

While there are many similarities between *The Urban Question* and *Grassroots*, (e.g., Castells is still critical of neo-Marxists' approaches other than his own), there is a significant shift in his views on the causal patterns between community and society. For example, in

Grassroots, he interprets the ghetto revolts of the 1960s more as responses by local black communities to poor schools and other substandard city services than to the national effects of the civil rights movements and the War on Poverty. Castells, in short, appears to be moving away from the traditional Marxist view of the community being merely a place where national or international economic forces determine events. If he is successful in moving neo-Marxist analysis away from the society being the "prime mover" in all local phenomena, it will be a major step toward making the approach more applicable to community change and development.

David Harvey: "Social Justice and the City"

English geographer David Harvey has approached the city in a manner that parallels Castells in a somewhat more humanistic way. Harvey's major work, *Social Justice and the City* (1973), contains two major approaches to the city: Part I, which is liberal, and Part 2, which is conflict. Like Castells, his distinction between them is based on a Marxian concept of ideology:

> I leave it to the reader to judge whether Part I or Part 2 contains the more productive analyses. Before making this judgement there are two points I would like to present. First, I recognize that the analysis of Part 2 is a beginning point which opens up new lines of thought. The analysis is rather unfamiliar (of necessity) but its freshness to me may have made it appear at times rather rough and at other times unnecessarily complicated. I beg a certain amount of indulgence on this score. Second, Marx gives a specific meaning to ideology—he regards it as an unaware expression of the underlying ideas and beliefs which attach to a particular social situation, in contrast to the aware and critical exposition of ideas in their social context which is frequently called ideology in the west. The essays in Part 2 are ideological in the western sense whereas the essays in Part I are ideological in the Marxist sense (Harvey 1973, p. 18).

Although the reader is invited to choose between liberalism and Marxism, Harvey clearly prefers the neo-Marxist perspective developed in Part 2. He argues that liberal approaches are probably insufficient and that a new conflict approach based on Marxism should be considered.

As a geographer, Harvey's major concern is with how social processes are expressed in spatial forms. His thesis in Part 2 is that the spatial patterning of capitalist cities reflects the exploitative injustices inherent to capitalism. These spatial patterns are dynamic because the dialectical contradictions of capitalism require constant adjustments to maintain the system.

In a later article, Harvey (1978a) illustrates how capitalism changes urban spatial patterns in an attempt to save itself from its own excesses. In order to maximize profits, individual capitalists produce more than can be consumed, leading to glutted markets, falling prices, and rising unemployment. This problem can be temporarily solved by switching investment from "primary circuits" (production) to "secondary circuits" (warehouses, offices). By reinvesting in their capital, they are able to temporarily reduce production, and at the same time, of course, they are remaking the urban environment through expansion and construction. Eventually, however, production is increased to even higher levels. The recurring problems of market glut are now exacerbated by the demolition of structurally sound buildings for new, but now largely vacant, blocks of offices. Thus, the physical patterns of urban structure and growth reflect the exploitation, development, and contradictions of capitalism.

Harvey's analysis is better suited to pointing out the injustices and inefficiencies of capitalist cities than to projecting the changes necessary to create a more just city. Harvey ends *Social Justice and the City:*

> An urbanism founded upon exploitation is a legacy of history. A genuinely humanizing urbanism has yet to be brought into being. It remains for revolutionary theory to chart the path from an urbanism based in exploitation to an urbanism appropriate for the human species. And it remains for revolutionary practice to accomplish such a transformation (Harvey 1973, p. 314).

Since the publication of Harvey's book, neo-Marxist analysis of local phenomena has expanded considerably, now including many American sociologists (Gordon 1978; Tabb 1978; Friedland, Piven, and Alford 1978; Block 1981; Bloomquist and Summers 1982). However, the neo-Marxist approach remains much as it was over a decade earlier: (1) pointing out the contradictions and exploitation of urban capitalism, and (2) accounting for the survival of capitalism in spite of these contradictions and exploitations. The "revolutionary practice" still awaits the development of "revolutionary theory."

Chapter Six

The Multiple Approaches to Community

We have now examined four approaches to the community. There could have been more. Roland Warren (1978) distinguishes between six approaches and later expands it to eight (Warren 1983). Dennis Poplin (1979) employs six. Jessie Bernard (1973) lists two general and seven more specific approaches to (or paradigms of) community. There is no complete and exhaustive list, but whatever "magic" number specifies the totality of community approaches, it will probably be substantially less than the total number of community definitions. Remember that Hillery (1955) found almost a hundred separate definitions of community, and even more have been added since then (Sutton and Munson 1976). Still, there is a causal relationship here. Since the community can be defined in such a large number of ways, it can be approached in different ways as well.

MULTIPLE DEFINITIONS YIELD MULTIPLE APPROACHES: EXAMPLES WITH AREA, COMMON TIES, AND SOCIAL INTERACTION

We can illustrate the degree to which the multiple community definitions produce multiple community approaches by referring to Hillery's three most common types of definitions: those including (1) area, (2) common ties, and (3) social interaction.

Defining the community in terms of people in a specific geographic area implies focusing on the physical environment of the community, emphasizing the relationship between the population and the physical environment and the resultant spatial patterns. Thus, it is not surprising that those who employ an ecological approach to community are likely to define the community as a specific territorial entity. The classic human ecologists of the Chicago School, neo-orthodox ecologists such as Hawley and Duncan, sociocultural ecologists like Firey, and modern applicants of factorial ecology all define community in terms of specific and important geographic boundaries. In short, conceiving of the community as a geographic area is likely to lead to an ecological community study.

A similar relationship exists between defining the community in terms of common social ties and the typological approach. Common social ties are a basic component of *Gemeinschaft* (Tönnies), mechanical solidarity (Durkheim), the folk society (Redfield), and diffuse relationships (Parsons). Conversely, the absence of such ties would be characteristic of *Gesellschaft*, organic solidarity, urbanism, and specific relationships. If a community is defined as people who identify and interact with one another, then the amount of identification and interaction and the reasons for the growth or decline in identification and interaction become important. The typological approach supplies a particularly relevant perspective for such concerns.

As a final example, a definition of community that emphasizes social interaction fits well with systems theory, especially the interactional field and network analysis variations. For example, the community as an interactional field approach focuses primarily on community-related social interactions. Note again, Kaufman's definition (from Chapter 4) of a community being an "interactional field" that is "one of several interactional units in a local society." Without these types of locally relevant interactions, there is no community. And network approaches, of course, are based on measuring the level and type of interaction that occurs in the community.

Certain community definitions, then, are especially well-suited for particular community approaches. And this is one reason there are multiple approaches to community. There is another, equally important reason for the multiplicity of approaches, however, and it has nothing to do with the special definitional characteristics of community. Rather, it involves the special nature of paradigms in sociology.

SOCIOLOGY AS A MULTIPARADIGMATIC SCIENCE

Ever since Thomas Kuhn's *The Structure of Scientific Revolutions* (1962), the idea of sciences being built around paradigms has become common and widely accepted. Although the exact meaning of paradigm is debatable,[1] we can take it to mean something very much like a combina-

---

[1] If the reader, by this point, is beginning to feel that the definitions of most words are debatable, the feeling is certainly understandable and probably correct. To follow the paradigm debate, see Masterman's (1970) discovery of twenty-one separate uses of the term by Kuhn. Various applications of the term in sociology can be found in Friedrichs (1970) and Ritzer (1975). Jessie Bernard (1973) provides one of the most important uses of the concept of paradigms in community sociology.

tion of "definition" and "approach" as they were used in the preceding section. A paradigm is "a fundamental image of the subject matter within a science. It serves to define what should be studied, what questions should be asked, how they should be asked, and what rules should be followed in interpreting the answers obtained" (Ritzer 1975, p. 7). For example, when a certain definition focuses attention on certain elements of community and predisposes the selection of a complementary approach to community, which in turn guides the choice of community research techniques, then that is a community paradigm.

It was Kuhn's thesis that science progresses not in an inexorable, cumulative march toward greater understanding but rather through abrupt scientific revolutions in which the current paradigm is found to be insufficient and replaced by a new one. Because Kuhn's examples always dealt with natural sciences possessing single paradigms, he inferred that the social sciences, with their lack of a single viewpoint, had yet to reach even an initial paradigmatic stage. Thus, as long as the social sciences cannot agree on a single paradigm, they will be unable to develop the "normal" science that followed the appearance of paradigms in the natural sciences.

Yet, more and more it is becoming recognized that the social sciences in general and sociology in particular do not fit Kuhn's model of scientific development. There is no hegemonic paradigm in any social science. Rather, within each social science, there are multiple paradigms, and no single paradigm appears capable of establishing hegemony over the discipline.

The three major paradigms in sociology are typically labeled: (1) structural functionalism, (2) conflict sociology, and (3) symbolic interactionism. These three labels are not universally accepted and are not always viewed as the only major paradigms. What is becoming universally accepted, however, is the position that sociology is and will remain a multiparadigmatic discipline. A phenomenologist, Alfred Schutz, was one of the first to recognize this phenomenon:

> What is happening at the present time in sociology is that different schools are each choosing . . . levels of interpretation as a starting point. Each school then develops a methodology suitable to that level and initiates a whole new line of research. The level of structure of meaning which was the starting point soon gets defined as the exclusive, or at least the essential, subject matter of sociology (quoted in Ritzer 1975, p. 32).

Since the 1960s, the perception of sociology as a multiparadigmatic science has become common (Friedrichs 1970; Effrat 1972; Ritzer 1975).

The Implications of Being a Multiparadigmatic Science

If sociology continues as a multiparadigmatic science, then no single paradigm will win out and become the dominant and unquestioned sociological perspective. Accordingly, then, the typically bitter conflict between proponents of competing paradigms will not be resolved through one paradigm achieving hegemony. And if there is no promise of conflict resolution, the desirability of political in-fighting among the supporters of various paradigms is questionable.

George Ritzer (1972, p. 201) assesses the problems stemming from interparadigmatic conflict:

> Because there is no dominant paradigm in sociology, sociologists find it difficult to do the highly specialized work needed for the cumulation of knowledge. Instead of concentrating on their specialty, they must spend a good portion of their time defending their basic assumptions in the face of criticisms from those who accept other paradigms . . . . Sociology is dominated by the highly-unprofitable process of trying to annihilate opposing paradigms with verbal assaults.

Ritzer continues his analysis of interparadigmatic conflict by describing the tendencies of paradigmatic proponents to exaggerate the explanatory power of their perspective and to downgrade the contributions made by rival paradigms. He concludes that a willingness to "bridge" paradigms and use multiple approaches to a social phenomenon is sorely needed. We can draw similar conclusions for community sociology.

REFLECTIONS IN COMMUNITY SOCIOLOGY

There are multiple approaches to the study of community, and most reflect basic paradigmatic splits within sociology itself. Further, the competition between paradigms in sociology is reflected in similar competitions by community sociologists. In the preceding chapters, we have witnessed conflict between classical, sociocultural, and then neo-orthodox ecologists, between conflict and structural-functional systems theorists, and in subsequent chapters there will be conflicts between supporters of a mass society view of community and those who argue for the community's continued relevance (Chapter 7), and between elitist and pluralist approaches to community power (Chapter 12).

Unfortunately, the often bitter and usually dysfunctional conflicts between paradigms continues in community sociology. For example, while the battle for community power between elitists and pluralists has subsided to a standoff, new competitions are appearing as conflict approaches are being brought to local phenomena and as the interactional field approach is being reasserted with new methodologies under the general heading of a network approach. Judging by the claims of the advocates of these new approaches, they are the forerunners of the long-awaited, all-explaining paradigm. Note, as an example, how William Tabb and Larry Sawers (1978, p. 6) contrast their newly applied conflict approach to the more traditional (liberal) perspectives of local phenomena:

> The Marxist political economist finds not only liberal solutions but liberal analysis to be inadequate and believes that it will be virtually impossible to remedy urban ills without a fundamental alteration of the political economic system. The liberal reformers' programs are destined to fail not because we do not know enough but because their programs do not address the systematic nature of the problem.

Barry Wellman and Barry Leighton (1979, p. 365) state their claims for the superiority of the new network analysis approach over the ecological perspectives that focus on the community as a specific place (an urban neighborhood) in slightly less critical terms: "The entangling of the study of community ties with the study of the neighborhood has created a number of problems for the analysis of the community question." And after detailing problem after problem with an ecological approach, they state: "We urge, therefore, the study of the community question be freed from its identification with the study of neighborhoods." In its place, of course, should be their new network perspective.

Yet, there presently is little reason to believe these newly emerging network and conflict paradigms will achieve hegemony. Thus, the paradigmatic battles will continue in community sociology, and there will continue to be multiple approaches to community.

CHOOSING THE BEST APPROACH

How, then, is a community to be studied? If there are a number of competing approaches, all claiming at least adequacy and usually superiority, which one is to be used? Roland Warren (1983), in a recent address to the Community Section of the American Sociological Association, suggests that since no single community paradigm can establish dominance:

> let us have a multiplicity of paradigms. Those which endure, despite their shortcomings, will find supporters and utilizers only because they can do some things—though not all things—better than can their alternatives. Let us have a kit of good tools; but why use a screwdriver when we need a saw, or why use a hammer when we need a foot rule?

Most students of community would probably agree with Warren, but his conclusion leads to another set of questions. Which approach is to be used when? When do we need a hammer rather than a saw? Are community researchers to take turns, choosing one approach and then another until all are exhausted? Or are they to somehow combine all approaches into one all-encompassing package of community theory and research? There are no easy answers to these questions, but it is possible to develop some general guidelines for applying different community paradigms to different community phenomena. For example, each of the four basic approaches outlined in the preceding chapters tends to be better suited for some research areas than for others.

The Typological Approach

The large body of theory and research that has built up around Tön-nies's original *Gemeinschaft/Gesellschaft* distinctions has proven applicable in several areas. It has the ability to account for change, especially in relation to the individual lifestyle changes that occur as a society is transformed into a modern *Gesellschaft*-like state. Possibly no other approach can so effectively combine a macro theory of social change with micro descriptions of individual behavior.

The typological approach is also a powerful tool for quality of life studies. Descriptions of the blasé urban way of life and the resultant "quest for community" continue to strike a responsive cord in urban America. It would be impossible to fully understand the American animus toward cities, our movement to and now beyond the suburbs, the continuing appeal of rural communes, and our nostalgic yearnings for a simpler, more *Gemeinschaft*-like time (even if it never existed) without an appreciation of the typological literature. Research on the degree of primary group relations, neighboring, and neighborhood identification (Chapter 7) demonstrate the continuing relevance of this approach. Philosophical questions about the quality and, ultimately, even the meaning of life appear here as well. The trade-offs of communalism for urbanism, of integration for independence, are fateful ones, and it is the stuff of which penetrating sociological, psychological, and philosophical insights are made.

Finally, considerable discussion has developed around applying the typological approach to studying and even guiding third-world modernization efforts. Remember that the chapter on typologies was introduced with a quotation from Robert Nisbet arguing that while the approach may have developed to account for social change in an industrializing Europe, it is applicable to other situations as well. Jessie Bernard (1973, pp. 113–14), in a book devoted largely to criticizing the dominant paradigms in community sociology, concurs by observing that

> The situation of blacks conformed in almost archetypical fashion to the scenario of the Gemeinschaft-Gesellschaft paradigm. In fact, the history of blacks in the United States in the twentieth century was such a precise, almost exact, demonstration of this paradigm as to look almost like a caricature. In less than a century blacks had been catapulted literally

from a feudal to an urban society, from a folk community to Gesellschaft. Frazier had called the great trek to the city a flight from feudal America. These migrants had had little experience with Gesellschaft—especially with money—or with its emphasis on achievement and the Protestant ethic.

As in the case of folk of whatever color, the effects of urban migration were to uproot old ways of life, destroy folkways and mores, and create confusion in thought and contradictions in behavior. As Booth and his predecessors had reported of London and other cities in the nineteenth century, as Chicago researchers had reported of Chicago in the 1920s, and as all later studies here and in the Third World had shown with such monotonous consistency, so also among black people in city slums researchers found juvenile delinquency, family breakdown, and unconventional sexual behavior. It was a painfully familiar scenario, independent of time, place, ethnicity, or race. The consistency with which the same conditions produce the same results may be reassuring in validating the legitimacy of the social sciences; at the same time it is disheartening to learn how little we profit from this knowledge.

In sum, the typological approach, although it is the oldest approach to community, would still seem to have much to offer.

The Ecological Approach

Although the theoretical base of the ecological approach may not have the sophistication or acceptance that it had when human ecology reigned at the University of Chicago, its *methods* are more sophisticated and widely accepted than ever. With the increasing amount of statistical data about urban phenomena, the mathematical techniques developed by urban analysts to explain city placement, population growth, density, and land-use patterns borrow heavily from the aggregate urban data approach pioneered in human ecology.

City placement. The question of why a city is where it is rather than someplace else has long intrigued urban ecologists. And with the traditional focus on environmental influences on spatial patterns, a number of theories have been proposed to account for the location of cities. Three of the best-known are: (1) *break-in-transportation theory* (Cottrell 1951; Ruben 1961), positing that cities are most likely to develop at points where one form of transportation stops and another form begins; (2) *specialized function theory* (Ogburn 1937; Ullman 1941), positing that some cities develop where and how they do because they are near a natural resource (e.g., mining or resort towns); (3) and especially *central place theory* (Christaller 1933) positing that since a certain amount of land is required to support a city, the size and location of a city is determined by the size of its trade area, its "hinterland." The result is a centrally placed city surrounded by a hexagonally shaped trade area that borders the adjacent city's hinterland.[2]

Population growth. Estimating population growth has become a major subfield within itself (indeed an industry within itself, since the demand for population projections is strong from both government and business). And whether the growth projections are based on standard census data,[3] administrative records (e.g., building permits, utility hook-ups, tax records), sample surveys, computer simulations (Foot 1981), Social Area Analysis (Goldsmith, Jackson, and Shambaugh 1982) or some combination of these techniques, ecological units of analysis and ecological methods of combining aggregate data are predominate.

Density. Ever since Wirth's "Urbanism as a Way of Life," urban ecologists have been interested in population density. Generally, ecologists have focused on two density-related phenomena: (1) the density-distance relationship, and (2) the various pathologies associated with high levels of density.[4]

The basic density-distance model simply states that as distance from the center of the city increases, population density experiences an exponential decrease (Clark 1951). Figure 6–1 illustrates this relationship for two hypothetical cities. The comparisons of variation in density over time and between cities have allowed the development of elaborate models of density-distance patterns and projections for urban growth patterns in both industrial and nonindustrial societies (Hawley 1971).

This preoccupation with such precise measures of population density is typically justified by the assumption that density affects human behavior. Since Wirth's classic work, widely publicized research with rats ("the behavioral sink" in Calhoun 1961, 1962) and into various social pathologies in Honolulu and Hong Kong (Schmitt 1963, 1966), and Chicago (Galle, Grove, and McPherson 1972) have supported a number of theories. *Social overload* (Altman 1975; Saegert 1978) posits that high levels of density lead to interference with and confusion in normal social processes. *Territoriality* (Ardrey 1966) posits that density

---

[2] This theory applies especially well in flat terrains such as in Kansas or Nebraska but must be modified considerably for environments dominated by mountains or lakes. See Berry and Pred (1961) for a detailed review of central place theory and an annotated bibliography of research on its applicability.

[3] The Census Bureau regularly makes projections for over thirty thousand different places.

[4] This discussion of ecological approaches to density is based upon Schwab (1982, Chapter 11) and Bardo and Hartman (1982, Chapter 10).

FIGURE 6–1   Urban density and distance

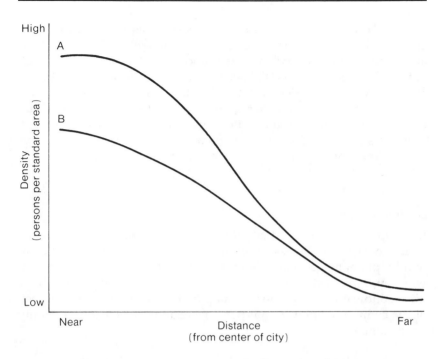

The density-distance curve for City A shows substantial density near the Central Business District and then a rapid reduction as one moves toward the fringe. Such a pattern is typical of Northeastern cities that developed prior to the mass production of the automobile. The curve for city B shows a less-dense center with and a more gradual decline in density toward the fringe. This is a typical Southwest pattern.

creates stress since human beings, like other animals, have a territorial instinct, while *stimulus overload* (Milgram 1970; Mitchell 1971) posits that crowded conditions are overly stimulating and thereby create anxiety and withdrawal, and *personal space* (Hall 1966; Sommer 1969) posits that, for cultural reasons, individuals need "space bubbles" surrounding them and that high density violates this personal space. Finally, *spatial constraint* (Saegert 1978) posits that high density can limit traditional behavior patterns to the extent that psychological stress results.

Most ecological research on these density → pathology theories concludes that there simply are no negative consequences of high residential density (Freedman 1975). However, some studies by urban ecologists (Gove, Hughes, and Galle 1979) suggest that the relationship between density and pathology may be a real one. In either case, the effects of density will probably continue to be a researched and debated topic in urban ecology.[5]

Land use. Finally, perhaps the most basic application of the ecological approach involves land use. The classic models of Burgess, Hoyt, and Harris and Ullman still have relevance to urban planning schemes. Later refinements such as William Alonso's "Theory of Rents" (Alonso 1965), moving (Rossi 1955; Wolpert 1965), and suburbanization (Greer 1962; Schnore 1965; Farley 1976; Schwirian 1977) are all squarely within the ecological focus on spatial patterning. This research, along with the references above to research in population growth, city location, and population density points out areas in which the ecological approach is particularly relevant.

Systems Theory

In Chapter 4 we argued that although systems theory has achieved wide acceptance in the social sciences, its specific applications to community phenomena remain limited. Still, it can be demonstrated that when systems theory has been applied to the community, it has been directed toward some of the most important issues in community sociology: community power, interpersonal relationships, and community development.

Community power. Power can be conceptualized as either an individual or structural phenomenon. Most of the community power research reported in Chapter 12 focuses on individuals, and the few times it has been treated as a structural phenomenon, it has been typically approached from an ecological perspective. However, there is a relatively new structural approach to community power that is based on a variation of systems theory: network analysis. Network analysis shares with systems theory a common focus on boundary maintenance and systemic linkage and is becoming something like a mathematical, computer driven update of Long's "Ecology of Games" approach (discussed in Chapter 4, page 57).

Building on the earlier and simpler network analyses of communities by Floyd Hunter (1953) and Herman Turk (1970), this new method combines individual and organizational linkages to provide multidimensional maps of local exchange networks. It views the community as being comprised of numerous linked organizational systems. Joseph Galaskiewicz (1979, p. 33) explains that network analysis assumes

---

[5] Much of the debate centers around: (1) what measure of density is most appropriate, (2) which pathologies should be considered, and (3) what variables should be used as controls.

"that organizations are open systems, and that, consequently, they must continuously engage in boundary interchanges with other organizations in their environment." Thus, network analysis maps the distribution of local power by measuring the intersystem linkages of money, information, and political support.

Interpersonal relationships. Another systems-related variation of network analysis also has been used to address the question of how much *Gemeinschaft* remains in our increasingly *Gesellschaft*-like society. Again focusing on linkages in social systems, Barry Wellman and Barry Leighton (1979, p. 364) have used this technique to study "how large-scale divisions of labor in social systems affect the organization and content of interpersonal ties." Their research into interpersonal linkages leads them to conclude that the locality-based *Gemeinschaft*-like community persists in our *Gesellschaft*-like society, "but only as specialized components of the overall primary networks. The variety of ties in which an urbanite can be involved—with distant parents, intimate friends, less intimate friends, co-workers and so on—and the variety of networks in which these are organized can provide flexible structural bases for dealing with routine and emergency matters" (Wellman and Leighton 1979, p. 388). In short, they argue that the territorial community retains a part, but only a part, of our interpersonal ties. We now are able to have close, *Gemeinschaft*-like relationships that are not territorially based.

Network analysis, then, has direct application to one of the most fundamental questions in community sociology: the *Gemeinschaft/Gesellschaft* issue. Systems theory also has provided the basis improving the local quality of life by providing a guide for community development.

Community development. Just as Wellman and Leighton were concerned with the degree to which interpersonal ties are locality based, a systems theory approach to community development shares a similar focus. The concern here is with locality-based community fields, which are social fields in which actions relating to a broad range of local interests are coordinated. And from a systems theory perspective, any actions that strengthen the structure of the community field are also actions of community development. For example, Kenneth Wilkinson (1972) has developed a field approach to community development that stresses the need to increase the generalization potentials of local interactional relationships. Thus, actions such as establishing an organization to coordinate community action projects or even simply introducing a leader in one local interest field to a leader in a different field would constitute community development because both are attempts to strengthen the structure of the community field by increasing the scope or generalization of local interaction.

In a similar vein, Roland Warren (1978, p. 325) defines community development as "a deliberate and sustained attempt to strengthen the horizontal pattern of a community." Warren's horizontal pattern is very much like Wilkinson's community field, and actions that strengthen the structure of Wilkinson's community field should strengthen Warren's horizontal pattern as well. Warren, however, gives major emphasis to actions strengthening those local organizations that provide "major locality relevant functions" —organizations such as the chamber of commerce, school boards, the city council, a local council of churches, or a United Way chapter.

With either Wilkinson or Warren however, the principle is the same. Namely, systems theory allows the definition of what a community is and does—and what actions are most likely to strengthen it. Hence, systems theory has substantial relevance to community development.[6]

Conflict

The application of a conflict approach to local phenomena became common only in the 1970s. It is not surprising, then, that one of the most popular local subjects for conflict analysis was the severe fiscal crisis that beset many American cities in that decade.

The urban fiscal crisis. Castells's (1977) analysis of these economic problems was reviewed in Chapter 5, but there have been many others (Friedland, Piven, and Alford 1978; Hill 1978; Tabb 1978; Kennedy 1983). Although there are variations in these conflict approaches, they share a common focus on extracommunity causes of local difficulties. From the conflict perspective, contradictions within the national capitalist system led to a local fiscal crisis. Since the city's economic problems stem from the capitalistic structure of American society, the city can do little to help itself.

Urban renewal. A similar body of analysis emerges from a conflict approach to urban renewal. Castells (1977), Harvey (1973), Mollenkopf (1978), and Beauregard (1981) have analyzed America's urban renewal programs from a conflict perspective. And although their separate analyses contain important differences, they all conclude that urban renewal was a *national* political response to a *national* economic prob-

---

[6] Systems theory also relates to community development via the analysis of local service delivery systems. See Garkovich and Stam (1980, pp. 163–70) for an overview of this input/output approach to community development.

lem. In other words, just as with the fiscal crisis, the cause lies in the structure of society; the effect occurs in the community. In fact, the neo-Marxist versions of the conflict approach typically view the national economic structure as the fundamental cause of local phenomena (Saunders 1981).

Is it always the national economic structure that matters? If the neo-Marxists are correct in assigning the basis for local events to the national economic structure, then the local environment doesn't matter very much. This means, then, that a neo-Marxist application to community phenomena typically focuses on national analysis rather than local change, since short of a fundamental restructuring of society (a proletarian revolt leading to a socialist society), little can be done to assist the community.

The lack of local applications for neo-Marxists' structural approaches has been noted before,[7] and as long as the cause of the local phenomena is invariably the national economic structure, this problem will remain. This can account for David Harvey's comment (see Chapter 5): "It remains for revolutionary theory to chart the path from an urbanism based on exploitation to an urbanism appropriate for the human species." And it accounts for the potential significance of a more locally oriented book like *The City and the Grassroots* (1983) by as influential a neo-Marxist as Manuel Castells.

This is not to say, however, that a neo-Marxist focus on extracommunity structure is necessarily irrelevant to producing social change. It is possible that such analysis can sufficiently raise the consciousness of the exploited and eventually lead to a restructured, noncapitalist society. William Tabb and Larry Sawers (1978, p. 19), for example, believe that the neo-Marxist analysis presented in their book *Marxism and Metropolis*

> shows the key to solution of the crisis of capitalism and its cities, is gaining steadily in influence both in the United States and throughout the world. The ideas in this book are being used as a guide for many who go on to work for fundamental social change. The popular forces for change are building even as the crisis of capitalism deepens. We do not await this 'inevitable' occurrence. We put our scholarship at the service of the class forces which will bring about this transition.

---

[7] Roland Warren (1971), for example, argues that although community poverty can be explained in terms of a national economic structure that produces poverty, this explanation has no accompanying means for combatting local poverty. More recently, see Katharine Coit's (1978) explanation of why the low level of American class consciousness has inhibited local participation in neo-Marxist community-action groups.

The transformation, of course, is a transformation of the national economic structure because from the neo-Marxist perspective, it alone is the major cause of local phenomena.

Still, there are *non*-Marxist conflict approaches that do not grant such preeminence to the national economic structure. Coleman's (1957) and Gamson's (1966) analyses of community conflict were considered in Chapter 5, but for the present purposes, it is sufficient to simply remember that both men argued that local characteristics influenced local conflict. Thus, both have community applications that do not require a restructuring of society.

A similar case can be made for Harvey Molotch's (1976) analysis of "The City as a Growth Machine," which will be considered in Chapter 12. However, it is important to note here that although he argues that national capitalism fuels the local drive for community growth, Molotch believes that local antigrowth forces can wrest control from the community's capitalists and thereby improve the local quality of life. In other words, Molotch employs a conflict approach that views state capitalism as an important but not overpowering variable.

Finally, an example can be drawn from the community development literature that will be reviewed in Chapter 8. Saul Alinsky (1971), a major figure in the field, developed an explicitly conflict-laden methodology for community organization and change. We will look at his methods in Chapter 8, but for our present purposes, it is sufficient to note that for Alinsky, the community is the locus for significant social change.

Choosing the Approaches That Work Best

It should be clear by now that the community is probably viewed best from several perspectives and that each approach has merit and relevant local applications. Each paradigm offers a different and important vantage point. The most accurate description and most complete understanding of the community comes from employing multiple approaches, but this conclusion is easier to draw than implement. Usually, the community researcher has a special affinity for a particular approach, and usually the local research topic is better suited to one approach than another. So, we tend to use an approach that corresponds to both our own perspective on the community and the particular topic of research within the community.

Broad research questions on large-scale social change, industrialization-modernization, and the quality of local life in a mass society lend themselves to the *typological approach.* Conversely, more specific, more technical questions about city placement, population growth, density, and land use are particularly well suited for the *ecological approach. Systems theory* has direct applications for community development because of its ability to locate the local community systems within the larger network of national systems. And when dealing with the interpersonal relationships within a community, systems-based *network analysis* is particularly effective. Finally, the *conflict approach* has proven popular for the analysis of local economic problems such as the recent urban fiscal crises.

In a sense, then, community researchers use whatever works best. If a lot of demographic data are available and the research question is a technical one, an ecological approach is almost assured. On the other hand, a broader, more critical concern with the unequal access to local goods and services is tailor-made for a conflict approach. Such pragmatism may seem to be unethical or at least disloyal to the one "true" paradigm; but remember, sociology has no dominate paradigm, and there is none on the horizon. Hence, attempts to stretch a perspective into areas for which it isn't applicable are unnecessary. Why stand on our head to explain violent crime from a radical, conflict perspective, or urban riots with a conservative systems theory?[8] Or, in Warren's (1983) terms, "let us have a kit of good tools," and use a tool that is appropriate for the job.

---

[8] This is not to say that it is impossible to fit together seemingly contradictory paradigms and problems, only that it is difficult, and requires a considerable amount of skill. Actually, when it is done well, the results are often outstanding. Note, as examples, Ryan's (1971) treatment of the urban criminal as a "victim," or Banfield's (1970) explanation of the motives of urban rioters as "fun and profit."

Section II

COMMUNITY AND THE QUALITY OF LIFE

Community sociology, in both its theory and application, has been especially concerned with the nature and quality of our lifestyles. The typological theorists focused squarely on how *Gemeinschaft* life differs from *Gesellschaft* life, often pointing to problems associated with moving from one type to another and sometimes concluding that the quality of life may decline in our increasingly *Gesellschaft*-like society. The ecologists focused initially on the low quality of life during the period of rapid urbanization and social disorganization in Chicago by associating various pathologies with demographic variables such as density. Systems theory has direct applications for improving the quality of local life through community development, and the conflict approach typically focuses on how capitalism reduces the quality of urban life.

While concerns with the quality of life were indirectly reflected throughout the chapters in Section I, they are the primary focus of the chapters in Section II. In Chapter 7, the theory and research that relate the community with the quality of life are reviewed, as well as attempts to reestablish the *Gemeinschaft* qualities of an earlier time.

The community theories or paradigms that make up Section I also influence the attempts to improve the quality of local life described in Chapters 8 and 9. Chapter 8 shows that how one goes about community development depends on the paradigmatic assumptions one makes concerning what a community is, what its problems are, and how those problems are best addressed. Chapter 9, on planned communities, is based on three of the approaches predominate in Section I: the typological, ecological, and conflict approaches. A careful comparison of these first two sections shows that community theory and applications are so closely intertwined that even the most abstract theory can influence local applications and even the most pragmatic community developer or planner will be indirectly influenced by some theoretical views of community.

Chapter Seven

The Loss of and Quest for Community

Our lifestyles, the reasons for our lifestyles, and especially the quality of our lifestyles have been major issues in community sociology since Tönnies's *Gemeinschaft und Gesellschaft*. We saw in the previous chapter how Tönnies, Simmel, Wirth, and, to a lesser degree, Durkheim, Marx, and Weber all concluded that, on balance, the quality of life is reduced when a society becomes more urban, more industrial, more *Gesellschaft*-like. Often, then, attempts to determine or improve the quality of life in modern-day America have dealt with the "eclipse of," "decline in," "loss of," or "quest for" community.

THE LOSS OF COMMUNITY

While only a few attempts have been made to measure the decline of *Gemeinschaft*-like relations in the United States, there is nonetheless a wide acceptance of this decline and numerous prescriptions for appropriate remedies to restore the lost quality of life. In this chapter, we will look first at the small body of research that has plotted the decline in *Gemeinschaft*-like relations, then we will examine attempts to guide our quest toward reestablishing them.

The Holistic Studies

The first evidence of a major movement from *Gemeinschaft* to *Gesellschaft* in the United States came from the early holistic community studies. In a book aptly titled *The Eclipse of Community*, Maurice Stein (1960) showed how the classic studies of Middletown, Yankee City, and Chicago could be combined to trace the transformation of America into a society much nearer the *Gesellschaft* end of the continuum. Stein used the Chicago studies of Park et al. to illustrate the effects of urbanization on our lifestyles, the two Middletown volumes of Robert and Helen Lynd to document the effects of industrialization, and the five volumes reporting W. Lloyd Warner's study of Yankee City to describe the growing impact of bureaucratization. These three processes (urbanization, industrialization, and bureaucratization), Stein concludes, combined to produce a mass society that eliminated many of the *Gemeinschaft*-like relationships associated with community:

> All of these studies during the 20's and 30's, then, show increasing standardization of community patterns throughout the country with agencies of nationwide diffusion and control acting as centers of innovation. Intimate life patterns become susceptible to standardized change as the mass media begin to inform each age group about new fashions and styles. Thus, the conditions for the formation of a mass society were found in these previously examined social processes, even though more advanced forms had not yet appeared. (Stein 1960, p. 108).

More recent holistic studies such as Vidich and Bensman's *Small Town in Mass Society* (1958) illustrate the "more advanced forms" of mass society referred to by Stein. We find in Vidich and Bensman's study of Springdale, a small village in upstate New York, a community that has become politically impotent, economically dependent, and culturally subservient when compared to the larger, more powerful, national society. They conclude that "[a] central fact of rural life then, is its dependence on the institutions and dynamics of the urban and mass society" (Vidich and Bensman 1958, p. 101). Thus, in addition to the psychological alienation described by Tönnies and Simmel, another important consequence of the growing influence of the more *Gesellschaft*-like mass society is the diminishing importance of the territorial community.

The Loss of Community as both a Psychological and Territorial Phenomenon

In the first chapter, we developed a working definition of community that included a specific geographic area, an identification by the residents with that area, and social interaction among the residents. Thus, when sociologists speak of the "decline" or "loss" of community, there are at least two distinct meanings. One meaning focuses on the social interaction dimension of the community and analyzes the psychological alienation that can come from the mass society. The other meaning focuses more on the territorial components of the community definition, with analysis of the economic dependence and political impotence of the local community in the mass society. Both meanings are related in that they see the same primary source for the loss of community—the mass society—and both describe a similar problem—a resultant lower quality of life at the individual and community levels.

The decline or loss of community, then, refers to two separate but related phenomena, each based on different elements of community. One is based on the social interaction part of community and focuses on the psychological alienation, isolation, and anomie that come from increasingly *Gesellschaft*-like relations. Our discussions of Tönnies, Simmel, Weber, Durkheim, Marx, and Wirth in Chapter 2 are elaborations of this theme. The other meaning of the loss of community is based more on the territorial conception of community. As the mass society becomes increasingly dominant, the local community ceases to be a place that matters very much. More important than decisions made in Middletown or Springdale are decisions made in New York, Washington, or other centers of the mass society.

Although the two types of community that are "lost" can be conceptually distinct and are treated as separate phenomena in most literature, they are, nonetheless, closely related. Robert Nisbet, in the preface to the more recent printings of his famous treatise on individual alienation in the mass society, *The Quest for Community* (originally published in 1953), relates the decline in identification with the place and property of the territorial community to the more psychological alienation from close, personal interaction.

> Similarly, I think alienation from place and property turns out to be, at bottom estrangement from close personal ties which give lasting identity to each. Native heath is hardly distinguishable from the human relationships within which landscape and animals and things become cherished and deeply implanted in one's soul. The same is true of property. It is not hardness or softness of property; it is the kind of relationship within which property exists that is crucial. If it is a close and significant relationship, the sense of ownership will be a vital one no matter what the form of property (Nisbet 1976, p. xii).

In short, the decline in the relevance of and identification with the territorial community is related to the decline in *Gemeinschaft*-like interpersonal relations; both reinforce one another, and both are symptoms of a mass society.

Surprisingly little empirical research followed these holistic studies in documenting the rise of the mass society and concomitant decline of the territorial and psychological community. Usually, the most influential evidence was of a more deductive, philosophical, even moralistic nature and directed toward the alienation and isolation common to *Gesellschaft*-like societies (Nisbet 1962; Slater 1970; Castells 1976). Typically, this analysis was an extension and revision of Stein's conclusions, occasionally including normative prescriptions to aid in overcoming the inherent psychological deficiencies of the mass society.

Some of these solutions to the perceived problems of the mass society will be considered in this chapter, but first some of the few research efforts that did attempt to document a loss of community will be considered, beginning with the evidence for a decline in relevance of the local, territorial community.

Research on the Loss of Relevance for the Territorial Community

We will use three research areas to illustrate the empirical evidence that argued for a diminished role for the territorial community: local versus national stratification, urban race riots, and community power.

Local versus national stratification. The early studies of American stratification patterns were almost exclusively within the province of community sociology. Warner's pioneering studies of inequality in Yankee City (and to a lesser degree the Lynds' work in Middletown) began an approach to stratification based on how residents in the community ranked other local residents. However, as sociology embraced the concept of America as a mass society, the focus for stratification research became national rather than local. Sociologists began using national samples with class rankings determined by only one criterion: occupation.

Warner's early community studies used a more personal and holistic approach to stratification. Warner's respondents ranked people they knew in the community by their occupation and also by any other individual characteristics they thought were important, such as family background, race, gender, age, and neighborhood. Unfortunately, with a national sampling, such a personal approach is impossible since the respondents do not know one another. Thus the respondents from national samples are asked only to rank occupations, not people. This technique of standardized national evaluations can be reliable only if: (1) people are increasingly evaluated not by who they are in the community, but what they do, i.e., their occupation; and (2) evaluations of occupations do not vary by community. Both of these conditions should exist in a *Gesellschaft*-like mass society, and, accordingly, the use of standardized occupation scales has become the accepted method of class identification in American stratification research.

Some criticisms of these national occupation scales have appeared. However, most of the complaints are based on the appropriateness of the scale for women (e.g., Sorensen 1979) or, more generally, whether occupational prestige is a meaningful component of stratification when compared to power or income (e.g., England 1979). Very few sociologists have questioned whether the move away from the community as a stratification research site was a wise one. Instead, most analysts of

American class structure have accepted the contention that stratification is a mass phenomenon.[1]

The acceptance of a mass society stratification model occurred without substantial supporting evidence. In fact, it was not until the publication of Richard Curtis and Elton Jackson's *Inequality in American Communities* in 1977 that an extensive body of research addressed the question of whether stratification models could be independent of intercommunity variation. They examined the structure and dynamics of local stratification in six different American communities, and their findings came down clearly on the side of the mass society. Curtis and Jackson (1977, p. 331) reported no significant intercommunity variation in either "the process of rank attainment" or in "the rigidity of the class system," and their explanation of the lack of differences among the six communities is expressed in concepts drawn directly from the mass society:

> If the same kinds of goods are available everywhere, then wealth can be converted into the same sorts of consumption in all communities. The distribution of information by the mass media naturally encourages and strengthens this unifying process. Indeed, the mass media are the major system of distribution for many ideas and attitudes, so that as individuals of somewhat different educational levels partake of somewhat different sorts of mass media information throughout the country, attitudinal differences between educational levels tend to become uniform nationwide. The end result is that not only are ranks translated into other ranks in a similar fashion across the society, but rank levels are also more or less uniformly translated into styles of life. For these reasons, American communities tend to be similar rather than unique arenas for rank attainment and status display. (Curtis and Jackson 1977, pp. 341–342)

There is the possibility that Curtis and Jackson's research design predetermined a measure of support for stratification as a mass society phenomenon. The variables they analyzed are the same as those used in most national studies. Potentially important local factors such as the distribution of power and the intracommunity patterning of classes, races, residences, and businesses were not included, and had they been, it is possible that the intercommunity variation in stratification would have been more important (Form 1978). Still, Curtis and Jackson's research is one of the very few attempts to document the rise of the mass society and the concomitant decline of the local community. And until future research includes local variables such as the distribution of power or races, *Inequality in American Communities* will remain among the most convincing arguments for the rise of the mass society in the American class structure.

---

[1] See Barber (1961) as a notable exception who argues *for* the relevance of local variables such as community and family in stratification models.

Urban race riots. In Chapter 1, we traced a revival of interest in the community in the late 1960s and 1970s. This renewed interest in the community was not based entirely on the growing scientific evidence in support of a more circumscribed view of the mass society. Americans were forced to turn their attention back to the local community when hundreds of minor and scores of major race riots exploded on to the urban scene in the late 1960s.

As might be expected, an aftermath of the rioting was a renewed public concern for "community development," more "local control," and other similar watchwords of that turbulent period. And when the public became concerned with the condition of its local communities, government interest and money soon followed. And where government money is available, sociologists and other scientists can be expected to appear, costly research designs in hand. Such was the case with the community. Increased government and private foundation support for community research, spurred by fears engendered by racial rioting, contributed in no small part to the revival in scientific interest in the community. It is ironic, then, that one of the major investigations into the race riots of the 1960s provided widely cited evidence for a decline in the relevance of the territorial community.

Seymour Spilerman published his research on "The Causes of Racial Disturbances" as the lead article in the August 1970 *American Sociological Review.* Evaluating a number of separate hypotheses involving various explanations of the riots, Spilerman concluded that most community specific variables such as the local levels of social disorganization and black deprivation were largely unimportant. Instead, the number of riots a community experienced appeared to be influenced only by the local percentage of nonwhite population. The higher the proportion of black residents in a community, the more likely the occurrence of urban riots. His explanation of this lack of relevance for most community variables borrowed liberally from the tenets of the mass society:

> Each of these factors—the national government, television, and the development of black solidarity—has served to expose Negroes to stimuli which are uniform across communities. It is not that local conditions do not differ significantly for the Negro, rather it is that these variations are overwhelmed by the above considerations (Spilerman 1970, p. 646).

The causes of the rioting, then, were not to be found among communities. The urban race riots were a mass society phenomenon that only impacted at the community level.

Three years after the publication of Spilerman's article, the *American Sociological Review* presented additional evidence based on not only the frequency of riots (Spilerman's only dependent variable), but also on the precipitating conditions and severity of the rioting. In this new article, William Morgan and Terry Clark (1973) claim that local community characteristics did indeed have significant impact on urban rioting, reversing the mass society conclusions of Spilerman.

Research findings in the social sciences are almost always tentative, and a full understanding of why the riots appeared in the 1960s and disappeared in the 1970s remains beyond our grasp.[2] Still, Spilerman's research, like the stratification analysis of Curtis and Jackson (1977), remains one of the few empirical documentations of the rise of the mass society, and it takes on special importance when we remember that Spilerman was investigating a phenomenon that had helped to refocus our attention to the community.

Community power. Our last example of empirical evidence on the decline of the geographic community comes from community power research. No longer content with simply describing the distribution of power in various communities, researchers in the late 1960s and early 1970s turned to "why" certain communities have certain power distributions and then on to "what difference the local distribution of power makes" in the communities.

A common answer to why different communities had different distributions of power was found by viewing America as a mass society. Robert Lineberry and Ira Sharkansky (1978), in a review of research efforts from many different communities, concluded that local politics was becoming more pluralistic as a response to increasing absentee-ownership, greater reliance on technical experts, and more government control and influence from Washington. In short, those communities that had been most integrated into the mass society were the most pluralistic.[3] Michael Aiken (1970), in a similar research effort, concluded that the largest cities were probably the most decentralized because they were the most integrated into the larger mass society. Thus, a trend toward increasingly pluralistic local politics was discovered and attributed to an increasingly dominant mass society. However, if this trend toward greater local pluralism does exist, the degree to which the mass society has permeated various communities must be uneven because other researchers have discovered substantial variation in the type and distribution of local power (Bonjean 1971; Clark 1971). Still, we find in much of the research on "why" communities have certain power structures further empirical support for the rise of the mass society.

---

[2] For example, subsequent reanalysis by Spilerman (1976) presents further evidence for rioting as a mass phenomenon. See Lineberry (1971) for an insightful overview of the conflicting data from the urban race riots.

[3] Also, see Walton (1967, 1970) and Liebert (1976) for further support of the growing influence of the mass society on local politics.

More support for the dominance of the mass society came with the research into "what difference the distribution of power makes." If one community has a largely pluralistic power structure while another is more elitist, what differences in local policies can be expected to result? Most studies pointed to a surprising answer: variations in community power have little or no effect on variations in local policy outputs. For example, after surveying the small statistical correlations between community power and participation in federal programs, Aiken (1970, p. 517) concludes "that the community power perspective as it now exists, is simply not the most appropriate model to use." Analyzing similar results, Larry Lyon (1977) points to the rise of the mass society as an explanation for the lack of association between power and policy:

> One possibility is that community power is simply not as important an explanatory variable as it once was. Walton (1970, 1973) among others, has shown how increasingly dominant vertical ties (i.e., the interrelationships of the community with state and national systems) have functioned to make the community power structures more pluralistic. If we follow Warren's original statement of the horizontal ties vs. vertical ties thesis, the trend toward stronger vertical ties should also make the community decision-makers less autonomous and thereby the particular form of local power distribution less important in determining policy outputs. Thus, while there may be considerable knowledge to be gained through studying the causes and dynamics of community power structures, if one's goals are to predict local policy outputs, it might be more efficacious to focus on the federal and state agencies that are vertically linked with the community (Lyon 1977, p. 429).

We find then, in the unsuccessful attempts of Aiken and Lyon to link community power with policy outputs, indirect evidence supporting the increasing dominance of the mass society.[4]

The idea that current conceptualizations of community power have little bearing on local events is still a common one (e.g., Walton 1976; Lineberry and Sharkansky 1978), but as we will show in Chapter 12, recent analysis questions that lack of association. Still, much of the community power research during the 1970s became evidence for the rise of an American mass society.

---

[4] Indirect proof via the absence of statistical association is becoming an increasingly common, but questionable research technique in sociology. Note that Spilerman's (1970) analysis of urban rioting and Curtis and Jackson's (1977) work in community stratification also employ this method. Perhaps the most widely cited and controversial use of this technique is Christopher Jencks's *Inequality* (1972). Two potential problems with assuming that the lack of statistical correlation indicates the absence of a causal association are measurement error and the omission of important variables. For example, some of our measures of community power may be unreliable (Nelson 1974), and we noted that Curtis and Jackson (1977) may have omitted key local variables.

Conclusions about research on the loss of the territorial community. Research on the decline in relevance for the territorial community appears inconsistent. Spilerman's (1970) evidence for urban rioting as a mass society phenomenon was subsequently contradicted by Morgan and Clark's (1973) finding that local community structure significantly influenced the severity of these riots. Likewise, significant intercommunity variation in power distribution remains, in spite of a mass society trend toward pluralism, and the absence of statistical relationships between local variations in power and policy now appears to be overstated. Only the stratification research of Curtis and Jackson (1977) has remained without contradiction, and even their conclusion about stratification as an exclusively national structure and process is questionable because of the variable selection. Given our discussion in Chapter 1 concerning how sociologists initially overestimated the effects of the mass society, it is not surprising that more recent data are suggesting a viable role for the territorial community. These inconsistencies in research findings, then, can be seen as reflecting community sociology during a time when we were beginning to reassess the effects of the mass society on the relevance of the territorial community.

Research into the Loss of Psychological Community

There is little inconsistency in the empirical evidence concerning the loss of the psychological components of community because there is virtually no direct, empirical evidence to support the claims of individual isolation, alienation, and anomie that are supposed to accompany a movement toward a more *Gesellschaft*-like society. Although major theorists from Tönnies to Parsons have subscribed to various aspects of the *Gemeinschaft/Gesellschaft* typology discussed in Chapter 2, the preponderance of research shows that psychologically significant neighboring (Kasarda and Janowitz 1974; Hunter 1975; Gans 1962; Greer 1962) and considerable territorial identification (Hunter 1975; Guest 1982) continue to exist. Other research (MacDonald and Throop 1971; Lystad 1969; Seeman et al. 1971; Fischer 1973) has failed to find the higher levels of isolation, anomie, and alienation thought to be associated with more urban (and therefore more *Gesellschaft*-like) populations. In short, while there are extremely powerful theories associating various psychological problems with a mass society, these theories have virtually no empirical research support.

Why is there no empirical support? There are at least four possible explanations for this inconsistency between theory and research. The most obvious explanation is that the *"Gemeinschaft/Gesellschaft*—mass society"* theories are wrong. Such a conclusion is possible, but its acceptance entails rejecting what many feel to be one of the most extensive, consistent, and powerful bodies of theory sociology has ever developed (McKinney and Loomis 1958; Nisbet 1966, Bernard 1973). Indeed, the deductive logic of these theories is so compelling, so widely accepted, that they are substantially insulated from inductive evidence to the contrary. Thus, a more accepted variation of this explanation argues that the theory was correct for a while but is no longer relevant. While there may have been substantial *Gesellschaft*-like anomie and alienation in the past (especially in the rapidly urbanizing and disorganized Chicago of the 1920s that so captivated Park, Burgess et al.) such pathological adaptations are no longer a distinctive characteristic of urban environments (Wilensky and Lebeaux 1965; Bell and Newby 1972; Kasarda and Janowitz 1974; Poplin 1979; Spates and Macionis 1982). In other words, the "loss of psychological community" theories described a condition unique to periods of rapid urbanization. While this would explain why the ethnographic descriptions and ecological explanations of urban deviance by the Chicago School no longer apply, it would not account for the existence of "loss of community" theses long before (e.g., Tönnies 1887) and after (e.g., Nisbet 1953) the period of rapid urbanization described in the Chicago studies.

A second possibility is that the dominance of the mass society has become so total as to obliterate any significant urban-rural differences (Greer 1962; Sjoberg 1965), rendering urban-rural comparisons of alienation and anomie levels useless. While this would explain why populations that are more urban do not possess more *Gesellschaft*-like characteristics, it would do little to explain why significant amounts of typically *Gemeinschaft*-like activities (neighboring, community identification) remain in our supposedly mass society.

A similar problem exists with the third explanation. It is argued that *Gemeinschaft*-like relationships have been reestablished in our mass society through voluntary organizations (Webber 1963; Rubin 1969). While voluntary organizations probably have become more important, their existence still does not account for the residential neighboring and identification that continue to turn up in community research.

A fourth and personally preferred possibility is that the *Gemeinschaft/Gesellschaft*—mass society theories are not wrong, only overstated. In other words, while significant components of *Gesellschaft* have been introduced to American society, much *Gemeinschaft* remains. It is important to understand that this fourth explanation does not directly dispute these classic theories, and in some ways it follows them more closely than a total loss of community thesis. Tönnies's *Gemeinschaft* and *Gesellschaft*, as well as all the related typologies such as Durkheim's mechanical and organic solidarity or Parsons's pattern variables, can be seen as forms of Weber's ideal types; that is, they do not exist in the real world but are only used for comparison with real world phenomena. All societies, the United States included, are between the typological extremes. Such a conception would cast the community question in the same terms as in Chapter 1. Namely, "What is the local mixture between community and society?" and "How might that mixture be modified for a higher quality of life?"

If the effects of the mass society have been overestimated, then the same must be said for the loss of community. It is hardly a total loss, and quests for community should bear this in mind. As we shall see in the next section, however, that has not always been the case.

THE QUEST FOR COMMUNITY

Numerous problems beyond the decline in the psychological and territorial community have been attributed to America's transformation into a *Gesellschaft*-like mass society. The irrelevance of traditional religion (Cox 1965), urban crime (Jacobs 1961), suburban sterility and artificiality (Whyte 1956), campus unrest (Lipset and Altbach 1967), labor-management conflict (Warner and Low 1947), worker exploitation (Castells 1977), and even America's involvement in Vietnam (Slater 1970) have been explained, at least in part, as a result of losing community. Thus, many who would lead us to a new community-based society are utopian in their approach. There is the implied promise that most social problems will disappear with the successful completion of our quest for community.

Utopian-Radical Quests

We will begin by examining two of the most utopian solutions to the loss of community problem: counterculture-type communes and Marxist socialism.

Counterculture communes. All the various quests for lost community—save one—are based on changing at least some of the alienating characteristics of our increasingly *Gesellschaft*-like society. The single exception is the counterculture commune. This approach argues that society is beyond redemption and that devotees of *Gemeinschaft* must physically remove themselves from society and form a new, separate, truly communal community. Typically, commune dwellers believe that while the *Gemeinschaft*-like community existed in the past,[5] it has virtually disappeared in urban, industrial American; but rather than try to reverse society's movement toward *Gesellschaft*, they believe small groups (of approximately twenty to two thousand) can recapture more intimate social relationships in the counterculture commune.

---

[5] See Raymond Williams (1973, Ch. 2) for examples of how the "perfect" *Gemeinschaft*-like community seems to have always existed a generation or two in the past, century after century, all the way back to Eden.

Communes are often called "purposeful" communities because they are consciously created to achieve a specific purpose (Poplin 1979). Communes have existed for centuries in many different societies, some with different purposes than others. The purpose of current communes in American society, however, is, virtually without exception, to provide a refuge from our *Gesellschaft*-like culture. And in most cases, the refuge comes in the form of a small commune with decidedly *Gemeinschaft*-like characteristics. For example, most American communes include:

1. A communal sharing of goods.
2. An emphasis on the group over the individual.
3. A common and unifying ideology.
4. Shared and unspecialized labor.
5. Emotion and intimacy.
6. A corresponding reduction of rationality and objectivity (Zablocki 1971, 1980; Kanter 1972; Redekop 1975; Berger 1981).

Not surprisingly, these characteristics are similar to the characteristics of Tönnies' *Gemeinschaft* because they represent a conscious attempt to reestablish the lost *Gemeinschaft*-like community (Redekop 1975).

Not all seekers of *Gemeinschaft* chose the traditional response of rural communes. During the late 1960s and early 1970s, there were substantial numbers of anti-*Gesellschaft* Americans who chose to remain in society,—the hippies.[6] Most hippies did not physically remove themselves from the *Gesellschaft*-like culture they opposed. Rather, they lived among the "straights" and hoped to change society by example (Howard 1974). Hippies were the ones who changed, however, because it may well be impossible for a counterculture to exist within a dominant culture if there is the high level of interaction that occurred between hippies and straights. The dominant culture's ability to discourage deviant behavior is too great. Thus, the hippie movement was short-lived, and predictably so.[7] Most hippies were absorbed by the

---

[6] Despite popular stereotypes, the hippies were never a homogeneous population of young whites seeking instant gratification. Howard (1974), for example, identifies four basic types of hippies (visionaries, freaks, marginal freaks, and plastic hippies) with numerous cases of group variation within each type. Still, most hippies rejected the major values of conventional *Gesellschaft*-like culture; thus the term counterculture was often used to describe hippie norms and values (Roszak 1969).

[7] There were analysts who correctly predicted the demise of the hippie movement. However, the demise was not always accounted for by the difficulties of maintaining a counterculture within the dominant culture. Note, for example, that Havighurst (1975) predicted a decline in emphasis on the anti-establishment norms and values of young people simply because of the coming decline in the proportion of young people in the United States.

dominant culture, and the ones who were able to hold on to their *Gemeinschaft*-like lifestyles were those who reduced the interaction with straights by leaving the *Gesellschaft*-like city and starting or joining rural communes (Berger 1981). This probably produced an increase in the number of communes during the early 1970s (Kanter 1972; Zablocki 1980).

The *Gemeinschaft*-like communes that survived the demise of the hippie counterculture represent an exciting experiment in the purposeful construction (rather than "natural" evolution) of community. There is much to be learned from their study. Practically, however, communes' utility for restoring elements of *Gemeinschaft* at the societal level are limited. It is difficult to conceive of a society in excess of 240 million based on communal, rural, *Gemeinschaft*.[8] Rather, the closest case studies we have to a society-wide attempt at communal living are the descriptions and analyses of communist nations.

Marxist-socialist quests. The association of capitalism with the loss of community is a common one. From Tönnies, Simmel, and Marx and through more recent analysis such as Eric Fromm (1941) and Manuel Castells (1977), a capitalistic economy is seen as a major (sometimes *the* major) contributor to the various pathologies of a *Gesellschaft*-like society. It is not surprising, then, that the elimination of capitalism is often given as the way to establish a new form of *Gemeinschaft*-like relationships.

Does Marxist socialism provide for a more *Gemeinschaft*-like society? Fortunately, there are a number of nations that can provide insight into the effect of communism on community. The Soviet Union, other urban industrial societies in Eastern Europe, and preindustrial, third world nations such as China and Cuba are all examples of Marxist-socialist societies.

Much of the analysis available to us suggests that the Soviet Union and its Eastern European allies have cities that are physically structured much as those in Western Europe (Osborn 1970). And, just as in the West, social interactions such as neighboring appear to be declining (Frolic 1970). In fact, the key to both the psychological and physical structure of the socialist community seems to be *industrial efficiency* (Sallnow 1983). Psychological identification is stronger with fellow workers than with neighbors, and cities are planned (to the degree they are planned at all) to increase industrial productivity. This is strikingly similar to capitalistic societies. (Note, for example, how the ecological models of urban structure that were developed to explain the growth of American cities are based on principles of efficiency and the

---

[8] It is only difficult, not impossible. Consider fundamentalist Islamic societies such as Iran and see also Reich (1970) and Slater (1970).

maximization of industrial output.) In short, communism in Eastern Europe and the Soviet Union has produced cities that are not as planned or communal as they theoretically should be. They appear to be much like their capitalistic counterparts, probably because both capitalist and communist cities serve industrial-economic ends before human-social ends (Frolic 1976).[9]

Objective sociological research from third world nations like China and Cuba is rare, and, accordingly, our conclusions about the level of community in these societies must be tentative. It does appear, however, that these nations have been more successful than industrial communist nations in establishing elements of *Gemeinschaft*. After describing the immense problems of overurbanization in pre–Castro Cuba, David Barkin (1978, pp. 334–35) glowingly describes the evolving communist society:

> The history of capitalist societies is a growing chasm between town and country, between mental and manual labor, and between classes. The Cubans attacked this problem frontally from the very beginning. The earliest redistributive measures forced a reallocation of resources from the urban areas to the countryside. . . . The residential structure of the population is gradually changing with the creation of a large number of smaller cities. Havana's population is growing only as fast as that of the country as a whole . . . . Just as important, the 'social disorganization so characteristic of cities in capitalist countries' is no longer a problem, and 'Cuban streets are clean and safe, and rarely populated by drunkards.' . . . In this way, Cubans also suggest that the transition to socialism is only a way station on the road to communism.

Similar successes are reported for the Chinese. Larry Sawers (1978, p. 360), after comparing Soviet and Sino cities, concludes that while the goal of Russian urban planners is *efficiency*,

> the key theme of Chinese spatial planning is *engagement*—all of the Chinese policies are consistent with the goal of integrating disparate segments of society into a single community. Regional planning has attempted to merge the city with the countryside through a number of policies. Within the cities, planning has sought to build a sense of involvement within neighborhoods.

It is possible, perhaps even probable, that a measure of the Cuban and Chinese success in maintaining community is a result of research that is less common and less objective than Soviet and Eastern European reports,[10] but there also seems to be a genuine level of political

---

[9] But see French and Hamilton (1979) for a dissenting view.

[10] And, in fact, there is research (e.g., Whyte 1983) that disagrees with Sawers' hypothesis and argues instead that Chinese cities are more separated than ever from the countryside.

decentralization and psychological communalism that is lacking in the Soviet Union and Eastern Europe. If this is true, it implies the *Gemeinschaft* is more threatened by industrialization than capitalism (and the recent Chinese experiments with doses of capitalism will provide an interesting test). Capitalism is limited in all communist societies, but only those lacking a strong industrial base appear to have substantial elements of community input in decision making and predominately *Gemeinschaft*-like social relations.[11] Even if industrial communism can be structured in a way that allows more *Gemeinschaft*-like relations, the likelihood of its implementation in the United States is slim, at least in the foreseeable future. Thus, it is the less utopian but more achievable quests for community that we now consider.

Less "Radical," Less "Utopian" Quests

The more "conservative" ways in which lost elements of community can be reestablished vary between two main schools of thought. One view argues that with considerable work by community development specialists, it is possible to reestablish, at least in part, the lost sense of community. The other position maintains that little work in community development is necessary since the structure of mass society guarantees new bases of communal feelings through voluntary organizations.

Community development. Although community development is traditionally associated with attempts to "modernize" rural American communities and third world villages, a recent and ironic twist has seen the term applied to combating the effects of modernization in the small towns and urban neighborhoods in America. During the 1950s and 1960s, community development models were created to battle the effects of modernization by transforming socially isolated, politically impotent individuals into organized, territorially based neighborhoods pursuing common goals. Unfortunately, our review in the next chapter will show the track record of community development is at best a mixed one, with its most notable victories often being short-lived.

Although there were a number of difficulties that beset attempts at community development, a major problem, one that is particularly relevant here, was an uncritical acceptance of the mass society thesis. Some community organizers approached neighborhoods, especially

---

[11] Gideon Sjoberg's *The Preindustrial City* (1965) implies a similar conclusion about the role of industrialization in producing a *Gesellschaft*-like lifestyle. For a summary of Sjoberg's as well as other support for the industrialization leading to *Gesellschaft* thesis, refer back to Chapter 2.

poor neighborhoods, as places devoid of local ties and social organization. In fact, a primary reason for the relative success of famed community organizer Saul Alinsky (1946, 1971) was his recognition that local
neighborhoods retained important elements of a socially organized
community:

> The ghetto or slum in which the organizer is organizing is not a disorga-
> nized community. It is a contradiction in terms to use the two words
> 'disorganized' and 'community' together; the word community itself
> means an organized communal life; people living in an organized fashion
> (Alinsky 1971, p. 115).

Alinsky's strategies for community development are usually viewed as
among the most successful attempts ever made at practical neighborhood organization (Bailey 1972; O'Brien 1975; Lancourt 1979; Reitzes
and Reitzes 1982), and a key to his success was the recognition of
indigenous community organization and the ability to combine and
build upon these local organizations (O'Brien 1975).

Still, as we shall see in Chapter 8, Alinsky's strategies are difficult
to implement. They require vigorous, time-consuming, and continuous efforts on the part of shrewd community organizers, and even
then their success is limited. Thus, Alinsky shares with other community development specialists the view that in a *Gesellschaft*-like society,
a *Gemeinschaft*-like community can be produced only with substantial
effort. Without such effort, the community surely will remain politically impotent, economically dependent, and probably populated by
fragmented residential groups possessing the various pathologies associated with the *Gesellschaft*-like mass society. There is, however, a
school of thought that believes new forms of *Gemeinschaft*-like social
relations will occur naturally (i.e., without assistance from community
development programs) in a mass society.

Voluntary organizations. While community organizers such as
Saul Alinsky promote the establishment and strengthening of voluntary organizations as major parts of a community development program, the organizations they promote are territorially based and in
need of considerable support and maintenance. Urban planner Melvin
Webber was among the first analysts to suggest that the concern for the
lost local community is unnecessary and that attempts to revive the
territorial community are misplaced. In an article, subtitled "Community without Propinquity," he argued that the concerns of analysts
such as Nisbet over the standardization and centralization of the mass
society are unfounded because "rather than a 'mass culture' in a 'mass
society' the long term prospect is for a maze of subcultures within an
amazingly diverse society" (Webber 1963, p. 29). However, the basis
for this subcultural variation is not the territorial community. Rather,

"Americans are becoming more closely tied to various interest communities than to place communities" (Webber 1963, p. 29).

A similar observation is made by Israel Rubin (1969, p. 116):

> The romantic theme that modern man has "lost" his community is fed by the common observation that the neighborhoods, towns, and cities have ceased to serve as significant foci of identification for the mobile man of industrial society. However, from our vantage point we see no reason for saddling the concept with the territorial element.

Rubin, like Webber, believes that the territorial community has become irrelevant.

While Rubin is not as optimistic as Webber in assessing the degree to which voluntary organizations can supply the needed sense of belonging in a *Gesellschaft*-like society, he maintains that when community research moves from "romantic daydreaming" about the lost territorial community and begins investigating more thoroughly the integrative functions of voluntary organizations, "we might be able to pinpoint realistically the extent and locus of alienation" and evaluate potential solutions.

So, while there are some differences between Webber and Rubin on the ability of voluntary organizations to meet the psychological needs of community in a mass society, both agree that the territorial community now possesses little relevance for attempts to raise the local quality of life. In this regard, however, they are in fundamental disagreement with community development practitioners and are at odds with the research that shows continued importance for the territorial community.

The idea that voluntary organizations can replace the territorial community as the primary basis for the psychological feelings of community is questionable. A minimum level of community rises naturally from propinquity. While professional associations, labor unions, religious groups, and other voluntary organizations can provide a measure of *Gemeinschaft*, the territorial community seems certain to remain a primary basis for the psychological community. For example, Benjamin Zablocki (1978, p. 108) maintains that a psychological community requires an "infrastructure" of interpersonal interactions to maintain itself and observes that while a voluntary organization "must nourish this infrastructure out of a surplus of its members' vested resources, if any such surplus remains after the manifest goals of the organization are met," in the territorial community, "proximity itself provides for the greater part of the maintenance of this infrastructure without the deliberate intention of the individuals involved." In other words, when people live near one another, a level of interaction and common identification is forced upon them. Voluntary organizations can supplement the territorial community, but it is difficult to foresee a time when *Gemeinschaft* is no longer associated with the territorial community.

Although the extreme position of Webber and Rubin—that the psychological feelings of community are possible (and even common) without a relevant territorial community—is in direct contrast with community development strategies intended to strengthen the local community, both voluntary organization and community development strategies represent "quests" for community. The method through which the "lost" community is "found" varies, but the common concern with the local or individual quality of life remains. In the next two chapters we will examine more closely attempts to improve the quality of community life through community development and urban planning.

Chapter Eight

Community Development

In the preceding chapter, community development was linked to quests for the economic, political, and psychological relevance of the community that are thought to be lost in a *Gesellschaft*-like, industrial society. In this chapter we can be more specific and explore various community development strategies for such quests. The exploration will be limited to American community development efforts because in less industrialized societies the concept can have a very different meaning (i.e., the hastening of *Gesellschaft*). Even in other industrial societies, there is less of the local political autonomy that distinguishes community development in the United States. Hence, even though community development is an area of international concern, the focus here is on community development efforts in this country.

AN OVERVIEW OF COMMUNITY DEVELOPMENT

Community development became both an academic discipline and applied profession in the latter half of this century. Beginning with the "community dynamics" program of William Biddle at Earlham College, Indiana, in 1947, the field has grown to include community development courses at over eighty universities and colleges, some with specialized graduate programs in community development. Professionally, the Community Development Society was established in 1970 and after ten years had grown to over a thousand members (Christenson and Robinson 1980). Members are employed by universities as teachers, researchers, and extension agents; by governments as technical advisors, planners, and managers; by private industry as counselors and consultants; and by neighborhoods as advocates or organizers. The academic training of the community development agent varies from sociology to psychology to social work to urban planning to physical education to home economics to agricultural economics. In short, it is a new and broad field, but beyond that, what exactly is community development?

Defining Community Development

Community development is yet another of those important, widely used but variously and differently defined concepts. Surprisingly little of the ambiguity surrounds the first term—*community*—which is usually defined as it is in the initial chapter of this text. James Christenson and Jerry Robinson Jr. (1980, p. 6), after reviewing the major uses of the term, conclude that in community development "a community is defined and best described by the following elements: (1) people, (2) within a geographically bounded area, (3) involved in social interaction, and (4) with one or more psychological ties with each other and with the place they live."

Development, however, requires more elaboration. "Perhaps no single word has been more widely and frequently used in so many countries of the world today than the term development" (Kim 1973, p. 462). Generally, it is a dynamic, value-laden concept that implies positive change. Perhaps the most common use is economic, where the focus is on technological transformations that increase economic productivity. Nationally, a common measure is the Gross National Product (GNP). The value-laden implication here is that transformations resulting in a higher GNP are desirable. As a similar example, political development would entail changes that result in a more representative government. Democratic politics, in this example, is the favored way of distributing and justifying governmental authority. In other words, development is regarded as a desirable change in social condition (Kim 1973). The ambiguity, of course, comes in distinguishing desirable from undesirable change. We will consider that problem shortly, but for now it is sufficient to simply combine "community" and "development" and come up with a working definition of the concept.

Task versus process. Two basic dimensions of community development exist in the literature: task and process. While they are not incompatible, they differ considerably in emphasis. Task conceptions focus more on a tangible goal (e.g., a new hospital, a school, or water treatment plant), while process conceptions emphasize the more abstract goals of strengthening community ties and local autonomy. Again, borrowing from Christenson and Robinson (1980, p. 12), we can define the *task* orientation to community development as: "(1) a group of people (2) in a community (3) reaching a decision (4) to initiate a social action process (i.e., planned intervention) (5) to change (6) their economic, social, cultural, or environmental situation." More succinctly, Roland Warren (1978, p. 325) refers to the *process* aspect of community development "as a deliberate and sustained attempt to strengthen the horizontal pattern of a community."

As an example of the difference between these two approaches, consider a large corporation locating a branch plant in a community in response to a request from the local chamber of commerce. From a task perspective, community development clearly occurred since the goal of securing a new factory was successfully reached. From a process perspective, however, the verdict is not so clear. If the chamber's activities were episodal rather than continual and if the new factory's presence increases the dependence of the vertical patterns while weakening local ties and identification, then community development did not occur. The difference is one of emphasis and value. Is the local quality of life enhanced by the new factory? From the task perspective the answer clearly is affirmative, but from the process perspective, it is possibly negative.

The best of all possible worlds occurs when a specific task is accomplished and the horizontal ties are simultaneously strengthened, but when pursuit of the task is likely to weaken local ties, the approaches are in conflict. We will employ both definitions in this chapter and try to reconcile their differences when they occur.

APPROACHES TO COMMUNITY DEVELOPMENT

In a review of the first ten years (1970–79) of publication of the *Journal of the Community Development Society,* James Christenson (1980) identified three approaches to community development: (1) self-help, (2) conflict, and (3) technical assistance.[1] As we have come to expect, one's definition of community development has a lot to do with how one goes about community development. We will see that the task definition is particularly well-suited for the technical assistance approach, while the conflict and self-help approaches are usually preferable from a process perspective.

Self-Help

The self-help approach is based on democratic principles of self-determination. The a priori assumption is that "people can become meaningful participants in the developmental process and have considerable control over the process" (Littrell 1971, p. 3). The community development agent is primarily a "facilitator." The local residents take primary responsibility for: (1) deciding what needs to be in the community, (2) how it is to be done, and (3) doing it. The goal of the community

---

[1] Similar typologies of approaches to community development can be found in Rothman (1968) and Warren (1977).

development agent is to enhance the horizontal pattern of decision making and implementation. The specific *task* is almost irrelevant. It can be directed toward any goal selected by the community. The most important part of this approach is the *process* of bringing local residents together.

Application. The process of strengthening horizontal patterns within the community is both difficult and complex. One of the first obstacles to overcome is the fatalistic apathy among local residents (Littrell 1980). The idea that ordinary people in the community can affect the local quality of life is often hard to sell to a justifiably skeptical public. Such apathy, of course, is supposedly a symptom of our *Gesell-schaft*-like mass society. Thus, an initial task of the community organizer is instilling the *Gemeinschaft*-like conditions of mutual assistance and collective action.

From the self-help perspective, the community development agent's role in this process of building *Gemeinschaft* is a limited one—very much like what group theorists have referred to as the "mainte-nance functions" of a group (Thibaut and Kelley 1959). Robert F. Bales and his associates at Harvard (Parsons and Bales 1955) found in their research that groups typically require two types of leaders: a *task* leader who proposes actions and assigns roles and an *expressive* leader who notices how people feel and works to sooth the tensions that develop within the group. The local change agent role can be seen as that of an expressive leader. The task leader, on the other hand, should be some-one indigenous to the community since only local residents are quali-fied to set the group's goals.

Task/process relationship. Although the process of strengthening horizontal patterns is given precedence over the task of achieving a specific goal, the task remains an important component of the self-help approach. In fact, it can often gain too much importance. That is, the task can become the primary reason for being, and when it is accom-plished, the local organization that was formed to achieve the task fades away.

Christopher Sower and his associates (1957) describe how various local agencies banded together to form a community health council. The initial task of the council was to gather local health data, and the council was active and growing throughout the data gathering activi-ties. When the report of local health statistics was finally prepared, it was presented at a banquet attended by fifty persons, but the comple-tion of that task was also the last action of the health council. The newly elected council president called a regular meeting, and no one came. When the task was completed, the health council was unable to sustain the horizontal pattern of integration necessary for continuance.

In fact, Sower (1957, p. 266) concludes that community development is impossible without special local tasks:

> One possible hypothesis is that there is almost no way to justify and legitimize a council type of organization in the structure of the average American community. Basic to any organization is that it must have some legitimate reason for existence, it must be justifiable. Churches, for instance, save souls, maintain moral standards, and generally do good; schools educate children; lodges provide insurance and meeting places for their members; athletic clubs provide recreation and keep down waistlines.

This emphasis on task to the exclusion of process is a problem that is especially common to community development. Bureaucracies, in contrast, often give more emphasis to preserving the organization than to accomplishing a specific task. A "goal displacement" occurs in which most of the bureaucracy's energies are directed toward maintaining the organization itself rather than accomplishing the original goals of the organization (Sills 1957). Roland Warren (1978, p. 331) maintains that exactly the opposite situation develops for community development organizations. Although the community development organization begins with the goal of strengthening the horizontal pattern,

> the organizational goal becomes displaced as the task accomplishment usurps it. This reverse goal displacement should not be surprising when we recall that community development, like community action episodes through which it takes place, involves an activation of the horizontal pattern of the community in ways in which it is not customarily activated. (If it were, the "community development" would not be necessary.) Thus, the community, as a social system, has not been made to pay the price of bureaucratic goal displacement largely because it has not received the values that bureaucratic organization affords. When it attempts to achieve these values through a rational, administered approach to creating or restoring a strong horizontal pattern in a deliberately "administered" fashion, this goal is easily displaced by the more immediate task goal of the action episode involved—be that a new school bond issue, a community center, the attraction of a new industry, an urban renewal program, or whatever.

Still, the achievement of specific tasks does not have to be as detrimental to strengthening horizontal ties as Warren implies. It can be beneficial, perhaps even necessary to the maintenance of the horizontal patterns. Allan Edwards and Dorothy Jones (1976, p. 161), after reviewing numerous attempts at community development, conclude that

> failure to achieve goals in a community action effort tends to weaken the *esprit de corps* of participants and to leave the community's members

less able to work together in subsequent actions. Conversely, the achievement of goals tends to boost community morale and increase the participants' facility for working together.

With the self-help approach to community development, then, there is a constant tension between process and task. The successful completion of a task aids in building support for the community development process, but too much emphasis on the task can divert energies from maintaining horizontal patterns. A tightrope must be walked, and a tilt too far in either direction can be fatal to community development efforts.

Evaluation. When does the self-help approach work best? Under what conditions should one expect difficulties? What kinds of difficulties? How can they be overcome? The research necessary to answer these questions has yet to be done, but it is possible to make some broad suppositions about the efficacy of the self-help approach.

First, the self-help approach probably works best in a homogeneous community. To the degree the community encompasses different groups (family status, race, social class) with different needs and values, a democratic approach to community development may become hopelessly deadlocked (Warren 1978).

Second, predominately middle-class communities may be best suited for a self-help approach since it assumes that local residents have the power, predilection, and resources to help themselves. For often powerless and sometimes apathetic lower-class residents, this may be a naive assumption. And upper-class residents, since their interest is more likely to be on extralocal events (Wellman and Leighton 1979), may be more difficult to organize around local issues.

Third, communities with a pluralistic power structure should have a tradition of open and democratic decision making conducive to the self-help approach. Communities with a covert elite decision-making structure may have little experience with, and little existent structure for, the type of politics associated with the self-help approach. Further, the ruling elite may perceive (quite accurately) this type of community development as a threat to their power.

Finally, this approach will probably be easiest to implement in relatively isolated, autonomous communities (Littrell 1980). Since the self-help process emphasizes local residents' assumption of responsibility for their environment, communities with strong vertical (and weak horizontal) patterns will be less receptive to the self-help approach. Of course, this comes close to saying that the self-help approach works best where it is not needed. A more accurate assessment, however, would be that those communities with weak horizontal patterns will present difficulties for community development from a self-help approach, but they will also be the communities most in need of community development; hence, they will also be the communities that will benefit most from a self-help approach.

Although, each of these four propositions is open to further research and revision, collectively they imply that the self-help approach will be more effective in some situations than others. And in keeping with the eclectic approach of this text, it is reasonable to assume that other approaches might do better under other conditions. Thus, it is to the other two basic approaches we now turn.

Technical Assistance

In many ways, the technical assistance approach is the opposite of the self-help approach. Where self-help emphasizes the horizontal process, technical assistance emphasizes the vertically imposed task. Where self-help is based on reestablishing *Gemeinschaft*, technical assistance is often the product of increasing *Gesellschaft*.

The technical assistance approach is based on the presumed need for expert planners who, through their technical skills (e.g., grant writing, management, cost-benefit accounting, law, counseling), can guide and evaluate the community development process. Community development, from this perspective, typically includes tasks such as economic development (e.g., attracting new industry), improving social service delivery systems (e.g., ambulance services), and coordinating existing services (e.g., regional planning).

This is the most common form of community development, and as Larry Gamm and Frederick Fisher (1980, pp. 60–61) conclude in their review of the technical assistance approach, it is a direct result of the increasingly *Gesellschaft*-like characteristics of our society:

> The growth of the technical assistance approach to community development has been attributed herein to two general forces. One such force is the increasing complexity and specialization of and interdependence among institutions in modern society. This force or dynamic contributes to the community need for technical assistance in the performance of even those functions traditionally defined as community responsibilities. A second force is the assignment of new or expanded functions to communities by outside organizations. The proliferation of federal grant programs is the major source of assigned functions and associated technical assistance activities.

In short, what has variously been described as "the eclipse of community," "the great change," or "the rise of the mass society" is the type of condition that lends itself to the technical assistance approach.

Application. Beyond the generalities of the mass society, what, specifically, has accounted for the popularity of the technical assistance approach? Who decides when expert technicians are needed? Who decides who qualifies as an expert? Who designs the project or program that needs the technical assistance? In most cases, the answer to all these questions is an extralocal (typically federal) government. In short, the process of technical assistance is almost exclusively a vertically patterned phenomenon. The task will impact upon the community, but the impetus for the task originates outside the community.

Today, most community development programs (for education, law enforcement, the elderly, job training, transportation) are funded by categorical state or federal grants. The government funds these programs for specific community programs and often determines the basic qualifications of the experts (usually from state agencies, universities, or private consulting firms) who provide the technical assistance and evaluation. In other words, the technical assistant must meet the requirements of the state or federal government, and then the technical assistant helps insure that the state or federal guidelines are being followed by the community that receives the funds.

Task/process relationship. In most cases of technical assistance, the specific task takes total precedence over the process of strengthening horizontal ties. In fact, the task, because of its base in the vertical patterns of the community, may cause the horizontal patterns to atrophy. Technical assistance often leads local residents to look to the state or federal government or to outside experts rather than to one another for solutions to community problems.[2]

There are rare but important exceptions to this relationship. There are some cases where providing technical assistance can actually strengthen horizontal patterns. Leadership training programs have this potential. In this case, federal- , state- or foundation-supported programs employ consultants to teach local residents the analytic and management skills necessary for community development. Another example is the International City Management Association's provision of technical expertise to member cities. Under this plan, a local city manager can receive expert advice on similar problems that other cities have encountered (Gamm and Fisher 1980). Still, such programs are more the exception than the rule. And the general rule is that the task takes precedence over the process.

---

[2] Ironically, a recent inducement for local organization comes from what has traditionally been a major force for strengthening vertical community patterns: the federal government. Beginning with the Great Society's problem-specific grants to communities and continuing with the broader revenue sharing and community development block grants, a major reward for many local organization efforts is federal money.

Evaluation. There is little doubt that when community problems require only facts and funds for their solution, when both the problem and the solution can be clearly defined, and when the concern is largely and simply with delivering goods or services efficiently, the technical assistance approach is preferable (Rothman 1979). However, most local problems don't fit these criteria. Thus problems like crime or poverty, with their complex causes and controversial solutions, would seem to fall outside the province of this approach, but this has not proven to be the case. We often like to conceptualize the solutions to our complex problems as technical manipulations rather than structural change. Thus, technical assistance is by far the most common approach to community development, and even if it seldom solves the local problem it is meant to address, the very fact that we try the technical assistance approach so often means that it probably has more lasting local impact than the self-help and conflict approaches combined (Christenson 1980).

Still, the evaluation of this approach by community development professionals is always colored by the neglect of horizontal ties. Christenson (1980, p. 45) argues, for example, that local change agents who rely on the technical assistance approach

> end up working *for* people rather than *with* them. While planners and technical assistance workers may argue against this characterization, it is fairly well documented that this orientation has largely ignored public input or participation.

In a similar vein, Gamm and Fisher (1980, p. 59) believe that "the more we attempt to impose technical assistance from the outside, the more we come to realize it does not work either as often or as well as those involved had hoped it would." We return, then, to a conclusion much like that reached for the self-help perspective: the most effective community development programs are those that manage to successfully complete tasks *and* maintain horizontal ties.

Conflict

The conflict approach to community development is in many ways the opposite of the self-help and technical assistance approaches. While the latter two approaches are ostensibly value-free (with self-help assuming that values must originate from the local residents and technical assistance assuming that the technical advice provided is unrelated to the more philosophical concerns of values), the conflict-oriented change agent believes there is injustice in the current structure of the community and that conflict is necessary to restructure the community along more egalitarian lines.

Application. The conflict approach to community development is identified closely with the community organization efforts of Saul Alinsky (1946, 1971). This is a very popular approach to analyze, but, outside of Alinsky, it has not proven to be a very popular approach to implement. For example, Christenson (1980, p. 44) in his review of articles in the *Journal of the Community Development Society* notes that

> articles in the *Journal* tended to report the work done by such professional activists as Saul Alinsky and not the work of the contributors. Although confrontation is interesting to discuss, when it comes to practice it seems that most authors who write for the *Journal* do not use it.

The reasons it is not widely implemented will become apparent as the steps involved in this approach are presented: namely, the conflict approach requires the change agent to make difficult and subjective choices and often alienates the change agent from powerful groups within the community.

There are, of course, other important applications of the conflict approach besides those of Saul Alinsky (e.g., the civil rights and women's movements), but at the community level, his techniques are the most widely used and analyzed.[3] So, drawing largely from Alinsky, how does one do conflict-oriented community development?

The first step is for the outside professional community organizer to *receive a formal invitation* from local leaders. Alinsky typically required invitations from several segments of the community (e.g., white liberals, blacks, churches, unions) so that local acceptance and broad-based interest developed. If the formal invitations are not initially offered, the organizer must create the type of conflict situation that will generate the invitations.

The second step involves *field research* to identify salient elements of community structure: community norms, power structure, divisions, and potential leaders. Alinsky refers to this as the listening, observing, and learning period.

The third step requires the *mobilization of community-wide sentiment for change.* Usually, the strategy is to create adversaries that unite the community. During his work in Rochester, Alinsky (1971, p. 137) called a press conference and identified the major employer as an adversary by saying, "Maybe I am innocent and uninformed of what has been happening here, but as far as I know the only thing Eastman Kodak has done on the race issue in America has been to introduce color film."

Step four is the difficult processes of *reenforcing existing community organizations and creating a new organization that represents several local*

---

[3] For alternative conflict approaches, see Cloward and Elman (1966), Glasgow (1972), Bailey and Brake (1975), O'Brien (1975).

groups. Block groups are established and linkages are formed with existing groups such as churches and unions. Then a new community-wide organization is created:

> The purpose of the organization should be interpreted as proposing to deal with those major issues which no single agency is—or can be—big enough or strong enough to cope with. Then each agency will continue to carry out its own program, but all are being banded together to achieve sufficient strength to cope with issues that are so vast and deep that no one or two community agencies would ever consider tackling them (Alinsky 1946, p. 87).

The final step is *winning a confrontation and delivering improved services.* In order to convince local residents that there is power through organization and that their membership is worth the investment of time and energy, a confrontation must be won early in the community development process. Thus, the initial confrontations should be chosen carefully to insure that they are: (1) highly visible, (2) salient, (3) nondivisive and (4) winable (Alinsky 1971, pp. 114–59).

The steps come together as scenes in a morality play of community development:

> It's the kind of thing we see in play writing; the first act introduces the characters and the plot, in the second act the plot and characters are developed as the play strives to hold the audience's attention. In the final act good and evil have their dramatic confrontation and resolution (Alinsky 1971, pp. 115–16).

But when a play ends, the audience leaves and the actors move on to other roles in other plays. Unfortunately, this has usually been the case with Alinsky's organizations as well. After the tasks of creating a community-wide organization and winning the initial confrontations are completed, the process of maintaining the horizontal patterns of local identification and action usually has been unsuccessful (O'Brien 1975; Reitzes and Reitzes 1982).

Task/process relationship. Theoretically, the successful completion of the task should insure the continuation of the process:

> Once the stated objective has been achieved the clientele need an evaluation to determine what other changes they could realistically attempt in order to better their life situation. At this stage, the conflict agent will help the indigenous leaders assess their situation, assess what they have achieved, and assess where they might go from here. The agent's intentions of leaving the community should be reaffirmed. It is probably best if the agent phases out of the community picture as quietly as possible, leaving the administration and the recognition to the indigenous leaders. The experiences derived from the exercise of planning change through conflict should provide local community organizations with the confidence and ability to carry on in the future (Robinson 1980, p. 88).

The above description has not proven to be the case, however. Alinsky's repeated attempts to build a national coalition of community organizations were failures (Reitzes and Reitzes 1982), and even within the same city, those organizations that remained in existence would not aid one another (Lancourt 1979). Hence, the process of maintaining horizontal patterns has proven to be a major difficulty for the conflict approach.

Evaluation. As shown above, the process of maintaining the community development organization is a major problem since the conflict approach lends itself to episodal rather than continuous development. Although it is, perhaps, too psychologically and physically demanding to maintain continuous community conflict, the individual tasks that can be accomplished by this approach should not be discounted. The conflict approach can accomplish substantial change in a relatively short period of time (Christenson 1980).

In fact, the inability to maintain the community development process is hardly unique to the conflict approach. It is also a common shortcoming of the self-help and technical assistance approaches. In other words, the inability to maintain horizontal patterns cannot account for the relatively few applications of the conflict approach. Rather, there are two other difficulties that account for its lack of popularity among community change agents. One is the nature of the opposition in the conflict—typically the rich and powerful. Even if the change agent is willing to side against the establishment,[4] the resultant backlash from these vested interest groups may outweigh the fruits of the initial victory.

Beyond the difficulties associated with going against the establishment, there is an ethical problem with this approach. When does one intervene into community affairs? On whose side? James Laue and Gerald Cormick (1978, pp. 217–18) suggest that the professional change agent should always ask:

> Does the intervention contribute to the ability of relatively powerless individuals and groups in the situation to determine their own destinies to the greatest extent consistent with the common good?

In theory, an affirmative answer to this question would appear to resolve the ethical dilemma, but in practice it is more problematic. Suppose several black families want to move from their all-black neighborhood to an all-white working class neighborhood. The black families need organization to win the conflict, and the white neighborhood could be mobilized to resist the "invasion." Both groups are relatively

---

[4] Since the change agent is usually an "outside agitator" in this approach, there is less to fear from local elites.

powerless; both wish to determine their own destinies; and the common good is, in this case, undefinable. Many community organizers would feel uncomfortable using the conflict approach in such a situation, and such situations are common.[5]

Comparing Approaches

Although each of three major approaches aims at improving the local quality of life, each makes very different assumptions about community problems and solutions. Table 8–1 contrasts these approaches along several common dimensions of community development. Note that each appears better suited for some situations than others. Depending on the values of the change agent, the nature of the local problem, and the characteristics of the community, one approach to community development will be preferred over another. Thus, the skilled practitioner needs sufficient insight into self and community to know which approach is most likely to succeed. And, then, sufficient flexibility is needed to implement that approach:

> Our field studies have produced voluminous evidence that [various] roles are needed, but not always at the same time and place. The challenging problem, on which we have made a bare beginning, is to define more clearly the specific conditions under which one or another or still other types of practice are appropriate. The skill we shall need in the practitioner of the future is the skill of making a situational diagnosis and analysis that will lead him to a proper choice of the methods most appropriate to the task at hand (Gurin 1966, p. 30).

While Gurin has been proven correct in his call for the ability to choose between various approaches, in the years since his article, it also has become increasingly clear that these approaches are not mutually exclusive.

Mixing and phasing approaches. In an insightful article comparing the three basic approaches, Jack Rothman (1979, p. 43) calls for the "mixing and phasing" of self-help, technical assistance, and conflict since many "problems require such blending, and organizational structure may permit adaptations." Most critics of the technical assistance

---

[5] This discussion of the conflict approach has focused exclusively on techniques geared toward *promoting* conflict. In that regard it reflects the usual use of conflict for community development. However, the goals of community development also can be met through conflict *prevention* and *mediation*. See Robinson (1980) for a comparison of these three types of conflict approaches, and for an attempt to escape ethical dilemmas by choosing mediation over promotion or prevention.

TABLE 8–1 Comparisons of the three major approaches to community development

Approach	Values of change agent	Typical occupation of change agent	Perception of clients	Relationship to power structure	Ideal community characteristics	Task/process relationship
Self-help	Democratic	Social worker, VISTA volunteer.	Unorganized citizens needing assistance in strengthening horizontal ties.	Attempts to broaden decision-making, may be seen as threat to power structure.	Homogeneous, middle class.	Process takes precedence over task.
Technical assistance	Neutral	Sociologist, agricultural extension agent.	Untrained consumers needing more efficient services.	Works for power structure.	"Eclipsed" community dependent on extra-local assistance.	Task is everything, process irrelevant.
Conflict	Egalitarian	Community organizer, labor organizer, civil rights worker.	Exploited victims who must band together to forcefully change community structure.	Works against vested interest of powerful, definite threat to power structure.	Numerous working or lower class neighborhoods.	Task and process both important, task has proven more attainable than process.

approach, for example, believe it should be mixed with some of the local self-determination of the self-help approach.

Rothman notes, however, that not all blends are possible, with the conflict approach being particularly difficult to combine with others. In these cases, the approaches may be phased. A community might be helped best by one approach initially and then, at a later stage, by another. Conflict, for example, may be necessary for securing the power and organization sufficient for the successful introduction of a self-help approach.[6] In this case, the change agent must be able to determine when conditions are ripe for a transition from one type of community development to another. Not only is the mixing and phasing the approaches often the best strategy for effective community development, it is also becoming the most common practice for local change agents.

Current Status of Community Development

Community development is becoming decidedly eclectic. Just as multiple approaches to community development are being employed, the field itself is opening up to a broader range of professionals with a wider variety of skills. The "new federalism," with its retrenchment from social welfare programs, required communities to practice various forms of long-forgotten self-sufficiency. Remaining programs, such as community block grants and revenue sharing, provided impetus for local decision making about the proper course of community development, with different communities making different decisions.

Still, it would not be correct to say that just because the field is becoming more eclectic, all the approaches to community development are flourishing equally well. The conflict approach has especially lost favor in the conservative 1980s. As "radical" loses it "chic," Alinsky-type community organizers become less numerous (Spiegel 1980).

Additionally, as federal and foundation money for community development has become scarcer, there has been an accompanying increase in the demand for accountability.[7] This typically implies a method of program evaluation that produces measurable community outputs. Such evaluations will naturally favor task-dominated approaches to community development, since it is relatively easy to measure how successful one is in building a new school or renovating a

---

[6] The labor and civil rights movements have moved through similar modes of action.

[7] This loss of funds for community development has also reduced the growth rate for practitioners in this field. The Community Development Society had less than half as many members in 1985 as it did in 1980 (Christenson et al. 1985).

housing project. But how does one measure the strength of horizontal ties, and how, then, can process-oriented programs to strengthen these ties be evaluated and justified? Hence, the fiscal crunch of the 1980s has required communities to become more responsible for their own fate, but it has also made it more difficult to fund the process-oriented types of community development programs.

This may be the major task confronting community development today: the horizontal patterns of the community must be better conceptualized and measured so that techniques for their strengthening can be evaluated. The measurement of these horizontal patterns is considered in the third section of this text, but before proceeding to that final section, one more subject that goes considerably beyond community development requires attention: "planned" or "new" communities.

Chapter Nine

Planned Communities

Most communities just happen. That is, they are much more the product of various unanticipated, uncontrolled, local, and extralocal forces than they are the product of deliberate, planned local development. Some important exceptions do exist, however. A few communities are, at least in part, the result of rational planning. Rather than improving an existing neighborhood, as in Chapter 8, planned communities are new towns that are consciously created to improve the quality of life. In this chapter, we will: (1) examine the theoretical basis for planned communities, (2) look back at some of the pioneering attempts at planning and building new communities, (3) evaluate the progress of more recently developed planned communities, and (4) try to determine what can be learned from attempts to plan communities.

THE ORIGINS OF PLANNED COMMUNITIES: *GEMEINSCHAFT/GESELLSCHAFT,* CONFLICT SOCIOLOGY, SPATIAL DETERMINISM, AND EBENEZER HOWARD

The planned communities examined in this chapter emerged from the convergence of three classic community themes: (1) the desire to restore lost *Gemeinschaft,* (2) a somewhat muted conflict view of the industrial community, and (3) the belief that a community's ecological structure influences its social structure. Thus, one of the major theoretical underpinnings for community planning is Tönnies's original idea concerning *Gesellschaft* replacing *Gemeinschaft.* The goal of many early planners was to construct a new form of industrial city including features common to rural, preindustrial environments; in this way, the negative effects of *Gesellschaft* might be tempered by the positive elements of a *Gemeinschaft*-like environment. Note, as a primary example, the position of the most influential planner of new towns since the industrial revolution, Ebenezer Howard,[1] in his classic *Garden Cities of To-Morrow:*

> The two magnets must be made one. As man and woman by their varied gifts and faculties supplement each other, so should town and country. The town is the symbol of society—of mutual help and friendly cooperation, of fatherhood, motherhood, brotherhood, sisterhood, of wide relations. . . . The country is the symbol of God's love and care. . . . All that we are and all that we have comes from it. Our bodies are formed of it; to it they return. We are fed by it, clothed by it, and by it we are warmed and sheltered. . . . It is the source of all health, all wealth, all knowledge. . . . Town and country must be married, and out of this joyous union will spring a new hope, a new life, a new civilization (1898, 1965, p. 48).

While Ebenezer Howard shared a nostalgia for rural *Gemeinschaft* with Tönnies, Howard's critical view of life in industrial cities was similar to the conflict approach of Karl Marx and Friedrich Engels. Again from *Garden Cities of To-Morrow,* Howard (1898, 1965, p. 43) cites observers who believe that "cities tend more and more to become the graves of the physique of our race, can we wonder at it when we see the houses so foul, so squalid, so ill-drained, so vitiated by neglect and dirt?" Later in the book, he views London as "an eye-sore and a blot . . . a danger to health and an outrage on decency" (Howard 1898, 1965, p. 156). Such descriptions of London could just as easily have been made by Engels.[2]

Not only did Howard reflect Marx and Engels in his critical view of industrial cities, he also was somewhat of a socialist, advocating community ownership of all the land in his new cities. And though not a revolutionary, he was a social activist who played a major role in securing support for his ideas. So, while Howard (1898, 1965, p. 114) claims that "no reader will confuse the experiment here advocated with any experiment in absolute Communism," his plans are certainly experiments in *partial* communism, and his influential garden cities movement includes the Marxist tradition of economic criticism almost as much as the Tönnies's tradition of lost *Gemeinschaft.*

Howard believed that new, planned communities could free England from the urban ills that so distressed Marx and Engels. For

---

[1] Several major cities existing prior to industrialization reflect attempts at planning: Moenjo-Daro, in the Indus River Valley (2500 B.C.), Teotihuacan, the forerunner of modern Mexico City (700 A.D.), Peking, during the Ming Dynasty (1400 A.D.), Hellenic Athens (480 B.C.), and Imperial Rome (100 A.D.); but planning as an attempt to reverse the growing dominance of *Gesellschaft*-like relationships can be attributed to the pioneering works of Ebenezer Howard.

[2] For example, see Engels's descriptions of London quoted in Chapter 5, p. 66 of this text.

Howard, much like Louis Wirth in America, the physical urban environment creates urban lifestyles, and, going beyond Wirth, Howard believed that modifying the urban environment would modify the social environment. In the introduction to his chapter on administering his garden cities, Howard (1898, 1965, p. 89) quotes from Albert Shaw's *Municipal Government in Great Britain:*

> The present evils of city life are temporary and remediable. The abolition of the slums, and the destruction of their virus, are as feasible as the drainage of a swamp, and the total dissipation of its miasmas. The conditions and circumstances that surround the lives of the masses of the people in modern cities can be so adjusted to their needs as to result in the highest development of the race, in body, in mind and in moral character. The so-called problems of the modern city are but the various phases of the one main question: How can the environment be most perfectly adapted to the welfare of urban populations? And science can meet and answer every one of these problems.

Howard's plans for a new urban environment are based on the environmental determinism reflected in this quotation.

In the next section, we will see Howard's ideas put into practice, but now it is sufficient simply to note that his ideas for new towns flowed from the same theoretical streams that produced the classic works of Tönnies, Marx, and Wirth. And to the degree that we will uncover examples of Howard's influence on later attempts to plan new communities, we can see these classic traditions being the ideological basis for modern planned communities as well.

EARLY ATTEMPTS AT PLANNING COMMUNITIES

Since this book focuses on North American communities, attempts to plan communities in Europe (Herman 1971; Michelson 1977), South America (Epstein 1974), and Asia (Payne 1977) are not detailed here. Because of the strong influence of Ebenezer Howard's ideas on community planning in North America, however, we must examine his "New Towns" movement.

New Towns in England

As we found in the preceding section, Ebenezer Howard's new towns were a reaction to the growing *Gesellschaft*-like atmosphere of industrializing England. In response to the abject poverty, high disease rate, pervasive crime, and near-uninhabitability of many dwellings in London, Howard began to plan new towns incorporating elements of rural, natural *Gemeinschaft* within the city itself.

A new town with "green belts." To maintain a rural atmosphere within an urban environment, Howard planned for gardens, parks, and especially for "green belts" of forest land as integral parts of each new city. A major proponent of Howard's new towns, Frederick Osborn (1969, p. 28) describes the towns as

> a balanced mixture of all social groups and levels of income. Areas are worked out for the zones; public buildings and places of entertainment are placed centrally, shops intermediately, factories on the edge with the railway and sidings. Houses are of different sizes, but all have gardens and all are within easy range of factories, shops, schools, cultural centers, and the open country. Of special interest is the central park and the inner Green Belt or Ring Park, 420 feet wide, containing the main schools with large playgrounds and such buildings as churches.

Not only did Howard conceive of *inner* green belts that separated various parts of the city, but each city was to have also an encircling *outer* green belt of forests or open land that was owned by the town and could never be developed. The purpose of the outer belt was to limit the growth of the city. These green belts have become the most enduring aspect of Howard's plans. Today, virtually every planned city in Europe and North America includes such belts.[3]

Letchworth and Welwyn. Howard's plans were realized in 1902, when, with the financial aid of the Garden City Association, his first city was built at Letchworth, about thirty miles north of London (Osborn 1969). It was not planned to be merely a suburb of London, but rather a self-contained, self-sufficient city of thirty thousand residents living in a blissful, largely *Gemeinschaft*-like environment. Unfortunately, it never reached the state Howard and his supporters had envisioned. Financial problems, a lack of industry, and lower than desired population growth hindered the new town. In spite of these problems, however, a second city was begun in 1920, Welwyn Garden City; and while it encountered similar problems, Welwyn was more successful and is today an attractive community of 44,000 residents (Palen 1981).

Although Letchworth and Welwyn were the pioneering attempts, the real impetus for implementing Howard's ideas came with destruction of much of London during World War II. The New Towns Act of 1946 provided government sponsorship of self-sufficient new towns beyond a green belt that was to encircle London and thereby curtail its future growth. The new towns part of the Act proved easier to implement than a green belt around London (just as Howard had predicted), and now over thirty new towns have been built.

---

[3] The inner green belts are more common than the outer belts since the outer belts are designed to limit growth. Few communities, even planned ones, want to limit growth.

FIGURE 9–1   Howard's plans for a garden city.

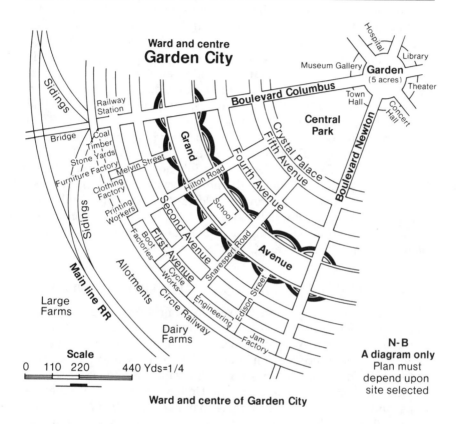

The "Grand Avenue" in these plans is an inner green belt while the "New Forests" comprise the outer green belts. From Howard (1898, 1965, pp. 52–53).

The Mark I and Mark II towns. The first of these new towns, called Mark I towns, were similar to Howard's plans for Letchworth and Welwyn. The Mark I town of Stevenage, for example, separated housing from industry and pedestrian traffic from autos and trucks, focused social life on the neighborhood, and emphasized single-family housing units. Later communities, Mark II towns, departed considerably from Howard's ideas: extending population limits to eighty thousand and beyond, dramatically increasing residential density, allowing more private ownership, emphasizing central shopping and recreation facilities rather than the neighborhood, and giving less emphasis to agriculture and green belts.

Although the Mark I and II towns did not follow all of Howard's plans for the ideal industrial community, they represent a large-scale experiment in community planning, an experiment that can be evaluated even if it is not a true test of Howard's ideas. How successful are these new towns? That is, do they meet either Howard's original goal of restoring the satisfaction of *Gemeinschaft* or the government's desire to relieve urban congestion and provide new housing? The general answer, on both counts, is no. Although residents of the new towns appear satisfied with their communities, their attitudes and lifestyles do not differ significantly from those of other Britons (Michelson 1977a). As for relieving London's congestion and providing new housing, the population limits on the new towns limited their impact on London's housing needs. Only 5 percent of Britain's housing constructed since World War II has been built in the new towns (Palen 1981). Yet, new towns based (however loosely) on Howard's plans were built, they survived, some even flourish, and, most important, they continue to influence community planning, as we shall see in the next section on planned communities in the United States.

PLANNED COMMUNITIES IN THE UNITED STATES

The idea of new towns came to America almost exclusively as a creation of private enterprise.[4] The lack of government support, planning, and control for new American towns is a unique social phenomenon, almost without precedent anywhere else in the world. As such, it shows how local communities reflect the values of the larger society. Capitalism is more developed in the United States than in other nations, and in the United States, more than in other nations, new towns were built to produce a profit. In fact, over one hundred new towns have been built in the United States by *private* developers since 1920, but among the most important attempts at constructing new communities are Radburn, New Jersey, Reston, Virginia, and Columbia, Maryland.

The earliest of these three major planned communities is *Radburn, New Jersey.* Henry Wright and Clarence Stein conceived of Radburn as a new, planned town near New York City, and the City Housing Corporation, a limited-profit group in New York, began development of Radburn in the late 1920s. Initially, Wright and Stein followed Howard's ideas closely, but added an innovative "super block" design that built houses facing a large public green space. The rear of the

---

[4] There were three unsuccessful exceptions. During the depression, three green belt towns were built by the government: Greenbelt, Maryland; Green Hills, Ohio; and Greendale, Wisconsin. In 1949, government support was ended for these towns and the Howard-inspired green belts that surrounded them were opened to private development.

houses faced dead-end streets, thereby limiting the vehicular traffic in residential neighborhoods. These superblocks have proven to be very popular. They now can be found in urban development plans from Adelaide, South Australia to Leningrad, USSR.

FIGURE 9–2   Wright and Stein's super block

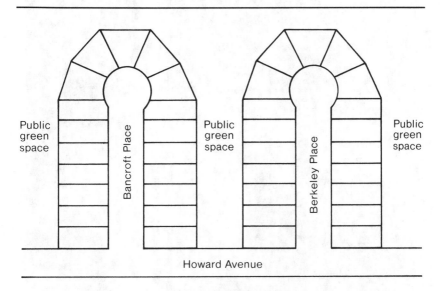

Radburn was clearly an architectural success, and economically it almost survived the Depression, in part because the emphasis on smaller and fewer streets held down construction costs. In fact, *Business Week* complimented Radburn in 1930 on its apparent immunity to the Depression, but in the long run, local communities rarely can resist national trends. In 1934, the City Housing Association declared bankruptcy.

When the City Housing Corporation lost control of development, it became clear that Radburn could never become an American version of Howard's garden city. It began as a place where middle-class families could raise their children, and it never changed (Stein, 1957). Early attempts by the City Housing Corporation to attract lower-income residents were unsuccessful. The planned green belt was not completed. Industry never moved to Radburn, and the idea of the community owning undeveloped land remained only an idea. Radburn became not a "garden city," but a "garden suburb" within the larger suburb of Fair Lawn. Radburn is a bit greener and better designed than many suburbs but not qualitatively different from other suburban communities in its local norms and values.

Reston, Virginia, possesses award-winning architectural designs. Reston is smaller than Columbia, the other planned community near Washington, D.C., but as a comparison with the photograph on page 138 shows, they have many similarities.

Reston, Virginia, was conceived in the 1960s by developer Robert E. Simon. While it is located only twenty-five miles from Washington, D.C., in Fairfax County, Virginia (about midway between Washington, D.C., and the Dulles Airport), it, like Radburn, was designed to have its own industry and thus be more self-sufficient than most suburbs. Simon planned it to have a population of over seventy thousand,[5] living in a decentralized city made up of seven villages separated by the Howard-inspired green belts.

Reston achieved stunning architectural success. With a mixture of various housing types (many designed by famous architects), green belts, office structures, lakes, and industrial sites, it became one of America's most attractive cities. However, it was a financially troubled city almost from the start. Planners assumed that thousands of families would move from Washington, D.C., to enjoy the architectural splendor of Reston, even if housing costs were appreciably higher. That was not the case, however, and Gulf Oil, Reston's principal investor, took over the development of the town in 1967 in an attempt to prevent further financial losses. Gulf, then, sold its holdings in Reston to Mobil in 1978.

The two petroleum conglomerates have been successful in bringing economic health to the community. In 1984, the number of jobs in Reston surpassed the number of households. It is a largely "white collar" community in which "high tech" industries such as GTE, Tandem Computers, and AT&T are especially predominant. Thus, Reston is no longer just a residential suburb for Washington, D.C., commuters, but some of the architectural quality, while still superior, may have slipped, and Simon's attempt to mix social classes by building middle-class and upper-class housing side by side has been abandoned (Palen 1981). In order to become profitable, Reston became more like other American communities.

Columbia, Maryland is another new town built near Washington, D.C., (midway between Washington and Baltimore), and it, too, plans to turn a profit while at the same time providing a superior community environment. James Rouse, the developer of Columbia, aimed "to create a social and physical environment which works for people, nourishes human growth, and allows private venture capital to make a profit in land development" (Bailey 1973, p. 16). Yet Columbia differed from Reston in one major way. While Reston reflected the plans of innovative architects, Columbia reflected the plans of innovative social scientists. While Reston tried to make an architectural statement, Columbia strove to make a sociological one. Columbia's founder hoped to demonstrate that he could provide "a richer sense of community among people if the physical place and the community institutions

---

[5] In 1985, Reston had forty thousand residents.

Columbia, Maryland, is one of the most successful of America's planned communities. Note the Howard-inspired green belts that separate the different land uses.

were all seen as opportunities to support and enable the growth of people" (Rouse 1978, p. 51). Rouse employed a large group of social scientists as regular consultants in the design of Columbia, and while Rouse (1978, p. 53) admits that the social planners "did not produce any brilliant new concepts or sociological breakthroughs," he does maintain that they developed a plan that "focused on producing a sense of community at various levels from the cul-de-sac or block to the neighborhood, to the village and to the city as a whole." Columbia is more in the tradition of Howard's garden cities in its planning, goals, and development than is Reston.[6]

Rouse plans for Columbia to have a metropolitan population of over 250,000, and since its initial development in 1963, it has grown to over 60,000 with a metropolitan area in excess of 100,000. Like Reston and Radburn before it, Howard's green belt concept is clearly evident in Columbia. Rouse's design attempts to give Columbia more characteristics of *Gemeinschaft*, i.e., more decentralization, more focus on neighborhoods, more economic and racial harmony and integration, and less use of the automobile. In some areas, Rouse's design has been successful. Subsidized housing is scattered throughout Columbia, rather than clustering in one area, neighborhoods have become the basis for a "town hall" type of government, and educational and medical facilities are convenient and of high quality. In fact, Columbia has been called "the most successful American new town" (Spates and Macionis 1982, p. 468), and it probably is.

However, one reason that Columbia has been regarded as such a success is because goals for new towns are so much more circumscribed than they were in Howard's day. Howard's plans called for nothing less than a truly *new* town: new in its architectural design and, most importantly, new in its quality of life, with substantial increases in *Gemeinschaft*-like relationships. In these two areas, Columbia has fallen short. Architecturally, Columbia is attractive, but its design is less harmonious and less innovative than Reston's (Palen 1981). The quality of life is perceived by its residents as high, but not much higher than in many other communities (Burby and Weiss et al. 1975). The automobile is still dominant, racial and class antagonisms remain (Palen 1981), and the feeling of *Gemeinschaft*-like community is probably no stronger in Columbia than elsewhere (Brooks 1974). In other words, Columbia, like Reston and Radburn, is a fairly typical American suburb. Columbia *is* more attractive and better planned than most suburbs—and that is no small achievement—but the similarities of Columbia to other unplanned American suburbs still outweigh the differences.

---

[6] To the degree that the two communities were competitive, it was suggested that one might want to live in Reston out of a sense of "duty," but one would want to live in Columbia because it was "fun" (Michelson 1977b).

EVALUATING PLANNED COMMUNITIES

How successful, in financial, architectural, and social terms, were these attempts to plan and build new communities? The majority opinion is that they were at least partial failures on all three counts. Financial difficulties always dogged the new towns. In America, especially, with new towns almost wholly dependent on venture capital, the inability to turn a profit has been a major obstacle. Accordingly, the profit motive has led to architectural problems. Columbia, for example, has increased its profitability by allowing various developers considerable freedom in design. John Palen (1981, p. 325) observes that "architecturally it [Columbia] is less successful; it resembles an ideal supersuburb, largely because the builders of the various sections were given a relatively free hand and built a mixture of their best-selling models." And since American attempts at new towns became places with suburban characteristics—making them indistinguishable from other suburbs—it should not be surprising that new towns have failed to innovate socially. Residents of American new towns live about the same way and have about the same perceived quality of life as residents in less-planned suburbs (Burby and Weiss et al. 1975).

Lessons from Attempts at Community Planning

So, what can be learned from these attempts to plan new towns? One lesson concerns the logical contradictions of differences in scale. New towns are scaled to be small, and the concentrations of urban populations are much larger. *If new towns are planned to be limited in their population size, then their effect on urban overcrowding must be limited.* If we believe our cities have several million too many residents, then a new town of 50,000 or even 500,000 won't make much difference. And, when it is remembered that most new towns grow at well below their anticipated rates, it is easy to see how critics like William Alonso (1970) can argue that new towns will have little effect on urban concentrations.

The disappointing growth rates of many new towns brings us to a second lesson—*the necessity of bringing people and jobs together at the same time.* Obviously, new towns have had a hard time providing jobs for their residents, but even if the jobs can be generated, the timing of industrial and residential growth is crucial. John Bardo and John Hartman (1982) point out that when industry was built before housing in Comotara, Kansas, workers settled in places outside the planned community of Comotara. On the other hand, developers in Flower Mound, near Dallas–Fort Worth, built homes before industry and businesses, and Flower Mound became an almost exclusively residential suburb.

Another lesson concerns what Roland Warren called the vertical patterns of community (in Chapter 4 of this text). For a town to be truly new and different, the social institutions must be new and different. Yet states have strict policies concerning the parameters of local education, government, taxation, and health care. Even local businesses and churches are usually accountable to a larger entity outside the community. *The ability of new towns to experiment, to differ from other towns, is limited severely by their vertical connections.*

The necessity for new towns (in America, anyway) to turn a relatively quick profit is a continuing problem. Community characteristics that enhance private profit are not always the same as characteristics that enhance the public good.[7] New towns, then, typically are smaller in size, more routine in design, and closer to a central city for one reason: to increase the chances of short-term profitability. *Planned communities end up looking very much like their unplanned counterparts because both must seek profits.*

The lessons drawn from new towns all seem negative. Together, they tell us that planned communities are hard to build, too small to do much good, and end up looking much like unplanned communities anyway. Practically, new planned towns don't make much sense. And, yet, we do not know what is practical until we try the impractical. In other words, the fact that new towns did not deliver the quality of life Howard and others had hoped for does not allow us to dismiss them simply as impractical, utopian dreams that hold no relevance for the "real" world. Even utopian dreams have a purpose; to paraphrase Goethe, we can attempt the possible only because we have postulated the impossible. Howard postulated the impossible: to create a community substantially different, substantially superior to the society in which it exists. We can now build the possible: a community, like Columbia or Reston, that may be a little better place to live than other places. The impossible dreams of Ebenezer Howard's garden cities led to the practical possibilities of Robert Simon's Reston and James Rouse's Columbia.[8]

---

[7] An example of this problem is the now-defunct federal program to encourage building new communities with a "proper balance of housing" (1968 New Communities Act) by race and income. Thirteen new communities were guaranteed loans, and all but one, The Woodlands, near Houston, defaulted. The failure to turn a profit often was attributed to the required housing mixture. One reason for the Woodlands' success may have been its continued resistance of HUD demands for more subsidized housing. Today, The Woodlands is about 2 percent black, while the Houston metropolitan area is about 25 percent black. Mixed housing may be in the public good, but it may not be profitable.

[8] And besides, pragmatism is an often overrated, oversupplied commodity in the 1980s. Adlai Stevenson once remarked in a similar time that "someone always cries out for practical men, and unfortunately, there always seem to be plenty of them around" (quoted in Hanson 1978, p. 25).

STUDYING THE COMMUNITY

Thus far, we have looked at how to define a community, how to make sense of it theoretically, and how to make communities better places to live. Our treatments of these important topics have been rather broad, with only the most important issues being considered in each chapter. In this section, however, the focus narrows. The goal of this text is more than to encourage an appreciation of the community; it is hoped that the research skills presented in this section encourage an active participation in studying the community as well. And since participation typically requires more detailed information than appreciation, Section III requires more specifics than abstracts.

These last chapters present both research skills and, when applicable, research findings. Most of the focus of Chapter 10 (Local Indicators) is on securing and interpreting indicators of the quality of community life. There is only brief mention of research findings concerning which communities offer the highest quality of life. The ratio of skills to findings is even more extreme with respect to community surveys (Chapter 11). Here we find a vast body of research techniques but virtually nothing in the way of accumulated knowledge about the community. A more even balance develops in the next two chapters on community power. Chapter 12 reviews the knowledge gained from our studies of local power distributions, and Chapter 13 presents a step-by-step guide to measuring community power. The ratio of skills to findings shifts even further in Chapter 14 (Field Research: Holistic Studies and Methods), where we see the most significant research findings in all of community sociology. Methodologically, however, we find in these holistic studies a conglomerate of techniques—including all the methods covered in the previous chapters in this section—as well as decidedly individualistic field methods. It is not easy to say exactly how one does a holistic study, but it is easy to see the enduring contribution of their findings.

If Section I sharpened our view of the community and Section II showed us how people have tried to improve the community, then these methods of community study should enable us to do the research that helps raise the quality of community life. But exactly what will the good community be like? Since there are no easy answers to that question, the final chapter considers possible answers in detail. In fact, we have encountered nothing but difficult questions in this text: What is a community? How should it be studied? How can communities be improved? Difficult questions, however, are usually the most important ones, and such questions are what make the study of community both difficult and important.

Chapter Ten

Local Indicators

The chapters in the preceding section are concerned with the quality of community life. In this section, while the chapters will focus more on various community *research methodologies,* the quality of life remains a concern. Beyond the academic worth of knowledge gained from community research, a very pragmatic goal of all the methodologies in this section is to analyze and improve the local quality of life. Indeed, concern with a community's quality of life was the very raison d'etre for developing the local indicators discussed in this chapter. Local indicators exist largely to indicate the local quality of life.

THE ORIGINS AND TYPES OF LOCAL INDICATORS

The concept of *local* indicators is not used as widely as the concepts from which it evolved: economic indicators and social indicators. Generally, anything that indicates the quality of local life can be a local indicator, but, more specifically, local indicators are typically divided into two types: *objective indicators* that measure actual events such as local crime rates, and *subjective indicators* that measure attitudes about events, such as community surveys on the fear of crime.

Most local indicators have evolved from objective types of measures. Economic indicators, which produced social indicators, which in turn produced local indicators, include objective measures like the Gross National Product, prices, earnings, inflation, and so on. By the 1960s, these objective economic indicators were being combined into econometric models that advised businesses or governments to pursue certain policies, such as cutting taxes that in turn would reflate the economy, as measured by the employment rate and gross national product. While the predictive success of these econometric models is debatable, their acceptance is not. Thus, the rise of what Otis Duncan (1969) called the "social indicators movement" was an attempt to develop a set of social indicators that might guide public policy in the same way that economic indicators are used currently.

Social indicators also tended to be objective measures, though not as exclusively objective as economic indicators. For example, the U. S. Government's *Social Indicators* (1973, 1976, 1980) are mammoth compendiums of objective statistics such as unemployment rates, crime rates, divorce rates, health care expenditures, disability and morbidity data, education levels, household size, and poverty rates. Subjective measures of opinion and perception are virtually nonexistent in the 1973 edition of *Social Indicators*, but there is an acknowledgment (p. xiii) that they probably should be included if they were "available" and "consistent":

> *Social Indicators* 1973 is restricted almost entirely to data about objective conditions. In only a few instances has information on people's attitudes toward or satisfaction with the conditions of their lives been included. Subjective information has been omitted in large part because it is rarely available on a consistent basis over time. As more attitudinal data become available, however, they will be considered for inclusion in subsequent issues.

And, as promised, the 1976 edition includes the results of a few public opinion surveys, but they are a minority of the data, and the 1976 introduction includes a lengthy introduction on the "quality" problems with survey data: sampling error, questionnaire design, falsified answers, coding errors, and inaccurate data processing. Still, there is movement toward including opinion survey data. The 1980 volume begins each chapter with a survey section entitled "Public Perceptions."

The ways in which subjective indicators are introduced in these volumes reflect a dilemma in social indicators research. On the one hand, there is the feeling that a major improvement in social indicators over economic indicators is the addition of the more subjective, qualitative survey data (Gross 1966), but at the same time, there is the fear that such "soft" data will not lend itself to the type of modeling practiced by econometricians (Sheldon and Freeman 1970). In short, the mixture of objective and subjective data in social indicators is an uneasy, awkward one, but a major difference between most economic and social indicators is that social indicators are much more likely to include subjective data such as public opinion surveys.

Local indicators are the logical extension of social indicators. If national statistics can describe the quality of life nationally, then community statistics can be used to describe the quality of life locally. As a further extension, just as social indicators are more likely to include subjective measures than are economic indicators, local indicators are even more likely to include attitude surveys than are social indicators.

The reasons for a greater reliance on surveys in assessing the local rather than the national quality of life are pragmatic. Local surveys are easier to do than national surveys, and, conversely, more objective data are available nationally than locally. In fact, some discussions of local indicators imply that they are exclusively surveys (e.g., Rossi 1972), but it is certainly possible and probably desirable to include both objective and subjective indicators in assessing the quality of local life.

There are advantages and disadvantages associated with both subjective and objective local indicators. Surveys have the advantage of directly measuring the state of the community as seen through the eyes of those who live there. And to the degree that the quality of life is a subjective perception of conditions more than the actual state of local conditions, surveys will provide a more accurate assessment of the quality of life. For example, if everyone in the community is afraid to walk the streets at night because of the perceived danger of crime, it may make little difference what the actual crime rate is. It is the *perception* of the magnitude of the crime problem that determines whether we venture out at night.[1]

Although surveys are the most direct measures of local perceptions, surveys are often hard to design, implement, and interpret. Thus, they are seldom comparable from one time or community to another. For example, Elizabeth Martin (1983, p. 729), after evaluating the use of surveys as quality of life indicators, concludes that the inherent difficulties "seem to leave us in a hopeless quandary." Still, her full conclusion is a bit more optimistic, arguing that *properly* designed surveys can be more comparable than most surveys are today. We will look at proper techniques of survey design in the next chapter, but for now the point is that while surveys are very valuable as local indicators, they also have problems of comparability. Comparability, however, is the strong point of more objective indicators.

Objective indicators are usually comparable from one time and community to another because of the impetus from community's vertical ties. The state and national governments require local reports to be comparable with previous reports and with reports filed from other communities. Local businesses, schools, churches, and charities are usually affiliated with extralocal organizations that require comparable standardized reporting. Thus, there are hundreds of measures in each community that are comparable to similar measures in other communities.

Beyond comparability, these objective indicators have other advantages. They are objective; i.e., they report actual conditions rather than

---

[1] Numerous surveys (e.g., Skogan and Maxfield 1981; Warr 1984) have shown that fear of crime tends to be highest among those who are the *least* likely to be victims of crime.

perceptions of the conditions. They are unobtrusive; i.e., it's not necessary to "bother" hundreds of people asking them survey questions. They are readily available, i.e., it takes relatively little time or money to gather these data. Libraries are full of them.

Objective local indicators are not without their problems, however. One of the difficulties comes from their availability. When hundreds of indicators are available, which ones should be used? And if several are selected, how should they be weighted? For example, if we are assessing the quality of local education, should we include student attendance rates, library size, standardized achievement tests, student-teacher ratios, educational expenditures, teacher experience, or teacher education? And if the answer is that all of these indicators should be included in an assessment of local education, then how are they to be combined? Which ones are more important indicators of educational quality than others?

Another problem with using objective indicators is that they are necessarily *indirect* indicators. In the above example, none of the indicators directly measures the quality of local education. Rather, they are a series of proxies—surrogate measures for an inherently unmeasurable concept. From these indicators, we can infer the level of educational quality, but it is not an inference that is made easily.

So, objective indicators, just like their subjective counterparts, possess attributes and defects. And community research that includes both types of indicators will almost always be superior to research that is restricted to only one. Thus, both objective and subjective indicators are considered in this text: objective measures in this chapter, subjective measures in the following chapter on community surveys.

THE USES OF LOCAL INDICATORS

Local indicators can be used in three ways: (1) to describe local conditions, (2) to evaluate local conditions, and (3) to prescribe changes for local conditions. A single local statistic can be used as an indicator in any of these three ways. As we shall see, its use depends on the assumptions we are willing to make regarding the local statistic.

Descriptive Indicators

The simplest, most direct use of local data is to describe the local quality of life. We could simply ask a random sample of local residents how they feel about their community. Or we might ask a special group of local elites to assess the community. Or census data can be used to provide local crime and poverty levels. Or, better yet, all these data can be combined to describe the overall quality of community life.

Yet description, while a necessary step to improving the quality of community life, seldom is sufficient by itself. Suppose we learn that 20 percent of the community believe it is an excellent place to live; all of the local elites believe more growth is needed; there were 18 murders and 180 stolen bicycles last year; and 10 percent of the local residents live in poverty. These are important data, and they tell us much about the community. Their interpretation, however, is difficult. How is the community to be evaluated with these data? Should we be pleased that 20 percent think the community is excellent, or is that percentage shockingly low? Do the elite interviews tell us that more growth truly is needed in the community, or do local elites always want more growth? Do we need to crack down on murders, or on bicycle thieves? Does the community have an alarming poverty problem; or should we rejoice in the 90 percent above poverty? Descriptive data, by themselves, cannot answer evaluative questions like the examples above. Evaluative questions require evaluative indicators.

Evaluative Indicators

The missing ingredient that allows descriptive indicators like those in the previous section to become evaluative indicators is a comparative benchmark. Descriptive indicators allow evaluation when they can be compared to other data. If we know that last year only 10 percent of the local residents felt the community was an excellent place to live, then the more recent 20 percent figure should please us. Further, if we know that almost all community elite surveys report a desire for growth, the local murder rate is twice the state's per capita rate, while the bicycle theft rate is three times the state average, and the poverty level is only half the national level, then we can evaluate the local quality of life. In these cases we have benchmarks that allow comparisons with other times, other communities, the state, and nation.

In these instances, we know where the community is doing well, and where it is not; and when such evaluations are determined, the next question is usually *why?* Why do people feel better about our community than they did last year? How can we get the "excellent" percentage even higher? Why are there so many murders and thefts? What can be done to increase the safety of people and bicycles? Is community poverty low because of the strong industries, the strong unions, or the strong United Way? These are questions of cause and effect. Hence, these are also questions about community change, since understanding why local conditions are the way they are should also allow an understanding of how local conditions can be changed.

Indicators for Causal Modeling and Community Change

The supreme use of local indicators is to: (1) explain why the quality of life is at its current level, and (2) prescribe changes in community structure that will improve the local quality of life. If we knew that for every police officer placed on patrol, ten fewer bicycles are stolen and one less murder is committed, then all it would take to make the community safe for people and their bicycles would be putting eighteen more law officers on the streets. This is the way in which one of the progenitors of local indicators—economic indicators—is used. At first, such elaborate models were enthusiastically envisioned for social indicators as well (e.g., Gross 1966; Bell 1969), but before long it became clear that such causal modeling is premature (e.g., Sheldon and Freeman 1970). The problems of measurement and the questions of multiple causation are too complex for our current skills.

The time may come when mathematical models of social change achieve a precision that allows concrete advice about improving the quality of life. Now, however, the thrust of most social indicators is evaluative (e.g., Duncan 1975), focusing more on simply comparing social conditions over time and place rather than accounting for changes in those conditions. And the same is true for local indicators. Most attempts to develop and employ local indicators have been pointed toward evaluative goals.

We aim for evaluation, then, because it requires considerably less ability in the use of local indicators than does causal modeling. Still, evaluation is far from easy. It is often difficult to create or locate local indicators. When the indicators are available, it is difficult to choose the best ones. And, finally, it is often difficult to compare the indicators across time or communities. Yet comparisons are almost always necessary for the evaluation of the local quality of life. So, in the following sections, we will consider techniques for: (1) creating and locating local indicators, (2) choosing the best local indicators, and (3) comparing the indicators for the purposes of evaluation.

SECURING LOCAL INDICATORS

There are two ways to secure the local indicators necessary to evaluate the quality of community life. The most direct way is creating the indicators from scratch, usually with community surveys. The local polling techniques required for community surveys are the subject of the next chapter. Here, however, we will consider a more indirect, more unobtrusive way of securing local indicators—using available statistics.

There are literally thousands of statistics available, with the U. S. Census being the major source, and the major source of local census data is the *County and City Data Book* (CCDB). Published by the U. S.

Bureau of Census, it includes data from the censuses of population, manufactures, governments, wholesale trade, retail trade, service industries, agriculture, other government data from sources such as the Bureau of Labor Statistics, and nongovernment sources such as Moody's Investors Service and the American Hospital Association. These data are combined and presented by nation, region, state, county, city, and place. Thus, one can easily compare a multitude of local data with other communities, the state, or nation.

Multitude is not much of a hyperbole. There are over two hundred county variables and almost as many at the city level—everything from the number of female-headed households to the number of dentists. And if the *CCDB* does not provide enough information, the sources that contribute to the book can provide even more. For example, *CCDB's* data on city government are drawn from *The Municipal Yearbook*, but the *Yearbook* also includes substantial amounts of local government data not included in the *CCDB* (e.g., the entrance salary for police, selection criteria for fire fighters, names and addresses of county and city officials). In short, while the *CCDB* provides an extremely wide range of local information, it still accounts for only a minority of the total data available at the community level, and is used typically as only a first step in securing local indicators.

WHAT INDICATES WHAT: CHOOSING THE CORRECT INDICATORS

Given that hundreds of measures exist for each American community, *finding* local indicators is often easier than *selecting* the most relevant local indicators. So, as a guide, it may be useful to look at some of the indicators' most common uses.

We can distinguish generally between two uses of local indicators: (1) *intra*community comparisons and (2) *inter*community comparisons. The intracommunity studies between neighborhoods are more common (Flax 1978), but the methodology for both types is similar. Both types, for example, rely heavily on census data. So, whether the unit of analysis is the block group or tract (for intracommunity comparisons) or cities, urbanized areas, counties, or MSAs (for intercommunity comparisons), the measures are often the same. This means that although the examples that follow are intercommunity comparisons, they can be used as guides for assessing the quality of life between neighborhoods as readily as between cities.

Dividing the Indicators into Groups

Since quality of life is such a broad concept, community indicators are typically grouped into various categories or dimensions of life quality.

For example, an early and widely cited University of Texas study (Community Analysis Research Project, 1973) developed eleven "dimensions" of life quality based on twenty-five community indicators (Table 10–1).

A more recent, more ambitious, and even more widely cited study by Ben-Chieh Liu (1976) groups 120 quality of life indicators into five "components": economic, political, environmental, health and education, and social components. Liu has weighted each indicator and combined them to give all American metropolitan areas a comparative quality-of-life score on each of the five components. And then by combining the component scores, the overall quality of life is assessed. So, where is the best place to live in America? According to Liu's data, Portland, Oregon, is the very best large metropolitan area. For smaller places, another Oregon community, Eugene, ranks first. These variations in extreme scores reflect a regional pattern throughout Liu's data with the highest overall quality-of-life levels in the West and the lowest in the South.

Other researchers have produced widely different rankings, many of which have become exceptionally newsworthy. For example, Boyer and Savageau's *Rand McNally Places Rated Almanac* (1985) identified Pittsburgh as the very best place in which to live and found the very worst to be Yuba City, California. All of these quality-of-life surveys use similar indicators, but the final rankings differ because different judgments are made about the weights of the various contributors. This is why the research by Marvin Olsen and Donna Merwin has such high potential. They claim to have a way of determining how much weight each indicator should be given.

Table 10–2 on pages 154–57 illustrates some of Marvin Olsen and Donna Merwin's (1977) massive multiple indicator research project. Olsen and Merwin's (1977) research was especially ambitious since it was attempting to accomplish two tasks considerably beyond most efforts. First, they developed a weight for each indicator based on perceptions from different segments of the community. Second, they attempted to develop a mathematically specified causal model of community change with these indicators. Thus, their research continued the original goal of developing community indicator models analogous to economic indicator models. However, Olsen and Merwin have not published any additional reports beyond the initial 1977 findings, suggesting that the ambitious reach for mathematical models of community change still remains beyond our grasp.

Comparing these various local indicator studies shows considerable overlap in both the general dimensions of life quality and in the specific indicators of those dimensions. The consensus choice for basic dimensions of the quality of community life are listed on page 158.

TABLE 10–1   Local indicators and dimensions of the quality of life: The University of Texas data set

Dimensions	Indicators
I. Economic base	1. Retail Sales: $ per 1,000 population
II. Education	1. Number of seniors taking college board exam (SATs) 2. Average per pupil expenditures
III. Employment opportunity	1. Occupational distribution: Number and percentage of census tract heads of households employed in various job categories 2. Percentage of heads of households within census tract claiming no occupation 3. Unemployment rate: Percentage of total work force
IV. Health and well being	1. Suicide rate: Number of suicides per 100,000 population 2. Communicable disease index: Number of cases of VD, TB, and hepatitis reported per 1,000 population 3. Infant mortality rate: Number of deaths of children under one-year per 1,000 births
V. Housing	1. Vacancy rate: Percentage housing units in an area which are vacant or abandoned 2. Median assessed value of single family units 3. Percentage total subsidized starts placed in each census tract
VI. Land use and recreation	1. Acres of park and recreation space available per 1,000 population
VII. Personal income distribution	1. Number of assistance payment welfare cases 2. Number of income tax returns claiming adjusted gross income: under $3,000; $3,000 to $5,000; $5,000 to $10,000; $10,000 to $15,000; $15,000 or more
VIII. Pollution	1. Percentage increase or decrease in concentration of particulate matter suspended in air 2. Percentage increase or decrease in concentration of atmospheric NO_2 and SO_2
IX. Public safety and justice	1. Type I crime rate: Number of cases of murder, forcible rape, robbery, and aggravated assault reported per 100,000 2. Type II crime rate: Number of cases of burglary, larceny ($50 and over), and auto theft reported per 100,000 population
X. Public service delivery	1. Number of complaints submitted to city sewer, water and garbage collection agencies per 1,000 population 2. General obligation bond rating
XI. Sense of community	1. Percentage voting in most recent local election compared to percentage voting in most recent state election
XII. Transportation	1. Percentage public street miles served by public transportation 2. Number of traffic accidents per 100,000 population

Adapted from *Community Analysis Research Project: Pamphlet 1.* Lyndon B. Johnson School of Public Affairs, The University of Texas at Austin.

TABLE 10–2   Local indicators and dimensions of the quality of life: Illustrations From the Olsen and Merwin Data Set

Dimension	Effect	Indicators
I. Demography	+ up to 500,000, − above that	1. Population size
	Unspecified	2. Population growth natural increase
	Unspecified	3. Population growth through net migration
	+ closer to 1%	4. Rate of population growth
	+ closer to 60–75%	5. Degree of county urbanization
	+ closer to 100	6. Population density of county
	+ closer to 20–50%	7. Population concentration of county
	+ the smaller the proportion	8. Age dependency in community
	+ closer to 1.0	9. Sex ratio of the community males to females
	+ the closer to 13%	10. Percent of the population nonwhite
	+ the closer to 2.0	11. Number of persons per household
II. Economy	+ higher proportion	1. Proportion of available unskilled jobs vacant
	+ higher proportion	2. Proportion of available semi-skilled jobs vacant
	+ higher proportion	3. Proportion of available skilled jobs vacant
	+ higher proportion	4. Proportion of available clerical/sales jobs vacant
	+ higher proportion	5. Proportion of available managerial jobs vacant
	+ higher proportion	6. Proportion of available professional jobs vacant
	+ lower proportion	7. Proportion of available jobs that are unskilled
	+ lower proportion	8. Proportion of available jobs that are semi-skilled
	+ higher proportion	9. Proportion of available jobs that are skilled
	+ lower proportion	10. Proportion of available jobs that are clerical/sales
	+ higher proportion	11. Proportion of available jobs that are managerial
	+ higher proportion	12. Proportion of available jobs that are professional
	+ greater amount	13. Gross county income per year
	+ higher rate	14. Percentage rate of growth in gross county income
	+ greater the proportion	15. Proportion of the labor force that is employed

TABLE 10–2 (*continued*)

Dimension	Effect	Indicators
	+ greater the proportion	16. Proportion of women in the labor force
	+ greater the proportion	17. Proportion of persons age 65 or older in labor force
	+ higher amount	18. Total value of assessed real property
	+ higher amount	19. Total value of assessed personal property
	+ greater amount	20. Amount of federal revenue sharing funds per year
	+ greater amount	21. Amount of direct federal aid to impacted areas per year
	+ greater amount	22. Amount of other federal monies per year
	+ lower the index	23. Community consumer price index
	+ greater amount	24. Total revenue by all community governmental units per year
III. Social structure	+ higher attainment	1. Median educational attainment age 25 or older
	+ high status	2. Mean occupational status of the work force
	+ high income	3. Median gross family income
	+ greater number	4. Number of unoccupied housing units per 1,000 population
	+ greater space	5. Mean dwelling unit size (sq. ft.) per person
	+ high proportion	6. Proportion of dwelling units that are single-family detached
	+ greater length	7. Mean length of occupancy of all dwelling units
	+ higher proportion	8. Proportion of all dwelling units that are owner occupied
	+ high circulation	9. Circulation of local newspapers per capita
	+ greater number	10. Number of television channels in area
	+ greater number	11. Number of civic associations per 1,000
	+ higher number	12. Total memberships per capita in all civic associations
	+ higher proportion	13. Proportion of persons registered to vote

TABLE 10–2 (*continued*)

Dimension	Effect	Indicators
	+ higher rate	14. Turnout rate in local election
	+ higher number	15. Total number of community governmental employees per 1,000 population
	+ greater amount	16. Total program budget of all community governmental units per capita
IV. Public services	+ lower number	1. Mean class size
	+ low ratio	2. Mean student-teacher ratio
	+ high level	3. Mean educational level of teachers
	+ greater amount	4. Educational expenditures per student per year
	+ greater number	5. Hospital beds per 1,000 population
	+ greater amount	6. Hospital expenditures per capita per year
	+ greater number	7. Number of mental health clinics per 1,000 population
	+ greater number	8. Number of physicians per 1,000 population
	+ greater number	9. Number of dentists per 100 population
	+ greater number	10. Number of psychiatrists and clinical psychologists per 1,000 population
	+ greater amount	11. Local governmental expenditures on public health per capita per year
	+ greater number	12. Number of public health workers per 1,000 population
	+ greater number	13. Number of sanitation employees per 1,000 population
	+ greater number	14. Number of fire employees per 1,000 population
	+ greater number	15. Local government expenditures on fire protection per capita
	+ higher the classification	16. Fire protection classification of the community
	+ greater number	17. Number of police employees per 1,000 population
	+ higher proportion	18. Local government expenditures on police protection per capita
	+ higher proportion	19. Proportion of all cases cleared by arrest

TABLE 10–2 *(concluded)*

Dimension	Effect	Indicators
	+ greater amount	20. Expenditures for public transportation per capita per year
	+ greater number	21. Number of miles of scheduled bus routes per capita
	+ greater number	22. Number of buses per capita
	+ greater amount	23. Expenditures for street maintenance per capita per year
	+ greater amount	24. Number of attorneys per 1,000 population
	+ greater amount	25. Budgets of legal services centers per capita
	+ lower number	26. Median months to trial in criminal cases
	+ lower number	27. Median months to trial in civil cases
	+ greater number	28. Number of professionals in all social service agencies per 1,000 population
	+ greater amount	29. Budgets of all social service agencies per capita per year
	+ larger number	30. Number of social service agencies per 1,000 population
	+ greater number	31. Number of movie theaters per 1,000 population
	+ greater number	32. Acres of public parks per 1,000 population
	+ greater amount	33. Governmental expenditures for parks and recreational facilities per capita per year
	+ greater amount	34. Governmental expenditures for recreational programs and activities per capita per year
	+ greater number	35. Number of books in municipal public library per 1,000 population
	+ greater amount	36. Budgets of all major museums per capita per year
	+ greater number	37. Number of publicly sponsored cultural courses per 1,000 population per year

Adapted from Olsen and Merwin in *Methodology of Social Impact Assessment,* edited by Kurt Finsterbusch and C. P. Wolf. © 1977 by Dowden, Hutchinson, & Ross, Inc. Used with permission of McGraw-Hill Book Co.

1. *Economics*, as indicated by measures of occupational distribution, retail sales, federal revenue and welfare expenditures.
2. *Education*, as indicated by per-pupil expenditures and measures of educational attainment.
3. *Health*, as indicated by measures of infant mortality, the availability of health care, and health expenditures.
4. *Housing*, as indicated by measures of residential crowding.
5. *Public safety*, as indicated by crime rates and levels of fire and police employment.
6. *Racial and sexual discrimination* as indicated by unemployment ratios.

Thus, most attempts to estimate the local quality of life should include these general dimensions, and many might also consider including less common dimensions such as *political activity, ethnic composition, transportation,* and *environment.*

While the indicators in these studies can provide an excellent point of departure, hundreds of other possibilities remain to be explored. For example, suppose it is important to assess the problem of alcohol abuse in the community. None of the indicators in these exemplary studies relate to alcohol abuse, but several indicators do exist (e.g., arrest rates for crimes such as driving under the influence of alcohol, public intoxication, and other liquor law violations, and medical records for alcohol-related diseases such as cirrhosis). Searching for such indicators is often difficult and always time consuming, but it is also an intellectually intriguing search that combines library, statistical, and political research skills. The skills of a reference or government documents librarian are an immense aid in determining what is available and how to find it. Statistical skills are required to select and interpret the correct indicator.[2] Politically, it often requires considerable authority or influence to obtain the needed data. Not all data are in the public domain, and even those which are legally available, may not be accessible without the assistance of a willing bureaucrat. So, while there are indicators for almost any local phenomenon imaginable, finding and selecting the best indicators is typically a difficult task.

INTERPRETING LOCAL INDICATORS: THE NECESSITY FOR COMPARISONS

Data do not speak themselves, and that is especially true for local indicators. Even when the correct indicators are selected, their inter-

---

[2] For example, *age-specific* cirrhosis data is preferred because a community with a high proportion of elderly will usually have a high cirrhosis rate regardless of the level of local alcohol abuse since it is a disease that results from continued abuse over a number of years.

pretation requires comparison with similar indicators from a different time or place. Thus, a necessary step in assessing the quality of life with local indicators is comparing those indicators with similar indicators from another neighborhood (usually, a census tract), another community (selected perhaps because it is similar in size, racial composition, economic structure, etc.), or a state or national average.

A general rule is "the more comparisons, the better." If the assessment is directed toward a census tract, compare the indicators with all other tracts in the community, similar tracts in other communities, state, and national indicators, and with indicators from earlier time periods. If unemployment is 10 percent in one tract, is that higher or lower than other tracts, other communities, and the state and national averages? Is unemployment growing or shrinking in this tract? What is it doing nationally? Are the trends the same?

It is possible, perhaps, that such comparisons are unnecessary if an absolute benchmark exists. If one decides that nothing less than zero unemployment is acceptable, then comparisons are not needed. The single indicator is sufficient. But in the "real" world, most of us are willing to settle for levels of unemployment, or crime, or alcohol abuse that are simply lower than another community's or lower than last year's, and that requires comparisons.

CONCLUSION: COMMUNITY INDICATORS AND THE QUALITY OF LIFE

In most cases the objective indicators of life quality discussed in this chapter need to be supplemented with subjective indicators. Likewise, the description and evaluation of the local quality of life is often only an intermediate step, with improvement being the final goal. Thus, while local indicators are closely related to concerns with the quality of life, they are insufficient for a satisfactory analysis without: (1) subjective indicators based on community perceptions and (2) an understanding of the local political conditions that must be dealt with to improve the quality of life. For example, if we learn that poverty is much worse in our community than in other communities, it is also important to learn if the community is aware of the problem (i.e., subjective indicators) and if those in power are willing to address the problem. The next three chapters consider these subjective and political aspects of the quality of community life.

Chapter Eleven

Community Surveys

While the social indicators in the preceding chapter allow indirect community assessment, a more direct approach is simply to ask local residents about their perceptions of the community. Rather than relying on test scores, drop-out rates, attendance levels, and other "indirect" indicators of the quality of local education, one can "directly" ask teachers, parents, students, and school district residents how good they believe the local schools are. And directly measuring subjective views of school quality can be as important as uncovering more objective indicators. For example, the outcome of a school's bond election will hinge more on the *perception* of local education's quality than on its *actual* quality.[1] This means, then, that community surveys can add important supplements to the information provided by community indicators.

In addition to being more direct and subjective, data from community surveys differ from community indicators in another way. Unlike social indicators, survey data are not as comparable to data from other communities. For example, standardized test scores are comparable from one community's schools to another community's schools, and, accordingly, a considerable body of knowledge is built on such comparisons (Coleman 1966; Coleman, Hoffer, and Kilgore 1982). However, there are no cross-community comparisons of how school quality is perceived via local surveys. Such comparative data exist only at the national level (e.g., the Gallup Polls reported in Gallup 1985). Similar situations exist for such topics as crime, health, unemployment, and divorce. Numerous cross-community comparisons exist for the objective local indicators, but survey measures of subjective perceptions of topics such as crime or health exist largely at the national level.

---

[1] This type of argument is based on W. I. Thomas' famous dictum: "If men define situations as real, they are real in their consequences" (Thomas and Thomas 1928, p. 572).

One reason for this lack of comparative community surveys can be attributed to the mass society view of America. When it became methodologically possible to survey a sample representing all of the United States, the use of the community as a sample of American perceptions virtually disappeared. Why study the opinions of Middletowners when with a similarly sized sample one can study the opinions of all Americans?

The position taken throughout this text is that researchers need not always choose between community and society. Rather, surveys should be made of local *and* national perceptions since both are important. And community surveys have made a comeback with thousands made each year. The annual surveys of Detroit, administered by the University of Michigan, and the surveys of Chicago performed by the University of Chicago and Northwestern University, many of which are reported in the University of Chicago's *Local Community Fact Book*, are prime examples. Unfortunately, however, the same question is seldom asked in the same way in several communities. Thus, no cumulative body of knowledge concerning cross-community variations in local perceptions exists.[2]

Clearly, the production of cross-community information on local perceptions is a sorely needed addition to our knowledge of American communities. Some promising steps are being made in the direction of greater comparability: more questions asked locally are now being phrased identically to those in national surveys, and attempts are being made to catalogue the various local surveys administered each year (e.g., American Public Opinion Index). For now, though, the absence of such information means that rather than including a cumulative body of knowledge gleaned from local surveys, this chapter must focus only on the techniques necessary to survey a community.

DESIGNING A COMMUNITY SURVEY

There is a variety of reasons for surveying a local population. Pragmatic concerns such as assessments of community needs (Is there a demand or perceived need for a rape crisis center?), determining the local perceptions of community agencies and institutions (Do residents

---

[2] This absence of published information from local surveys is especially striking when compared to the following chapter on community power. While hundreds of local elite studies have been published, widely analyzed and intensely debated, there are no comparable publications or analyses for local surveys of the general population. The great popularity of the local elite surveys in Chapter 12 is due in part to the methodological difficulties associated with national elite surveys. That is, power has been studied at the community level almost by default.

believe their police protection is adequate?), and estimates of the support for various community plans (Will the public support a bond issue?) often result in community surveys. Less often, traditionally academic concerns, such as the amount of neighboring (Fischer 1982), community identification (Hunter 1974), local stratification (Curtis and Jackson 1977), or community satisfaction (Baldassare and Protash 1982), result in community surveys. Regardless of the areas of interest, researchers use similar methodological techniques.

Choosing the Technique

There are three general techniques for community surveys: (1) face-to-face, (2) mail, and (3) telephone. For many years, the face-to-face interview was the exclusive choice of survey researchers, but more recent improvements in mail and especially telephone methodologies have made all three options viable.

Face-to-face interviews. Although there are several types of face-to-face interviews, the most common type is a relatively structured questionnaire administered by one interviewer in the physical presence of the respondent. Since the interview usually occurs in the respondent's home, face-to-face surveys require a larger investment of time, personnel, and money than the other two techniques. These investments, however, are much less for a community than a national survey. Still, in spite of the costs, the face-to-face interview remains a common technique. It is probably the most likely to come to the public's mind when surveys or polling is mentioned, and even in many academic circles it remains the preferred technique.

Much of this popularity reflects its traditional preeminence, but another reason face-to-face interviews maintain a favored position among surveyors is that certain questions are especially well suited to face-to-face interviews. For example, demographic questions, such as race or housing quality, which can be answered by the interviewer's observations are, therefore, less susceptible to error. And questions requiring the respondents to rank a series of statements typed on cards, to respond to pictures or products, or to consult their records or family members are best handled with face-to-face interviews.

Mail interviews. Mail interviews are sometimes referred to as self-administered surveys since the respondents must go through the questionnaires themselves and, in effect, interview themselves. This is their chief disadvantage since there is no one to explain the questions, probe for additional responses, or to be sure the desired respondent is actually the person completing the questionnaire. Hence, this self-administered approach to surveys has never been as popular as face-to-face interviews and now probably ranks well behind telephone surveys as well. Nevertheless, this approach does have the advantages of allowing respondents to answer at a time of their own choosing, to consult records, or to check with someone else who might assist in answering the question. For this reason, many surveys of organizations (rather than individuals) are conducted by mail because organizational surveys typically require complex numerical data that may require the investigation of several people. A self-administered survey allows respondents to gather the information at their convenience.

Telephone interviews In recent years, telephone interviews have become increasingly popular, even rivaling the traditional face-to-face interview. Naturally, a major advantage is reduced cost, but technological changes (e.g., the proliferation of residential phones) and methodological advances (e.g., random-digit dialing) have combined to make telephone surveys as reliable as face-to-face interviews (Frey 1983). And cultural changes associated with *Gesellschaft,* such as respondent reluctance to admit interviewers into the home, and interviewer reluctance to enter certain neighborhoods at certain times (American Statistical Association 1974) have made the telephone survey an attractive alternative to face-to-face interviews.

Comparing the techniques. No "best" technique exists, but some are "more appropriate" than others. Depending on the research question, and the resources of the researcher, one technique will usually be more appropriate. As the comparison in Table 11–1 indicates, if funds are limited, face-to-face interviews are probably out of the question; if visual aids are necessary, telephone surveys are inappropriate; and should it be important to probe for additional responses, self-administered questionnaires cannot suffice. Each technique has strengths and weaknesses, and no technique can be categorically rejected as inferior to another.

Still, it is my opinion that recent improvements in telephone methodology have made it the most *generally* applicable technique for community surveys. It is as reliable a survey instrument as traditional face-to-face interviews, it can be based on effective sampling techniques that probably exceed the other two approaches, and it is considerably quicker than mail-out surveys and cheaper than face-to-face interviews. Thus, the methodology that follows applies more specifically to telephone surveys than to face-to-face or mail techniques.

Designing the Questionnaire

Unlike the sampling procedure and data analysis techniques associated with survey research, questionnaire design remains more art than

TABLE 11–1   Comparison of three basic community survey techniques

Area of comparison	Face-to-face	Mail	Telephone
Cost	Worst	Best	Medium
"Turn-around time" from initiation of polling to analysis	Medium	Worst	Best
Response rate	Best	Worst	Best
Ability to probe	Best	Worst	Best
Ability to ask complex questions	Best	Worst	Medium
Ability to use visual aids	Best	Medium	Worst
Ability to allow respondent to seek additional data	Medium	Best	Medium
Ability to use long questionnaire	Best	Worst	Medium
Assurance that desired respondent completes questionnaire	Best	Worst	Medium
Ability to monitor interview process	Worst	Medium	Best

Best   This is a strong point of the technique. Neither of the other two techniques can surpass it in this area.
Medium   While the technique can be somewhat successful in this area, at least one other technique is superior.
Worst   This is a weak point of the technique. Both of the other techniques will surpass it in this area.

science. While there are a number of excellent primers on questionnaire design (Payne 1951; Warwick and Lininger 1975; Bradburn and Sudman 1979; Backstrom and Hursh-Cesar 1981; Sheatsley 1983), some of their general principles are contradictory, and few are based on systematic replications (Schuman and Presser 1981). The following prescriptions for questionnaire design, then, can and should be modified when circumstances dictate.

The introduction: "setting the hook." Most respondent refusals occur during the introduction. But if this phase is successfully completed, there is a very good chance that the entire questionnaire will be completed as well. In framing an introduction, it is a good idea to put yourself in the place of the respondent: the unanticipated call, the unknown caller, the anticipated sales pitch, the natural suspicion. The introduction must allay the respondent's fears and skepticism by providing assurances of legitimacy, and, most important, the introduction must make the respondent willing to participate in the survey. Otherwise, it makes no difference how well designed the questions are, how carefully the sample respondents are selected, or how sophisticated the data analysis is.

Surveyors disagree as to how much information should be included in the introduction, but it should *always* include: (1) the full name of the interviewer, (2) the research organization and/or its sponsor, (3) the general topics of the survey, (4) the selection procedure, (5) a screening technique, and (6) an assurance of confidentiality. It *might* also include: (1) the approximate length of the interview, (2) an opportunity to ask questions, and (3) an opportunity to refuse to participate.[3] In most cases, this additional information is not needed in the introduction. Naturally, the interviewer needs to be prepared to answer inquiries such as "How long will this take?" or "Why did you pick me," but it is not necessary to provide such information if it is not requested. Figure 11–1 illustrates an introduction that includes only the required information. It is the type of introduction I have found most successful.

FIGURE 11–1   A brief introduction to a community telephone survey

---

Hello. My name is _____ . I'm conducting a survey for the Baylor
                         (Interviewer's full name)
Center for Community Research. This phone number was selected by a computer and
I would like to get your opinions on some important local issues. Of course, your
opinions will be kept confidential. In fact, I don't know your name or address. So,
first of all, are you eighteen years of age or older?

Borrowing questions: It's better and easier. After the introduction comes the reason for the survey—asking questions. Whenever possible, don't write your own; use the same questions asked in other surveys. Borrowed questions have two important advantages. First, valid questions are very difficult to write. If other researchers have already wrestled with how to ask a person if he or she feels alienated and then tested, revised, and retested those questions, why not profit from their labors? The Survey Research Center at the University of

---

[3] Some federal agencies require surveyors to inform each potential respondent that participation is not required and that the contents of individual responses will not be released except as required by law.

Michigan, the National Opinion Research Center at the University of Chicago, various commercial polls, and hundreds of academic and marketing articles are excellent sources for questions.[4]

A second advantage of borrowed questions is comparability. When a question asked in one community is also asked in exactly the same way in other communities and at the state and national level, it is possible to analyze the responses in a relative context. For example, if we learn that 20 percent of the local residents express some feelings of alienation, is that a high percentage, low, or about as expected? If data are available from identical questions asked in other communities, then the local percentage becomes more meaningful. Likewise, if data are available at state and national levels, then the community's responses can be interpreted even more meaningfully. For example, Table 11-2 shows the "grades" Wacoans give their public schools. Existing without other comparisons, these ratings are difficult to interpret; but when compared to state and national data, it becomes clear that Wacoans give their schools higher marks than the national Gallup sample. A comparison with the Texas poll suggests this is a regional phenomenon rather than a local one. If the Texas and Waco polls had not borrowed their questions from Gallup, such comparisons would be impossible.

Developing original questions. In spite of the advantages of borrowing, local issues are often unique to a community, and it is usually necessary to custom-design questions. In designing your own questions several general rules apply:

1.   Vocabulary should be aimed at the "lowest common denominator." Since questionnaires are typically the result of formally educated researchers interacting with similarly educated community leaders, there is a tendency for the vocabulary of the questions to include terms such as "tax abatement districts," "discriminatory intent," "self-

---

[4] Sources of questions suitable for potential borrowing include: (1) the CBS–New York Times Poll, as indexed in *New York Times Index;* (2) *The Gallup Poll: Public Opinion 1935–1971* (Gallup 1972) and *1972–77* (Gallup 1978); (3) *General Social Surveys, 1972–80; Cumulative Codebook* (National Opinion Research Center 1980); (4) *Index to International Public Opinion, 1978–1979* (Hastings and Hastings 1980); (5) *Measures of Political Attitudes* (Robinson, Rusk, and Head 1969); (6) *Measures of Social Psychological Attitudes* (Robinson and Shaver 1973); (7) Opinion Roundup Section of *Public Opinion;* (8) Polls Section of *Public Opinion Quarterly;* (9) *Survey Data for Trend Analysis: An Index to Repeated Questions in U. S. National Surveys Held by the Roper Public Opinion Research Center* (Roper Public Opinion Research Center 1975); and (10) *Handbook of Research Design and Social Measurement* (Miller 1977). These sources will typically tell whether or not an acknowledgment or written permission is required to use the questions.

TABLE 11–2   Borrowing questions for local, state, and
national comparisons

Question: What grade would you give the public
schools in your community—A, B, C, D, or Fail?

Grade	Sample	Percentage giving each grade*
"A"	Waco	13%
	Texas	12
	Nation	6
"B"	Waco	33
	Texas	37
	Nation	25
"C"	Waco	34
	Texas	29
	Nation	32
"D"	Waco	5
	Texas	8
	Nation	13
"Fail"	Waco	5
	Texas	3
	Nation	7

* Percentages do not equal 100% because the "Don't know" responses were not included. Those percentages are 6 for the Waco poll, 11 for Texas, and 17 for Gallup.

Source: Baylor Center for Community Research Poll, March 1982; Texas Poll, December 1983; Gallup Education Survey, 1983.

actualization," "feasibility," "central city," "MSA," and so on. Need-lessly long words, complex phrases, and technical jargon will greatly limit the applicability of the survey.

2. The questions should be conversational, not condescending. Questions should be asked at a conversational level. While it is impor-tant to be "natural" in vocabulary choices, it is not necessary to "talk down" to the respondent. One can usually assume, for example, that local residents understand what a "mayor" is. Thus an explanatory phrase such as "The mayor, *who is the top-elected official in our city,* recently suggested . . ." should be avoided.

3. Avoid "double-barreled questions" that ask for opinions on two different issues in one question. For example, "How satisfied are you with the performance of our local police and fire departments?" will produce responses that are difficult to interpret. What if the re-spondent is positive toward police protection, but negative toward fire protection? Ask two separate questions instead.

4. Be specific. Asking "Are local taxes too high?" will yield little useful information (and, usually, a strong affirmative response). What

is too high: the sales tax, the property tax? Or is it too high for the respondent (who typically views him or herself as middle class) but too low for the rich?

5.   Avoid extreme terms such as "always," "never," "racist," "exploitation," and so on. You may indeed want to measure "exploitation" or find if the respondent "always" acts in a certain way, but such terms are typically so extreme as to bias the response. For example, levels of agreement with "Local businesses always exploit women workers" will be so low that they will probably be of no value; but a rewording of the statement to "Local businesses often take advantage of women workers by paying them less than men workers in the same jobs" will produce higher levels of agreement and specificity (i.e., the kind of exploitation is defined).

6.   Make it difficult for the respondent to acquiesce to statements. For a variety of reasons not yet fully understood, respondents are likely to agree with statements presented to them. Thus, when possible, a forced-choice question is preferable to agree-disagree versions. For example, when presented with a statement such as "The city should raise property taxes to build a new library" and asked if they agree or disagree, some respondents (especially those with little formal education) will agree for reasons other than supporting higher taxes for a library. If the question is reworded to force a choice such as "Should the city raise property taxes to build a new library or leave property taxes at their current level and do without a new library?" there is less chance for a biased response. When forced-choice questions are not possible, then increasing the variation of agreement (e.g., "strongly agree," "agree," "disagree," "strongly disagree") will help to minimize acquiescence-response bias.

7.   Finally, be careful, in the sense that care is taken to structure the questions logically, grammatically, and precisely. There could be a dozen more "rules" or "hints" to effective question construction (Frey 1983; Sudman and Bradburn 1982; Sheatsley 1983), but, generally, the carefully and thoughtfully constructed, pretested questionnaire will also be a valid and useful questionnaire.

Response sets: Open versus closed-ended. Questions naturally elicit answers, and as much care should be given to the structure of potential responses to questions as to the questions themselves.

There are two broad types of answers: open-ended and closed-ended.[5] Open-ended answers allow the respondent freedom to answer in any way he or she wishes. For example, "What do you believe are

---

[5] Often, it is the question rather than the answer that is referred to as "open" or "closed" ended. Technically, it is only the response set that is left open or closed (Sudman and Bradburn 1982).

the major contributors to the overall quality of life in our community?" Closed-ended answers require the respondent to choose between predetermined responses, such as "Which do you believe is the most important contributor to the quality of life here: (1) the local economy, (2) the climate, or (3) the size of the population?

The open-ended answer appears, at first glance, to be clearly superior. It allows the respondent to answer with less bias from the interviewer; qualifications and specifications impossible with closed-end answers can be attached to the responses; and an open-ended response requires more focused attention by the respondent. However, there are less apparent disadvantages associated with an open-ended answer. For example, it takes much longer to answer since a typical respondent will verbalize the thought process that produces the answer as well as the answer itself.

Interviewer: What do you believe are the major contributors to the overall quality of life in our community?

Respondent: I don't know. I guess there's a lot of good things about Waco. The lake is pretty, but I don't know if it's actually in Waco. Is it okay to mention it as a good point?

Interviewer: Yes. Our community includes the entire Waco/McLennan county area.

Respondent: Well, then, the lake. No, we really don't go there that much. It's hard to say, I guess the park is awfully nice, but we hardly ever go there either. Of course, my job is the main reason we live here; can that be a good point?

Interviewer: Yes, it can.

Respondent: Well, let's make that one of them. How many do I have so far?

How many indeed! Does the interviewer include the lake and the park? In addition to being time consuming, the responses are difficult to record and interpret.

Since all the open-ended responses must be categorized eventually and since the opportunities for subjective error in that process are considerable, why not let community respondents code their own answers from a list of categories? That is, why not use closed-ended answers exclusively? In practice, this isn't a bad rule to follow. *Most of the time, most of the questions should have closed-ended response sets.* Open-ended responses should be included in community surveys only when there is little agreement before the survey as to what the most common responses will be or when there is a clear need to probe for further analysis ("Why do you feel that way?" or "Why did you choose this over another?")

Ordering the questions. Order the questions in the following ways: "easy" first and last, "sensitive" last, and "transitions" in between.

Generally, the questions should be ordered in a logical, conversational sequence. The initial question should be: (1) related to the introduction, (2) interesting, (3) closed-ended and (4) easy to answer. For example, if the introduction refers to important local issues, questions about threats to world peace or relatively trivial city zoning changes are inappropriate.

Subsequent questions should be grouped by subject, and the interjection of an occasional opportunity for an open-ended response will not only give the respondents chances to express themselves more fully, but also provide an effective change of pace.

Particularly difficult questions (e.g., those requiring open-ended responses, choosing from long lists, or making difficult choices) should be placed toward the front of long questionnaires to reduce the effects of respondent fatigue. Easier questions (e.g., demographics, such as age or education) can be asked toward the end when fatigue is not so serious a bias. Potentially sensitive questions (e.g., income, candidate preferences) are also best asked toward the end of the questionnaire. Hopefully, sufficient rapport and trust will have been established with the respondent to overcome any hesitation, but in the worst case—the respondent terminating the interview—enough information may have been gathered by then to include it in the sample.

Transition statements (e.g., "Now I would like to ask you some questions about education") aid in the movement from one group of questions to another. They can also ease the movement from one response set to another (e.g., "Now I am going to read a series of statements about the local quality of life and would like you to tell me the extent to which you agree or disagree with them.") In either case, when the questions are grouped and ordered, transition statements will aid in moving the respondent from one part of the questionnaire to another.

Length of the questionnaire. Community surveys should be shorter than national surveys. Since considerable time is devoted to choosing the sample, training the interviewers, and contacting a desired and willing respondent, one naturally tends to try to get as much return on that investment as possible—in other words, to ask as many questions as possible. However, there is a point at which respondent fatigue makes further questioning unreliable; but what, exactly, is that point—ten minutes, an hour? The answer, typically is "It depends." It depends largely on the difficulty and interest of the questions. If we are asking complicated questions that hold little perceived relevance to the respondent (e.g., asking a random sample of community residents to choose between five different ways of treating sewage), try to keep the average interview under ten minutes. If we are asking relatively simple and overtly relevant questions (e.g., asking a sample of teachers if their classes are overcrowded), then the average interview might go as high as thirty minutes. There are surveyors who claim no problem with even longer telephone interviews (Colombotos 1969; Rogers 1976), but for the *community* telephone survey, questionnaires that typically take over thirty minutes to answer are probably inadvisable.

One reason that community surveys need to be briefer than state or national surveys is that the resource (potential respondents) is so much smaller locally and, therefore, more likely to be used up. If a community has 100,000 adults that are sampled four times per year (with a sample size of 500), after five years, we would expect that in our next sample approximately 10 percent of the respondents will have participated in previous local surveys and about 20 percent will live in a household that has been previously surveyed.[6] If the respondent's previous interview was tiring, boring, or in some other way unpleasant, he or she will be less likely to participate a second time.

In general, then, it is advisable to keep community surveys shorter (and less threatening and more interesting) than national surveys. If the community is surveyed regularly, the people you interview are more likely to be interviewed again, and, perhaps even more important, they are also more likely to know personally the surveyor or the client organization. Thus, long, boring, threatening questionnaires can do considerably more damage locally than nationally.

CHOOSING THE SAMPLE

Sampling is the cornerstone of the community survey because it makes feasible an accurate estimate of local opinion without asking for the opinion of each and every community resident. We take this marvelous shortcut for granted now, but systematic, representative sampling is a relatively new addition to social science methodology. As examples, in 1934, Robert Woodbury, (1934, p. 364) concluded that "it is so difficult to insure the representativeness of the sample that . . . complete enumeration is preferred,"[7] and even in the 1960s, Gerhard Lenski (1963, p. 12) referred to survey sampling as "a new research technique." By the 1980s, however, this "new research technique" has

---

[6] Given the movement of people into and out of the community, the exact level of overlap is impossible to predict from pure probability theory.

[7] The now-classic debacle of the *Literary Digest* predicting a victory by Alf Landon over Franklin Roosevelt shows that Woodbury's assessment of sampling techniques was indeed correct for that time. In a similar vein, pollsters' inability to predict the magnitude of Reagan's landslide victory over Carter in 1980 reminds us that while survey methodology has come a long way in a relatively short time, a distance still remains to be traveled before survey researchers predict with the precision associated with some of the physical sciences.

been developed quite extensively for local research, especially in light of recent advances in telephone surveys. This section, then, will provide an overview of the community sampling techniques necessary for an accurate local telephone survey.

Fortunately, community surveys typically require only the most basic, most accurate, and most simple form of sampling: *simple random sampling*. This means that while state and national surveyors must build complex modifications of simple random sampling methodology (e.g., stratified samples, cluster models, multistage designs), local telephone surveys possess one key element that is missing in national and even state surveys, the one element that always makes simple random sampling possible: a list of all units in the universe from which we wish to sample. In this case, of course, the all important list is the local telephone directory.

Using the Directory

The community is one of the largest groups for which a reasonably complete and accurate list of all members (or, more precisely, all members' households) is available. There are no such lists for states or nations. The presence of this list, then, is the reason a reliable community sample is so much simpler to obtain than a similar state or national sample. However, the phone directory does not solve all our problems. We cannot simply call every *n*th number in the book until we get our sample. Actually, if we did, the sample wouldn't be too bad, but there are better ways.

Why not rely completely on the directory? The most serious drawback for randomly selecting numbers from the directory is unlisted numbers.[8] Numbers are not listed in the directory for two reasons: (1) the person has recently moved into the community and is not yet in the directory, or (2) the person has chosen to have the number unlisted. In both instances, this can seriously bias the sample since these unlisted numbers have no chance to be selected. Combined, these two problems mean that a local directory will not list from a fifth to a third of the current households in a community.

Fortunately, however, two recent methodological improvements have enabled telephone surveyors to reach even households with unlisted numbers: Add-a-digit sampling (adding either a random or constant number to each number chosen randomly from the directory), and random-digit dialing (substituting the last digits of each number selected from the directory with a randomly selected set of digits).

---

[8] There are other, less serious, problems. For example, about 3 to 5 percent of American households do not have a phone (Frey 1983) and some households (approximately 3 percent) have more than one directory listing.

Add-a-digit dialing. The simplest method of adding unlisted numbers to a sample is add-a-digit dialing (Landon and Banks 1977). In this technique, numbers are randomly selected from the phone book, and a constant or random number is added to each one. For example, if the number 1 is added to each phone number, then a selected number of 776–4787 becomes 776–4788.

This technique is direct, simple, and hence intuitively appealing, but it has not been widely adopted in survey research. Perhaps the main reason is that it is tied too closely to listed numbers. For a number to be generated from this technique, its predecessor (the initially selected number) must be listed, and if unlisted numbers are not numerically close to listed numbers, then they are unlikely to be generated. As a result, add-a-digit dialing is most appropriate where there are relatively few unlisted numbers and new exchange banks are seldom opened. Since the phone company will almost never supply the information necessary to determine how numerically distant unlisted numbers are from listed numbers, and since rapidly growing communities are continually adding new banks of numbers, some form of random digit dialing is usually preferred over add-a-digit dialing.

Random-digit dialing based on a telephone directory. Assuming that the telephone directory includes numbers that have the same geographic boundaries as your community,[9] drawing a representative sample from the directory requires:

1. Determining how many phone numbers you need (see pp. 176–80).
2. Choosing a sampling interval (*n*).
3. Determining a random starting point.
4. Proceeding through the directory taking every *n*th number. But if the number selected is nonresidential, choosing alternately the preceding or successive number, and then returning to the original nonresidential listing before counting to *n* again.

For example, if you determine that 1,000 potential numbers are needed to complete your sample of 300, then to choose a sampling interval (*n*), simply divide 1,000 into the total number of residential listings. Fortunately, determining the total number of residential listings in a community is not as formidable a task as it might initially

---

[9] If the community is a small subset of those numbers listed in the directory or if it is a subset of two or more directories, then sampling based on Cross-Reference Directories is required in order to focus more efficiently on those numbers within the community. These directories are a valuable tool for many types of community research. The International Association of Cross-Reference Directory Publishers produces an annual catalog of these directories.

appear. Simply select a few pages from the directory, count the number of residential listings on each page, compute the average number of residential listings per page, and then multiply that average by the total number of pages in the directory. For example, if there is an estimated total of 125,000 residential listings, the sampling interval n will equal 125 (125,000 ÷ 1,000).

After the sampling interval is determined, start with the third, fifth, eighth (or whatever) phone number and then select every 125th listing thereafter until 1,000 telephone numbers are selected. When a nonresidential number comes up as the 125th listing selected, go back to the 124th the first time, take the 126th number the next time a nonresidential number appears as the 125th listing, and so on; but return to that original 125th listing to begin counting again, even if it was not a residential number.

At this point the 1,000 telephone numbers, while representive of the listed residential numbers, do not include unlisted numbers. To catch these unlisted numbers, replace the last two, three, or four digits of each phone number with random numbers. How many digits to replace is a judgment call. Replacing the last four digits is the most likely way to pick up banks of new numbers and unlisted numbers, but it is also the most likely way to pick nonresidential and nonworking numbers. A two-digit replacement, conversely, minimizes the nonresidential and nonworking numbers but maximizes the chances of missing new numbers and numerically distant nonlisted numbers. Since communities vary substantially in the degree to which new numbers are opened, the proportion of unlisted numbers, and the numerical distance nonresidential and unlisted numbers are from listed residential numbers, there is no substitution level that is appropriate for all communities. A general strategy might be to begin with a four-digit exchange. If that produces an intolerably large number of nonresidential and nonworking numbers, substitute only the last three on the next survey, and go down to a two-digit exchange, if necessary, on the third survey.[10]

Callbacks. Regardless of whether the replacement is two, three, or four digits, the end result will be a list of numbers that can be used to reach a random representative sample of households. However, not every number on the list will result in a completed interview. Some will be business numbers or nonworking numbers and are not really a part

---

[10] Another strategy for selecting the most efficacious exchange level is to peruse a cross reference municipal directory and determine the degree to which nonresidential numbers are separated from residential numbers. That is, are most business members separated from most residential phones by two, three, or four digits?

of the sample anyway, but some numbers will not answer, will be busy, or the person you need to interview will not be home. What is to be done with these numbers? Move on to another number? Try again later? *Yes*, to both questions: move on, but also call back at a later time.

Considerable bias can be introduced into the sample if there is not a strong attempt to reach those numbers that did not answer, were busy, or at which the required respondent was not available. If the caller moves on to the next number on the list and never returns to the busy or nonanswering number, then those kinds of people most likely to be talking on the phone or away from home will not have a chance to be interviewed equal to that of people who rarely talk on the phone or usually stay at home. The only way to equalize their probability of being interviewed is to call back, usually up to five times.

Again, there is a judgment call to be made here. It's generally advisable to complete a community survey as quickly as possible so that local events won't occur during the survey to bias those who answer after the intervening event. On the other hand, if the survey is completed in one night, there will be little opportunity to reach respondents through callbacks. So, if the survey lasts two or three days, the five callbacks should be equally distributed over the remaining time. The code sheet in Figure 11–2 illustrates how numbers are recalled during the length of the survey period.

FIGURE 11–2   Interview response codes for call back forms

X   interview complete
1   refused, no call back
2   incomplete, no call back
3   not working number
4   business number
5   no eligible respondent (e.g. lives outside McLennan County)
6   incomplete, call back (record time for call back and keep questionnaire)
7   line busy
8   no answer, or answering machine
9   respondent not available now, call back (record time for call back)

			Call number		
Phone number	1	2	3	4	5
776-4787	3				
662-5501	7	8	X		
705-1256	8	8	8	9 *8 pm Tues.*	X
882-6666	X				
666-5274	4				
776-2634	7	1			
705-2603	5				
...-....					

Screening within the household. The numbers selected by the techniques described above represent *households* rather than *individuals*. And since we are usually interested in individual opinions rather than household opinions, we must systematically sample among the residents in each household called during the survey. Usually, the surveyor is interested in adults, and there are several methods available to screen or filter the household for the desired adult respondent. The initial attempts at screening (e.g., Kish 1949, 1965) were designed to systematically select by age and sex within each household so that every adult in each sampled household would have an equal probability of being selected. The screens were successful, but they were also time consuming, cumbersome to administer, and better suited to face-to-face interviews than to telephone surveys. Subsequent modifications have typically sacrificed some degree of probability of equal distribution in selection for an increase in ease of administration. This has been particularly true in telephone surveys, where the traditional screening questions about the number of adult males and females living in the house were sometimes seen as threatening and too personal by the people being interviewed.

There has been a series of modifications in screening procedures for telephone surveys (Troldahl and Carter 1964; Bryant 1975; Groves and Kahn 1979; Hagen and Collier 1982), and, generally, they have moved toward less time-consuming and less intensive methods of selecting respondents. An example of such a screen, in Figure 11–3, lists a set of questions used to minimize respondent resistance (as measured by refusals to be interviewed) and to maximize representativeness (as measured by comparisons with census data). Theoretically, it is not as rigorous as it should be in systematically sampling by age and sex, but, practically, it works.

The screening questions in Figure 11–3 assume that: (1) no serious bias is introduced by not systematically asking for the youngest or oldest adult; and (2) women are more likely to answer the phone and participate in the interview. Comparisons of the age and sex distributions of samples with census data from the same communities indicate that these two assumptions are sound. Again, trade-offs are involved. Most screens are more systematic than the one in Figure 11–3, but they are also more likely to increase the refusal rate.

How Big Should the Sample Be?

Usually the first questions asked about any survey concern sample size: "How large is the sample?" "Why is it that size?" "How large should the sample be?" These questions about sample size are not as important as questions about the validity of the questions, the selection procedure for the telephone numbers, and the efficiency of the screen-

FIGURE 11–3   Screen for a community telephone survey

1. IF AN ADULT MALE ANSWERS, INTERVIEW HIM.
2. IF AN ADULT FEMALE ANSWERS, INTERVIEW HER, BUT THE NEXT TIME A FEMALE ANSWERS, ASK FOR AN ADULT MALE.

Hello. My name is _____ . I'm conducting a survey for the Baylor Center for Community Research. This phone number was selected by a computer and I would like to get your opinions on some important local issues. Of course, your opinions will be kept confidential. In fact, I don't know your name or address. So, first of all, are you eighteen years of age or older?

YES AND CORRECT SEX

YES BUT WRONG SEX OR
NO ——————→   In order to make sure we have a random sample, I need to speak to a male eighteen years of age or older from this household. Is there an adult male living at this residence I could speak to?

YES [IF AT HOME, REPEAT INTRODUCTION, OTHERWISE, SCHEDULE A CALLBACK]
NO ——————→   In that case I'm authorized to talk with a female. [IF UNDER EIGHTEEN, ASK FOR ADULT FEMALE AND THEN REPEAT FIRST PART OF INTRODUCTION] ———

1. Our first question deals with health services and problems. What do you . . .

ing questions. In other words, if these matters are not properly attended to, the sample size will make no difference. The survey will be scientifically useless as a measure of community opinions. Conversely, if the questions are reasonably valid, if the numbers are selected in a random, representative manner, and if the screen systematically samples respondents within the household, it doesn't make much difference whether the sample is one hundred or one thousand; the survey will be a reasonably accurate measure of community opinion. Sample size is not as crucial a component of a community survey as it first appears. Still, sample size is an issue. How big should the sample be?

Confidence levels and intervals. One of the major considerations in determining the size of a community sample is how precise one must be in estimating local opinion. If 60 percent of the sample believes the community is a good place to live, how sure can we be that 60 percent of the entire community feels that way? Naturally, it would be nice to be absolutely sure, but practically, most surveyors settle for a 95 percent *confidence level.* That is, we are willing to accept five chances out of one hundred of being wrong.

When a confidence level is specified, typically at 95 percent, it is then possible to specify a *confidence interval*, which is the range around the sample's response within which the community's response can be expected to lie ninety-five times out of one hundred. If the confidence interval was ± 4 percent, the confidence level 95 percent, and the sample response was 60 percent saying the community is a good place in which to live, then there would be a 95 percent probability that between 56% and 64% of the community believes it is a good place in which to live.

The computation of a confidence interval is relatively straightforward for community surveys because, unlike national surveys, local surveys typically use a form of simple random sampling and the statistics for computing a confidence interval for simple random samples are much simpler than for other forms of samples.

The formula for computing a confidence interval is based on the proportion of responses (A and B in the formula below) to the question, the confidence level (always 1.96 for 95 percent, since 95 percent of a normal distribution falls within 1.96 standard deviations around the distribution's mean), the number of potential respondents in the community (C) and the sample size (S). If, for example, 60 percent of a sample of 500 respondents from an estimated 100,000 adult community residents believe the community is a good place in which to live, the confidence interval would be between 56 percent and 64 percent (60% ± 4%).

$$\text{Confidence Interval} = 1.96 \sqrt{\left(1 - \frac{S}{C}\right) \frac{A \times B}{(S - 1)}} =$$

$$1.96 \sqrt{\left(1 - \frac{500}{100,000}\right) \left(\frac{60 \times 40}{499}\right)} = 4.29 = \pm 4\%.$$

If you experiment with various values in this formula, it will become clear that *the size of the community doesn't matter very much, the proportion of the responses matters a little, and the size of the sample matters a great deal* (up to a point). For example, if the number of adults in the community increased tenfold to 1,000,000, the confidence interval would increase to only ± 4.3; or in effect, it would often still be reported as ± 4 percent, and not change at all! Thus, sampling in a community is not much more efficient than sampling an entire state or nation.[11]

---

[11] Actually, the formulas used to compute community and national samples are identical even though communities should have more homogeneous populations and therefore less element variance. In other words, although community and national surveys may report identical confidence intervals, the community's confidence interval is probably narrower than the nation's, but it is impossible to estimate how much narrower.

Further experimentation will show the effects of variation in response proportion to the questions asked on the survey. The worst possible case is a 50–50 split, where the confidence interval would increase to ± 4.4. Narrower margins result from more uneven response levels, with a 90–10 split producing an interval of only ± 2.6 percent.

Finally, experimenting with sample size shows that a sample of only 100 produces a confidence interval of ± 9.6 percent, a sample of 500 = ± 4.3 percent, a sample of 1,000 = ± 3.0 percent, 5,000 = ± 1.3 percent, and 10,000 = ± .9 percent. Increasing the size of the sample will narrow the confidence interval, but the law of diminishing returns soon asserts itself. Note, for example, that adding 400 respondents to an original sample of 100 cuts the confidence interval in half, but adding 5,000 more to an initial sample of 5,000 hardly narrows the interval at all.

So, what do all these statistical exercises tell us about how large the sample should be? Simply this: *if a specific confidence interval is desired for the survey, adjust the sample size accordingly.* Assume a 50–50 split on the response proportion to the question (any deviations from that even split will narrow the interval) and determine the number of respondents necessary to reach ± 3 percent, ± 5 percent, or whatever confidence interval is required. As a general guide to selecting a sample size, the relationships in Table 11–3 should be helpful.

TABLE 11–3 Approximate relationship between sample sizes and confidence intervals

Sample size	Confidence interval*
10,000	±1.0%
1,500	±2.5%
1,000	±3.0%
800	±3.5%
600	±4.0%
500	±4.5%
400	±5.0%
300	±6.0%
200	±7.0%
150	±8.0%
100	±10.0%
50	±14.0%

* Rounded to nearest .5 percent, assuming a community size ranging from 50,000 to 1,000,000 and a 50–50 division on the responses.

Subsample analysis. Another and equally important consideration is the need to analyze the responses of various groups within a sample.

For example, it may be particularly important to separate and analyze the responses of males over sixty-five to a question on a proposed retirement center; but if only 5 percent of the adult community fits that category, then only about fifteen male respondents over sixty-five will come from a sample of three hundred. That produces a virtually useless confidence interval of about ± 26 percent! Unless there is a special procedure to oversample the older males, the entire general sample will need to be increased. For example, a general sample of 600 would reduce the confidence interval in this case to ± 18 percent, and a general sample of 1,500 would bring it down to ± 11 percent.

A subsample of only 5 percent is an extreme case, and in most instances (e.g., race, sex) the subsample will be proportionately larger, but the point should be clear: the sample must be large enough to allow required subsample analysis with reasonable confidence intervals. How large should a sample be, then? It should be large enough to be: (1) precise in its confidence interval for the entire community and (2) reasonably precise in the confidence intervals of relevant subsamples. The precision required to be "reasonable," depends on the researcher.

ADMINISTERING THE SURVEY AND ANALYZING THE RESULTS

After the questionnaire is developed and the telephone numbers are selected, the remaining tasks include scheduling the times to call, training and monitoring the interviewers, coding the responses, and, finally, analyzing the results. The administration jobs are sometimes shortchanged for the more "visible" or "sophisticated" tasks of sampling or questionnaire design, and there are fewer published guides to some of these "nuts and bolts" methods; but each administrative or analytic task is crucial to the successful completion of a community survey.

Scheduling the Calls

Obviously, not all days and times are equally well suited for telephone interviews, but which days and times are best for calling? That is, when will calls produce the most responses and the most representative responses? Usually, weeknights between 6:00 P.M. and 9:00 P.M. are best, and on weekends, Saturdays from 9:00 A.M. to 5:00 P.M. and Sundays from 2:00 P.M. to 9:00 P.M. will usually be the best times. A schedule that combines weeknight calls with weekend daytime calls can be expected to provide a more representative sample than an exclusively day or nighttime poll.

Since communities do vary, these times should be seen only as rough guidelines. Calls in a farm community may need to be stopped earlier at night than in an urban community. Special events such as sports or weather conditions can also affect surveys. One of our worst calling periods in Texas occurred when the Dallas Cowboys appeared on Monday Night Football; our best ever was when the community was snowed in.

Training the Interviewers

Telephone interviewing is not an easy job, and many people are not well suited for it. Not everyone has (1) the tonal qualities of voice, (2) the ability to read precisely, but also conversationally, (3) the mental "quickness" necessary to handle unanticipated respondent questions or comments, and (4) the tact and self-confidence to deal with refusals. But even potential interviewers who are ideally suited for telephone surveys will not do well without training and practice.

If the interviewers have no experience, the training process typically goes through three stages: (1) a general overview of telephone survey methods (open versus closed responses, probes, etc.); (2) question-by-question instructions on the actual questionnaire; and (3) a practice time when interviewers can actually go through the questionnaire and code the responses. If the interviewers have participated in previous surveys, much of the initial steps in the training process can be omitted, but in all cases, some training and practice are required before actual calls are made into the community. In fact, interviewer training is arguably more important for local surveys than for national ones since community surveys are more likely to encounter respondents who have participated in previous surveys or who know the interviewer, the research organization, or the client sponsoring the survey. Poorly trained interviewers can be more than just a threat to the reliability of survey results; for community surveys, they will damage the public image of the research organization and the sponsoring organization.

Monitoring the Calls

Interview training does not stop when the calling begins. Even interviewers who have gone through extensive training prior to the calling should be monitored during the interviews. There is some difference of opinion on whether or not it is a breach of confidentiality to "listen in" on the interview, but all agree that either one or both sides of the interview should be monitored.

Monitoring is possible only with a phone bank that centralizes the calling. The centralized facilities give phone surveys a distinct advantage in quality control over face-to-face interviews. Telephone interviews made from a central location can be checked to be sure the right people are asked the right questions in the way they were intended to be asked. Because face-to-face interviews are scattered throughout the community and because mail interviews are completed in isolation from an interviewer, telephone surveys are clearly superior here. A centralized facility, then, is the key to monitoring the interviews, and monitoring is one of the strongest links in the methodological chain of a telephone survey. In fact, James Frey (1983, p. 142), in his text on telephone surveys, lists fourteen advantages of centralized calling and then concludes: "It is difficult to imagine any telephone survey of quality being conducted from a facility other than one that was centralized." He is, I believe, correct in his assessment; thus it becomes almost impossible to justify any continuation of telephone interviewing as it was in the 1950s, i.e., a "cottage industry" with calls made from the interviewers' homes.

Coding the Responses

Just as almost all calls are made now from a centralized location, almost all responses now are coded for eventual entry into a computer. In fact, state-of-the-art telephone survey methods allow for *immediate* entry into the computer. Computer-assisted telephone interviewing (CATI) bypasses traditional pencil and paper techniques by having questions read from a video screen and directly keying the response into the computer as the respondent answers (Shanks 1983). CATI systems, however, are expensive, still being perfected, and typically required only for the big sample national surveys that demand almost immediate "turnaround" (e.g., ABC reported poll results on the second Reagan-Mondale debate during the half-time of the immediately following football game). CATI is still in the future for most community surveys, probably the rather distant future.

Still, community telephone surveys need to be designed in ways to ease the job of coding the responses into the computer. A coding method particularly well suited to community surveys is the use of optical scanners. If the interviewer codes the response on a "mark sense" or "optical scanning" sheet rather than on the questionnaire, it is immediately ready for computer storage and analysis. This takes only a little more time in the training and monitoring stages, and the payoff in reduced personnel cost and turnaround time is substantial. In other words, it offers many of the advantages of CATI at a price most community surveyors can afford.[12]

---

[12] The cost of the optical scanner varies, but it generally costs about as much as a microcomputer. Most mainframe computers will already have an optical scanner.

Analyzing the Responses

Assuming that the responses have been stored in a computer, the growing availability of preprogrammed software packages has made statistical analysis quick, easy, and accurate. Statistical packages such as SPSS and SAS are available on most mainframe computers and will perform more than enough analytic techniques for all but the most sophisticated researcher. For microcomputers, SPSS is now available for IBM compatible models, and other micros run software packages that will handle most descriptive analytic needs.

Relatively simple descriptive statistics are sufficient for most research questions, especially for those asked by nonacademic clients. That is, for the pragmatic questions of *who* feels *how* about *what*, computations of mean and modal responses, perhaps broken down by demographics such as age, sex, or neighborhood, will suffice. And almost all computers will run software that can quickly and easily provide such information. Only for more complex issues (such as causal modeling or analyzing latent structures) are sophisticated packages such as SPSS or SAS necessary.[13]

With the completion of the data analysis, it will be possible to answer those pragmatic questions referred to above. However, full pragmatism must include recognition that improving the local quality of life requires more than compiling a public "wish list," no matter how accurately the list is compiled. Discovering that the elderly want more public transportation or that the community as a whole supports the idea of a new park does not mean that the desired community changes will occur. There is a complex political process that must be successfully enacted—a process in which the opinions of some people are much more important than those of other people. And it is to the areas of unequal local power and community politics we now turn.

---

[13] It is beyond the scope of this text to explore either simple or complex methods of statistical analysis, especially since scores of excellent texts exist.

Chapter Twelve

Community Power

With the development of reliable methodologies for questionnaire construction, sampling, and interviewing outlined in the preceding chapter, it has become possible to measure the desires of the community. The ideology behind this community polling is democratic, sometimes naively democratic: if the will of the "people" is more clearly understood, then it can be followed more closely. This implies that all "people" are equal and that all wills are equally likely to be implemented. Of course the Lynds' description of the X family in Middletown illustrates the fallacy of that implication. "People" are not equal. Some have tremendous amounts of power, some have none, most are in between. Any successful attempt to improve the local quality of life must be cognizant of the unequal distribution of community power. In fact, the first systematic study of community power began with an attempt to improve the local quality of life.

FLOYD HUNTER'S *COMMUNITY POWER STRUCTURE:* THE REPUTATIONAL APPROACH TO MEASURING THE DISTRIBUTION OF COMMUNITY POWER

As noted in Chapter 1, Floyd Hunter's *Community Power Structure* (1953) is generally acknowledged as the providing the initial impetus for community power research. What has not been generally acknowledged, at least until recently,[1] is that Hunter's reason for studying community power was to improve the local quality of life by describing more clearly the processes by which important local policies are conceived:

---

[1] John Walton's insightful review of community power research in *Social Problems* (1976) was among the first to explore the pragmatic concerns of *Community Power Structure*.

It has been evident to the writer for some years that policies on vital matters affecting community life seem to appear suddenly. They are acted upon; but with no precise knowledge on the part of the majority of citizens as to how these policies originated or by whom they are really sponsored. Much is done, but much is left undone. Some of the things done appear to be manipulated to the advantage of relatively few (Hunter 1953, p. 1).

Hunter set out to discover the "real leaders" and determine how they were able to foist their will upon the community. His premise was that until the local power structure becomes visible, the chance for meaningful change remains remote:

If the basic issues which confront individuals and groups in the community are to be adequately met, it would seem necessary for the citizenry to be fully aware of who their real leaders are and how they are chosen. This would seem to be a first order of business for any individual who is interested in civic issues (Hunter 1953, p. 260–61).

But how can one discover who these "real" leaders are? Hunter's answer was a technique for uncovering the local leadership that came to be known as the *reputational approach*. He began with a list of 175 people who held positions of power in Regional City (his pseudonym for Atlanta). That list was submitted to the scrutiny of fourteen local informants. These informants, who were described as knowledgeable of local affairs and representative of various segments within the community,[2] were asked to select the ten persons from the list (or choose unlisted names) they felt were among the most powerful. This produced a group of forty reputational leaders who were subsequently interviewed by Hunter. In the course of the interview, each of the forty was asked the same principal question: "If a project were before the community that required a decision by a group of leaders—leaders that nearly everyone would accept—which ten on this list of forty would you choose?" The forty reputational leaders named twelve men consistently enough to convince Hunter that these twelve represented the top echelon of the community power structure in Atlanta.

None of the twelve top leaders held a public political office. In fact, only four of the original forty reputational leaders held a public office of any sort. Most were businessmen in the fields of banking, insurance, and manufacturing. Although these elite leaders held no political office, Hunter concluded that they managed to effectively control the local government:

---

[2] We are told very little about this aspect of Hunter's methodology. In an appendix to *Community Power Structure* (1953, p. 258), he describes similar informants as persons "who had lived in the community for some years and who had a knowledge of community affairs."

It is true that there is no formal tie between the economic interests and the government, but the structure of policy-determining committees and their tie-in with other powerful institutions and organizations of the community make government subservient to the interests of these combined groups. The government departments and their personnel are acutely aware of the power of key individuals and combinations of citizens groups in the policy-making realm, and they are loath to act before consulting and "clearing" with these interests (Hunter 1953, pp. 100–1).

Floyd Hunter, then, described a class-structured distribution of power in Atlanta that was very similar to the Lynds' earlier description of Muncie. When Robert and Helen Lynd wrote of Middletown's politicians as men of "meager caliber, [who] the inner business group ignore economically and socially and use politically," or when "the pervasiveness of the long fingers of capitalist ownership" was used to describe how the business elite maintained their local control, they could have been describing Hunter's Regional City as easily as their own Middletown. In both communities, there was a ruling class that used its economic dominance to structure the local cultural and political values and actions for their own advantage.

ROBERT DAHL'S *WHO GOVERNS?*: THE DECISIONAL APPROACH TO MEASURING THE DISTRIBUTION OF COMMUNITY POWER

Considerable response greeted Hunter's *Community Power Structure*, much of it critical. His techniques were questioned on scientific grounds, his findings on ideological ones. Political scientists, generally more conservative than sociologists and viewing Hunter and other sociologists as invaders of their academic turf, were among the most critical. This is hardly surprising since Hunter's findings could be construed to imply that: (1) democracy was not working well, if at all, on the local level, and (2) political scientists, by studying local politicians, were missing the true leaders and focusing, rather, on lower-level henchmen. Yet, it was not until Robert Dahl's *Who Governs?* was published in 1961 that an organized set of criticisms accompanied by an alternative theory of community power was presented as a response to Hunter's thesis. Dahl and his colleagues (Nelson Polsby and Raymond Wolfinger) in the Political Science Department at Yale University authored major criticisms of the reputational-elitist approach to community power, and *Who Governs?* was the theoretical and methodological linchpin.

The methodology for answering the question of *Who Governs?* in New Haven, Connecticut, (this time, thankfully, there was no pseudonym for the community being studied) was based on the detailed analysis of political decisions. While Hunter's focus was directed largely toward top *leaders*, with specific decisions analyzed only tangentially, Dahl focused primarily on what he felt were key *decisions* in New Haven and who made them.

Dahl, employing what came to be known as the *decisional approach*, analyzed decisions made in three areas: public education, political nominations, and, especially, urban renewal, which was "by most criteria the biggest thing in New Haven" (Polsby 1963, p. 70). He found an elected official, the mayor, to be the driving force behind urban renewal, and, with the exception of the mayor, leaders making decisions in one issue area were not found to be particularly influential in another. Dahl discovered an essentially pluralistic local power structure, with only the mayor able to move from one competing group to another and from one issue to another. In short, representative democracy was alive and reasonably well in New Haven:

> For more than a century, indeed, New Haven's political system has been characterized by well nigh universal suffrage, a moderately high participation in elections, a highly competitive two-party system, opportunity to criticize the conduct and policies of officials, freedom to seek support for one's views, among officials and citizens and surprisingly frequent alternations in office from one party to the other as electoral majorities have shifted (Dahl 1961, p. 311).

Although a careful comparison of *Who Governs?* with *Community Power Structure* will show considerably more agreement than the subsequent literature would suggest, it is possible to find in the works of Dahl and Hunter the beginnings of the polar extremes for the pluralist-elitist debate. Hunter analyzed local *opinions* to discover a largely *elitist* power structure based on *economic class structure*. Dahl analyzed local *behaviors* to discover a largely *pluralistic* distribution of power based on *formal political structure*.

METHODOLOGICAL DEBATE AND COMPROMISE

The Debate

The resulting debate between the elitists (typically and somewhat incorrectly conceptualized as sociologists employing reputational approaches) and pluralists (political scientists employing decisional approaches) was an interesting epistemological phenomenon.[3] In addition to competing methodologies, we are treated to the spectacle of interdisciplinary and ideological competition as well.

The pluralists strike back. Although the first blow was struck by Hunter, the next several years witnessed a strong counterattack from pluralists in general and political scientists from Yale in particular. Among the earliest criticisms of Hunter's reputational approach was that it assumed, without ever proving, the existence of a small group of powerful leaders. For example, Herbert Kaufman and Victor Jones (1954, p. 207) claim that "the major deficiency of Hunter's treatment of power in Regional City is his proneness to take for granted precisely what must be proved, and by this practice, to predetermine his findings and conclusions." If one asks for the names of local leaders, they are likely to be supplied. And if the next step is to call these names a community power structure, then, the pluralists maintained a serious methodological error is made because merely producing a list of names does not demonstrate the existence of a group of individuals working toward common objectives.

There is no simple solution to this problem. Even if the reputational approach is modified by incorporating an initial query such as, "Is there a small group which runs things in this town?" (Bonjean and Olson 1964), critics (such as Kaufman and Jones 1954; Greer 1962) could still reject the reputational approach because they maintain that "deeply embedded in the thought patterns of our culture" is the belief that a powerful elite is influencing important events. In other words, their contention is that while some respondents may believe that particular people possess power, such beliefs cannot be accepted as proof.

Based upon the contention that studying beliefs about community power is a poor substitute for actually studying the exercise of power,

---

[3] There was, during this time, a widely accepted belief that political scientists typically studied local power with decisional approaches and discovered pluralism while sociologists were likely to employ reputational approaches to uncover elitism. Two empirical studies of community power research purported to find support for these relationships between discipline, method, and findings (Walton 1966; Curtis and Petras 1970) and launched into epistemological treatises to explain the phenomenon. However, subsequent analyses (Clark, Kornblum, Bloom, and Tobias 1968; Nelson 1974) have shown rather conclusively that there is very little relationship among discipline, method, and findings. Still, the conception that academic discipline influences the choice of methodology that in turn precludes certain findings remains common in major summaries of community sociology (Bell and Newby 1972, pp. 222, 240–43; Warren 1977, p. 366; Sanders 1975, pp. 327–29). That this idea can retain acceptance without empirical support is an epistemological phenomenon in its own right.

pluralists (see especially Wolfinger 1962; and Polsby 1963) pointed out, quite accurately, that the reputational approach measures the *reputation* for power rather than power itself. They argued that power can be measured only by the careful analysis of important decisions made in key community issues (i.e., the decisional approach). Thus, the way to determine who has power is to study local decisions and find out who dominated those decisions. Otherwise, the researcher is dependent upon gossips who "distort reality" and "accept gossip as gospel and pass it on as the latter" (D'Antonio, Ehrlich, and Erickson 1962, p. 849).

At this point, the critical analysis of the reputational approach moves into more philosophical and epistemological domains concerning the nature of reality and how it is to be known.[4] For example, one reputational response is to build on the ideas of W. I. Thomas by arguing that "the way in which people perceive the power structure of the local political system affects the way in which they behave towards and in that system" (Ehrlich 1961, p. 926). This is only a small step from arguing that if respondents believe others in the community are powerful, then they become powerful. Reputed power may indeed lead to actual power, but as Polsby (1963) points out, there should be independent verification of that power, and the decisional approach appeared to offer such verification.

The pluralists falter. In the early 1960s, then, the pluralists were clearly on the offensive, largely due to the apparent superiority of the decisional approach to community power. It was during this decade, however, that the shortcomings of the decisional approach began to surface. Robert Presthus (1964) found that the decisional method identified several government officials as powerful when a more accurate and complete interpretation including a reputational method showed them to be only highly visible front men with very little decision-making power.[5]

Another criticism involved the absence of criteria by which the key local issues were selected (Dye 1970). Obviously, the selection of specific issues influences the findings since other local issues might produce entirely different findings. For example, leadership patterns for urban renewal issues may be very different from leadership patterns

---

[4] The debate also moved into more acrimonious areas that have been described as "ideological" (Walton 1976) and even "silly" (Bell and Newby 1972). With the advantage of hindsight, some of the exchanges between the pluralists and elitists probably can be seen as yielding more heat than light.

[5] Presthus was not arguing for the superiority of the reputational approach to power. Rather, he was advocating a combination of approaches, which, as we shall see, is the direction power research moved.

for public education issues. Yet, there is no clear method for selecting the correct issues for analysis.

Still another, and very pragmatic, drawback of the decisional approach became recognized during this time: it is extremely time consuming. In order for Dahl to write *Who Governs?*, Wolfinger (who was a graduate student at Yale at that time) camped in an amazingly gracious mayor's office for a year. Other researchers employing decisional approaches (e.g., Burgess 1962; Agger, Goldrich, and Swanson 1964) devoted even longer amounts of time to observing and analyzing community politics.

Perhaps the most telling criticisms of the decisional approach came from Peter Bachrach and Morton Baratz (1970). They argued that the decisional approach focuses too narrowly on formal, overt decision making. Using examples from race relations in Baltimore, they show that formal decision making, the kind analyzed by the decisional approach, is typically limited to "safe" choices that benefit vested interests. Key issues that might challenge dominant groups are never raised.

We find in the analysis of Bachrach and Baratz a criticism of the decisional approach of similar magnitude to Wolfinger's (and others') major criticism of the reputational approach. Just as measuring the reputation for power can bias the findings toward elitism, focusing on formal decision making can overestimate the role of public officials and the degree of pluralism. In short, both the reputational and decisional approaches to community power possess inherent methodological problems. Fortunately, however, many of their shortcomings can be offset through various combinations of the two approaches.

Compromise and Combinations

In the mid and late 1960s, one of the more positive developments in community power research occurred. The mutual condemnation society of the elitists and pluralists disbanded. In its place, a strong movement toward combining the reputational and decisional methodologies developed along two separate but related lines.

Employing both approaches. One of the combinational approaches was certainly the more straightforward and probably the more valid of the two: study the community with both a reputational and decisional methodology and use both sets of findings to describe the local power structure. An early proponent of this approach was political scientist Robert Presthus (1964). He found that the employment of both reputational and decisional methodologies revealed a much clearer picture of community decision making than either approach in isolation from the other:

In sum, the two methods of ascertaining power used in this study produce somewhat different results. In over 40 percent of the cases, the reputational method does identify individuals who by decisional test are found to be overtly powerful. It also identifies individuals who possess necessary attributes of power, but who escape the decisional net because they either do not choose to use their power, or, as in several of our Edgewood cases, use it "behind-the-scenes." However, as noted earlier, the use of both methods provides evidence of the existence and the use of the latter type of power. If one were to rely only upon the decisional method, he might well overlook these more subtle facets of community power (Presthus 1964, p. 127).

Sociologist Delbert Miller (1958, 1970) also used both methodologies and arrived at similar conclusions. Namely, the reputational leaders tend to be more concealed, more economically based, and possibly more important. Conversely, decisional leaders were more visible, more politically based, and probably more symbolic. The main conclusion of both Presthus and Miller was that the use of both reputational and decisional techniques is clearly more reliable than the exclusive use of either.

Combining the two approaches into one measurement technique. The other method of combining the reputational and decisional methodologies is to merge both into a single technique. Typically, this approach involves reputational questioning supplemented with a focus on specific decisions. Terry Clark's (1968, 1971) "ersatz decisional method" is a leading example of this type of combinational approach:

> Attempting to collect as much information as possible but to maximize reliability and validity while minimizing costs, we decided to interview eleven strategically placed informants in each community . . . [T]hese same informants were interviewed about the same four issues: urban renewal, the election of the mayor, air pollution, and the antipoverty program. These four particular issues were selected because they tend to involve different types of community actors in differing relationships with one another . . . (For each issue area we posed a series of questions inquiring essentially:
>
> 1. Who initiated action on the issue?
> 2. Who supported this action?
> 3. Who opposed this action?
> 4. What was the nature of the bargaining process; who negotiated with whom?
> 5. What was the outcome? Whose views tended to prevail? (Clark 1971, p. 296–97)

It is important to note that Clark refers to "minimizing costs" as a criterion by which his technique was developed. This is probably the primary virtue of this type of issue-specific reputational approach. As opposed to the "two separate approaches" methodologies employed by Presthus or Miller, this combinational approach is substantially easier, quicker, and cheaper. Whether or not it is as valid as the more time-consuming separate approaches is another, and yet unresolved question.[6] Still, Clark's inclusion of specific issues in the reputational approach is clearly a methodological improvement that incorporates one of the major tenets of the pluralist position. For example, in *Who Governs?*, Dahl (1961, p. 169) observed that "probably the most striking characteristic of influence in New Haven is the extent to which it is specialized; that is, individuals who are influential in one sector of public activity tend not to be influential in another sector." Unlike many reputational techniques, Clark's methodology can easily reflect such a segmented and specialized distribution of power. In other words, there should be little bias toward elitist findings with this combinational approach.

The similarities between the reputational and decisional approaches. It is not very surprising that the study of community power has moved to a complementary combination of the reputational and decisional approaches, like those of Presthus and Miller, or to a synthesis of key elements from both approaches, like that developed by Clark. In spite of the polemics on both sides of the debate, the methods of the reputational approach are amazingly complementary with the decisional approach. For example, a comparison of Hunter's (1953) methodology with that of Dahl (1961) will show that both make extensive use of interviews, historical documents, current news reports, and subjective impressions. Further, both approaches, in the final analysis, rely on someone's opinion about the distribution of power. In sum, since their methodologies are hardly mutually exclusive, attempts to combine them did not prove inordinately difficult.

As noted earlier in this chapter, the methods and findings of the two camps were more alike than one would suppose from the ensuing debate and controversy. Rather, the fundamental differences between *Community Power Structure* and *Who Governs?* lie in the interpretation and implication of their findings. It is not so much "Who governs New Haven, Atlanta or wherever?"; rather, it is "Why?", "How?", "For whose benefit?", and "What difference does the distribution of power make in the community anyway?" In order to answer questions such as these, community power researchers moved from case studies of

---

[6] At least it is unresolved for me. Lyon's (1977) initial analysis of Clark's methodology concludes that it is "superior" to other techniques, while a subsequent review of his methodology (Lyon and Bonjean 1981) suggests that it may be "superficial."

single communities to comparative research based on large samples of communities.

COMPARATIVE RESEARCH: THE CAUSES, CHARACTERISTICS, AND CONSEQUENCES OF COMMUNITY POWER

As long as community power research consisted of case studies, it was virtually impossible to validly generalize about the nature of local decision making. Generalizations were made, of course, but with questionable validity. Philip Trounstine and Terry Christensen, in a review of community power research, made the following observation:

> Power was studied community by community. From each case researchers strove to generalize about power to the universe of communities. The effort to generalize is apparent in the researchers' choice of titles for their works: The Lynds called their book *Middletown*, not "Uniquetown"; Hunter titled his *Community Power Structure*, not "Atlanta's Power Structure"; and Dahl wrote *Who Governs?*, not "Who Governs New Haven?" But even if we accept the reliability of each researcher's methods, are we willing to accept that all communities function like Middletown or Atlanta or New Haven? Would a biologist generalize from a single fruit fly to the species (Trounstine and Christensen 1982, p. 37)?

Naturally, one fruit fly is not enough, but fruit flies are considerably easier to collect and study than communities. Trounstine and Christensen (1982, p. 38) ask, "How could social scientists study enough communities to get a valid sample for generalization?" Their answer is direct and disappointing: "The simple fact is, it can't be done."

Fortunately, Trounstine and Christensen's position is slightly overstated. Studying the distribution of power in enough communities to provide a meaningful sample is indeed difficult, but not impossible. There have been several attempts to create such samples, with varying degrees of success.

Comparative Community Power Samples

Hawley's MPO. The first attempt to measure the distribution of power in a large number of communities was an ingenious ecological approach developed by Amos Hawley (1963). Hawley conceived of local power as more of a structural than individual phenomenon. He measured the distribution of power by computing a ratio between the total number of Managers, Proprietors, and Officials (positions of potential power) in a community and the size of its local labor force. The smaller this MPO ratio, the smaller the number of leadership positions, and, therefore, the more elitist or centralized the community power structure.

Hawley sought to establish the predictive validity of his measure by correlating it with success in participating in urban renewal programs. He found that the MPO ratio was lowest in cities that had successfully implemented urban renewal programs, highest in cities that never participated, and in between for those that began the process but dropped out of the program before completion. From this, Hawley inferred that communities with a low MPO ratio possessed a more concentrated power structure that was more efficient because of fewer problems with coordination and conflicting interests.

Since the necessary labor force data are available on virtually all communities at all times from the U.S. Census, the problem of securing an adequate number of communities for comparative research no longer existed. Thus, the ease of measurement and resultant wide availability of Hawley's measure appeared to be significant advances in community power research.

Unfortunately, later analyses of the MPO ratio raised serious questions about its validity. Does it really measure the distribution of community power, or does it measure only the local proportion of managers, proprietors, and officials? Straits's (1965) reanalysis of Hawley's data with multiple regression techniques concluded that much of the relationship between the MPO ratio and urban renewal was spurious. Later research by Aiken (1970) and Williams (1973) found that when the MPO ratio was computed for communities in which the distribution of power had been measured by the more traditional reputational or decisional approaches, the relationships were *opposite* to Hawley's propositions. Aiken and Williams found that communities with high MPO scores were more elitist, those with lower MPO scores were more pluralistic! Based on this reanalysis, Williams (1973, p. 241) concluded that the MPO ratio is not an adequate measure of power distributions, but rather "is nothing more than a weak measure of the middle class composition of a community." So, while a few researchers have continued to use the MPO ratio and other ecological constructs of community power (Lincoln 1976; Turk 1977), the MPO ratio did not deliver the methodological breakthrough that initially appeared possible with the publication of Hawley's article in 1963.

Walton's secondary analysis. The major advantage of Hawley's ecological approach was that it was easily administered. Since the usual case study approach to community power typically took months or even years, Hawley's ability to quickly measure the distribution of power in a large number of communities appeared to be a decided improvement. Another technique, developed by John Walton, promised to provide similar ease of measurement but without the validity problems of the MPO ratio. Walton (1966a, 1966b) reviewed the community power literature and selected thirty-three studies containing information on fifty-five communities. He grouped each individual description of local power distribution into one of four categories: (1) pyramidal, a monolithic elite; (2) factional, at least two durable groups competing for power; (3) coalitional, fluid coalitions that vary by issue; and (4) amorphous, the absence of any persistent local leadership patterns. In this way, Walton was able to produce a relatively large sample of communities that were measured with intensive reputational and decisional techniques. Additional case studies were added to the sample by Walton and other researchers (Walton 1970; Curtis and Petras 1970; Aiken 1970) so that by the early 1970s, this secondary analysis approach to community power seemed to have the best of both worlds. It produced relatively large samples with almost as much ease as Hawley's ecological approach, and it possessed the in-depth, direct measure of community power only found in time-consuming case studies.

Walton's secondary analysis technique, much like Hawley's earlier MPO ratio, seemed almost too good to be true; and just as we found for Hawley's ecological approach, it was. Michael Nelson (1974) reanalyzed the classifications made in the secondary analysis of Walton and Curtis and Petras. He wrote to the original researchers of the case studies and asked them to classify the distribution of power (again using Walton's four categories) in the communities they studied. In Walton's sample, Nelson found eighteen of thirty-three communities were classified differently by the original researcher than they were by Walton. For Curtis and Petras it was even worse, with thirty of the forty communities incorrectly classified. If that were not discouraging enough, there were even cases where the senior author of a case study would provide a different local power classification than a junior author of the same study! Nelson concluded that because community power is an extremely elusive, multidimensional concept, it is difficult, if not impossible, to group the various case studies into a single scheme such as the one developed by Walton.

The problems associated with the ecological and secondary analysis "shortcuts" imply that the only way to produce an adequate sample of community power structures is the hard way: i.e., to directly measure the distribution of power in a large number of communities with the same research methods and theoretical definitions in each community. Currently, there are only two such samples, one created under the direction of Charles Bonjean, the other under Terry Clark.

Bonjean's seventeen community sample. The technique Bonjean used was a "two-step" reputational approach that measures the *legitimacy* and *visibility* of local power. In the first step, a group of informants is asked to identify community leaders. Then, as a second step, those named as leaders are asked to supply their own list of local leaders. The visibility of the power structure is simply the proportion of leaders named in the second step that were also named in the first step. Also, the leadership list is analyzed to determine what proportion held political and/or associational office. The greater the proportion, the greater the legitimacy of the community power structure.

Bonjean, his students, and colleagues studied a total of seventeen communities with this technique between 1963 and 1971 and, as can be seen in Table 12–1, the proportion of legitimacy and visibility varied substantially by community. While this sample is a significant improvement over the case study approach, it is, nonetheless, an availability sample with a strong southern bias.[7] Thus, the randomly selected community sample of Terry Clark represents another methodological advance.

TABLE 12–1   The Bonjean sample: Legitimacy and/or visibility
seventeen communities

	Percent of leaders	
Community (investigator)	Legitimate†	Visible†
Tupelo, Mississippi (Preston, 1969)	100.0	88.0
Charlotte, North Carolina (Bonjean and Carter, 1965)	77.0	82.0
Winston-Salem, North Carolina (Bonjean and Carter, 1965)	75.0	80.0
Andrews, Texas (Spiekerman, 1968)	70.0	80.0
Natchez, Mississippi (Preston, 1969)	69.0	81.0
Victoria, Texas (Bonjean, 1971)	69.0	39.0
Burlington, North Carolina (Bonjean, 1963)	65.0	29.0
High Point, North Carolina (Bonjean and Carter, 1965)	62.0	38.0
Carlsbad, New Mexico (Bonjean, 1971)	58.0	27.0
Edinburg, Texas (Bonjean, 1971)	52.0	40.0
Crystal City, Texas (Spiekerman, 1968)	46.0	85.0
Alice, Texas (Bonjean, 1971)	43.0	43.0
San Marcos, Texas (Bonjean, 1971)	43.0	34.0
Austin, Texas (Bonjean, 1971)	40.0	29.0
Belvidere, Illinois (French and Aiken, 1968)	32.0	12.0
Bloomington, Indiana (Miller and Dirksen, 1965)	16.0	32.0
Barbourville, Kentucky (Sutton, 1970)	*	57.0

* Data not available

† Pearson's r between legitimacy and visibility = .651 $p < .05$, Kendall's tau = .53 $p < .05$

Source: Bonjean and Grimes (1974).

---

[7] Bonjean's academic career has been based at the University of North Carolina and the University of Texas. Those two states account for eleven of the communities.

Clark's fifty-one community sample. Clark's methodology, an "ersatz decisional" technique, was discussed earlier in this chapter as an example of a combinational approach to community power. Because his method is relatively quick and easy, he was able to administer it to a total of fifty-one communities that comprise part of the Permanent Community Sample of the National Opinion Research Center (Rossi and Crain 1968). The distribution of power (or, in Clark's terms, the degree of decentralization) in Table 12–2 shows a pattern of wide variation similar to the Bonjean sample.

Although only eleven respondents must be interviewed in each community with Clark's technique, a sample of this size and diversity still requires substantial effort and costs. And given current cutbacks in government support (via agencies such as the National Science Foundation and the National Institute of Mental Health) and the concomitant increase in demands on foundations, the opportunities for additional community power research of a magnitude similar to Clark's project are limited. Thus, considerable analysis and reanalysis has been made of Clark's data, and, to a lesser degree, Bonjean's as well. Such intensive analysis is appropriate since these two samples represent our only collections of "fruit flies." They are our best opportunities for comparative research into the "whats," "whys," and "effects" of community power.

The Characteristics of Community Power

What are the characteristics of community power? Is it largely an elitist phenomenon similar to the descriptions of Hunter and the Lynds, or is it more commonly found in relatively pluralist patterns, such as that described by Dahl? The answer is, as you might suppose, "It depends." It depends on both the definition of power and the community studied. However, it is possible to find agreement on at least two basic characteristics of community power.

1. Community power is multidimensional. There have been several attempts to specify the various dimensions of local power. One early and widely cited typology is the one by Bonjean and Olson (1964) shown in Figure 12–1. After a careful review of the community power literature, they concluded that four of the most important dimensions are legitimacy, visibility, ideology and consensus, and scope of influence or decentralization. And although these dimensions are all reflections of aspects of political pluralism and elitism, they remain conceptually distinct. This means, then, that a community could conceivably possess a power structure that is pluralistic on one dimension, elitist on another, and somewhere in between on others. Thus, it becomes

TABLE 12–2   The Clark sample: decentralization in fifty-one communities

Community	Number of decision makers per issue
1. Akron, Ohio	7.50
2. Albany, New York	6.63
3. Amarillo, Texas	3.33
4. Atlanta, Georgia	6.50
5. Berkeley, California	5.92
6. Birmingham, Alabama	5.88
7. Bloomington, Minnesota	4.45
8. Boston, Massachusetts	7.25
9. Buffalo, New York	8.67
10. Cambridge, Massachusetts	5.00
11. Charlotte, North Carolina	6.25
12. Clifton, New Jersey	5.90
13. Duluth, Minnesota	5.25
14. Euclid, Ohio	6.93
15. Fort Worth, Texas	6.75
16. Fullerton, California	6.45
17. Gary, Indiana	6.75
18. Hamilton, Ohio	6.00
19. Hammond, Indiana	7.75
20. Indianapolis, Indiana	9.00
21. Irvington, New Jersey	7.67
22. Jacksonville, Florida	6.25
23. Long Beach, California	4.75
24. Malden, Massachusetts	8.50
25. Manchester, New Hampshire	4.97
26. Memphis, Tennessee	6.38
27. Milwaukee, Wisconsin	7.75
28. Minneapolis, Minnesota	8.00
29. Newark, New Jersey	9.13
30. Palo Alto, California	6.50
31. Pasadena, California	5.50
32. Phoenix, Arizona	7.75
33. Pittsburgh, Pennsylvania	7.75
34. Saint Louis, Missouri	8.00
35. Saint Paul, Minnesota	8.50
36. Saint Petersburg, Florida	6.75
37. Salt Lake City, Utah	7.13
38. San Francisco, California	7.75
39. Santa Ana, California	6.50
40. San Jose, California	5.63
41. Santa Monica, California	6.33
42. Schenectady, New York	5.75
43. Seattle, Washington	7.50
44. South Bend, Indiana	7.00
45. Tampa, Florida	8.25
46. Tyler, Texas	7.67
47. Utica, New York	9.38
48. Waco, Texas	3.25
49. Warren, Michigan	5.50
50. Waterbury, Connecticut	8.75
51. Waukegan, Illinois	7.67

Source: Terry Clark (1971).

FIGURE 12–1   Four dimensions of power

Extreme plural structure	Dimension	Extreme elite structure
Leaders hold public or associational office	Legitimacy ←——→	Leaders do not hold public or associational office
Leaders are recognized by general public	Visibility ←——→	Leaders are unknown to general public
Leaders have widely conflicting political beliefs	Ideology and ←——→ consensus	Leaders hold similar political beliefs
Large number of leaders, each exercising power in one or a few policy areas	Scope of influence ←——→ or decentralization	Small number of leaders, each exercising power in most or all policy areas

Source: Based on model developed by Bonjean and Olson (1964) and extended in Bonjean (1971).

important to specify precisely what definition or dimension of community power is being used.[8]

In Table 12–1, we have the distribution of legitimacy and visibility and in Table 12–2, decentralization, or scope of influence. And while we could logically argue that in any particular community one dimension of power is likely to vary in the same direction as others, our experience with the tests of Hawley's MPO ratio shows the need for empirical proof of such propositions.

There is some evidence that the separate dimensions do vary together, at least to a degree. We know, for example, from Table 12–1 that the correlation between legitimacy and visibility is about 0.6. Likewise, Clark (1971) found a correlation of similar magnitude with decentralization and another indicator of pluralism.[9] In other words, our best inductive and deductive guesses would be that when a community is strongly elitist or pluralist on one dimension, it is likely to have similar variation on the other dimensions. Still, much more research is needed in this area, and until such research is attempted, conclusions about the characteristics of community power must remain tentative.

---

[8] It should be remembered that Nelson (1974) saw the multiple dimensions and conceptions of community power as the major obstacle to attempts at secondary analysis.

[9] Clark (1971) found a Pearson's *r* of .584 with Lineberry and Fowler's (1967) index of reformism. Similarly, that index is highly correlated with legitimacy and visibility in a direction that implies support for decentralization, legitimacy, and visibility all varying together (Lyon 1977). The index of reformism is discussed more fully as an antecedent of community power in the next part of this section.

2. *Communities vary substantially in the distribution of local power.* Both the Bonjean and Clark samples show wide intercommunity variation in power structures. This means, then, that the earlier debate over whether American communities are largely elitist or pluralist was misguided. Some communities appear to be very elitist (Bloomington, Indiana; Waco, Texas). Others are much more pluralistic (Charlotte, North Carolina; Newark, New Jersey). And this time the differences cannot be ascribed to the discipline of the researcher or the type of methodology.[10]

The Causes of Community Power

When we find that some communities are much more pluralistic than others, the obvious question is, Why? The size of our two community samples allows the kind of comparative analysis necessary to provide an answer. So, based largely on published analysis of the Bonjean and Clark samples, three causes of variation in community power are presented:[11]

1. *The larger the population size of the community, the more pluralistic the power structure.* Analyses of both the Clark (Clark, 1971) and Bonjean (Grimes, Bonjean, Lyon, and Lineberry 1976) samples support this proposition. Larger cities are more likely to have multiple groups with opposing interests competing for power. Similarly, as communities grow, they should become more difficult for one or two groups to dominate local decision making.

2. *The more economically diversified the community, the more pluralistic the power structure.* The logic here is similar to the proposition above. Economically diverse communities will be particularly difficult to dominate to the degree the X family was able to do in a one-factory town like Muncie. Again, analyses of both samples (Clark 1971; Grimes et al. 1976) support this association.

3. *The more "reformed" the formal political structure of the community, the more elitist the power structure.* City governments that include nonpartisan elections, a city manager, and at-large representation are more likely to have dimensions of elitism (Clark 1971; Grimes et al. 1976). Political scientists (Lineberry and Fowler 1967) have found

---

[10] This variation between communities also provides additional evidence for the limits of the mass society since there is clearly little standardization in community power structures.

[11] Beyond these three, there have been a large number of other propositions made about the causes or antecendents of community power (see Aiken 1970; Walton 1973; Lineberry and Sharkansky 1978), but many of them are supported by research from secondary analysis and are, therefore, subject to the potential validity problems associated with that technique.

that the reform movement that transformed many cities of the South, West, and Midwest into more "businesslike" governments also insulated them from the demands of the public they represented. This lessening of the public accountability appears to have increased the possibility for elitist power structures.

The Consequences of Community Power

After examining some of the contributors to the different characteristics of community power, the next logical consideration concerns the effects of variations in community power structure. That is, what difference does it make to the community for its power structure to be pluralistic or elitist? Often, the answer may be that it makes very little difference. Research based on the Clark and Bonjean samples (Lyon and Bonjean 1981) has shown that for many local phenomena, political elitism or pluralism is not very important. This appears to be because many local decisions (e.g., most municipal budget expenditures) are incremental in nature and more likely to involve midlevel administrators instead of top-level community leaders. Only the most visible or important local issues are likely to produce the active involvement of community leaders. Of course, what is important in one community may not be important in another. However, there is at least one issue that is crucial to virtually all local leaders: community growth.

Harvey Molotch (1976, p. 313), in a provocative article entitled "The City as a Growth Machine," maintains that "this organized effort to affect the outcome of growth distribution is the essence of local government as a dynamic political force. It is not the only function of government, but it is the key one and, ironically, the one most ignored . . . . This is the politics which determines who, in material terms, gets what, where, and how." Molotch argues that, in virtually all communities, a business-oriented elite exists that has population growth as a major goal. And a subsequent analysis of the relationship between community power and population growth in the Clark sample found a strong causal link between the power of local business leaders and population growth that was independent of environmental factors such as region of the country or size of the city (Lyon et al. 1981). Thus, we can list the following outcome of community power: *Communities in which business leaders have high levels of power are likely to experience relatively high levels of population growth.*

Community growth may be a very special local phenomenon that is an important issue in virtually all American communities. This would help to account for the fact that while community power is linked to growth, it does not appear to be closely associated with many other local phenomena. Most local issues are routine or administrative in nature and therefore of little concern to local leaders (Lyon and

Bonjean 1981), and, equally important, an issue that may be very important in one community may be of little consequence in another (Bonjean 1971). So with few exceptions (such as growth), those few issues that are important enough to involve top-local leaders will vary by community. In sum, *the structure of community power matters most for those issues that matter most in the community, and those issues vary from one community to the next.*

Since the degree to which local leaders influence community phenomena typically varies by both issue and community, it follows that the practical applications of community power measurement techniques should be issue- and community-specific as well. While there may be a few local issues, such as population increase or economic growth, that are important in virtually every community, the more common situation is for local issues to vary in importance by place and time. Thus, it may be that the major lesson to be learned from comparative community power research is that much of community power is a locally unique phenomenon and that the causes and consequences of community power can vary accordingly. This would indicate, then, that the proper study of community power should once again be based on the case study approach.

FROM COMPARATIVE RESEARCH BACK TO CASE STUDIES

The above conclusion about the unique nature of community power is similar in some ways to the conclusion John Walton (1976) drew in a review entitled "Community Power and the Retreat from Politics: Full Circle after Twenty Years?" Walton felt that the major lesson to be drawn from comparative community power research was the need to return to it origins: namely, Hunter's *Community Power Structure.* As we pointed out earlier in this chapter, Hunter's concern was to learn more about the power structure of Atlanta so that pressure might be applied efficiently on those who mattered in order to improve the local quality of life. Sociology and political science moved rather far from that pragmatic goal with the academic debates on methodology that followed, but the twenty (or now thirty) years of research that followed Hunter were not entirely circular. We have returned to the case study approach in the 1980s with a considerably more sophisticated understanding of community power and its measurement than existed in the 1950s. For example, *power* is now defined with more precision, usually as a multidimensional phenomenon with clear distinctions between the various dimensions. Likewise, the techniques for measuring these dimensions reflect this definition of power; techniques are almost always combined in order to avoid the inherent difficulties in any single approach. Further, the findings are generalized to other communities (if at all) with clear disclaimers and warnings about the variations in power between communities. Instead of having relevance to some general model of community politics in a mass society, the findings are seen more commonly today as relevant to establishing a higher quality of local life.

Recent Examples of the Case Study Approach

Hayes's **Who Rules in Oakland?** There are three examples of these new community power case studies that are worth noting at this point. The first is Edward Hayes's *Power Structure and Urban Policy: Who Rules in Oakland?* (1972). In an ironic change of roles, Hayes, a political scientist, studied Oakland with goals reminiscent of sociologist Floyd Hunter's research in Atlanta. It was Hayes's (1972, p. xi) desire to determine "the extent to which certain major economic interests, primarily real estate and manufacturing, have come to influence public policy." Relying largely on available data (newspaper reports, published histories of Oakland, census data) and supplemented by personal interviews, Hayes reaches conclusions very similar to Hunter's. After analyzing major local issues, such as the model cities program, the Bay Area Rapid Transit System (BART), and assorted poverty programs, he concludes:

> these programs which the government has undertaken have been undertaken in such a way as to guarantee benefits for the affected businessmen and, often but not always, to minimize possible benefits for the laboring poor. Indeed, it is accurate to say that the public policy process generally has tended to *increase* the incomes of the rich and the nonincomes of the poor, quite the opposite of any redistribution effect (Hayes 1972, p. 198).

And sharing with Hunter the desire to use community power research as a tool for community change, Hayes (1972, p. 199) presents "the need for informed opposition to the present system," with the information being supplied from community power research. Hayes's research in Oakland, then, represents an attempt to move away from the methodological polemics that followed *Community Power Structure* and back to Hunter's original goals of practical research geared toward transforming the community into a more efficacious democracy.

Trounstine and Christensen's **Movers and Shakers.** A second and in some ways similar example is *Movers and Shakers: The Study of Community Power* (1982), a joint effort by journalist Philip Trounstine and political scientist Terry Christensen. Like Hunter and Hayes, one of the goals of their case study of San Jose, California, is to increase local citizens' understanding of how the "movers and shakers" control community events and, thereby, increase community residents' ability to form more responsive power structures. In addition, Trounstine and Christensen also attempt to insure a wider dispersion of community power information than previous researchers.

One method by which community power findings of *Movers and Shakers* are communicated to a larger audience is through the inclusion of a journalist in the research team. Trounstine and Christensen make a convincing case for the special skills journalists can bring to community power research. The journalists' contacts with important sources of information, their superior writing skills, and their ability to get the findings "out of the library and into the public forum" can contribute substantially to a higher public awareness of community power research.

Another way in which Trounstine and Christensen hope to spread the influence of community power research is by "demystifying" the methodology of community power and thereby making it more available to the average person. They have provided in *Movers and Shakers* a methodological primer on the reputational approach to community power that encourages local citizens to undertake the challenge of discovering the true patterns of leadership in their own community. Thus, *Movers and Shakers* continues the legacy of *Community Power Structure* by more accurately informing citizens about local leadership so that a power structure more responsive to the needs of all the community can be created.

Galaskiewicz's Exchange Networks and Community Politics. Not all of the new case studies of community power are such pragmatic reflections of Floyd Hunter's legacy. Some, like Joseph Galaskiewicz's *Exchange Networks and Community Politics* (1979), are much more in the academic-methodological tradition. Using local organizations as the primary unit of analysis rather than individuals, Galaskiewicz intensively interviewed spokespersons for over a hundred formal organizations in "Towertown" to gather information on its interorganizational networks of money, information, and support. For these three important resources, the centrality and dominance of different organizations were then established, which allowed him to test hypotheses about the structure and dynamics of community-based organizations. These hypotheses generally supported a conclusion that "organizations which controlled more resources and had an interest in maintaining local institutions tended to be more central in each of the three networks" (Galaskiewicz 1979, p. 154). This conclusion, in turn, supports a "market model" of community decision making in which organizations compete for power in areas viewed as crucial to their own self-interests. The winners are those organizations that are most central in the transactions of money, information, and support.

Galaskiewicz's analysis is in the tradition of classic community field research, i.e., an intensive study of a small, isolated community with little emphasis on issues or organizational links in the larger society. It differs from its predecessors in its explicit focus on organizations and its sophisticated statistical methodology. And it represents along with *Who Rules in Oakland?* and *Movers and Shakers* a movement away from large-sample, comparative community research and back to the intensive case studies common in the *Community Power Structure—Who Governs?* era.

Chapter Thirteen

Measuring Local Power

Hunter, Hayes, and Trounstine and Christensen believe that improvements in the local quality of life are more likely when there is a clear understanding of the structure of community power. If they are correct, it behooves those interested in improving a community's quality of life to invest some time and energy in mapping out the patterns of local power. The following is a general methodological guide for determining who governs in the community. The measurement techniques will work equally well as a technique for uncovering a community-wide distribution of power or for focusing on power patterns within a single area of community affairs. For academic and journalistic goals of general description and explanation, a broad study of power throughout the entire community (or at least through several issue areas) is the common approach. However, for the more pragmatic concerns of community development and change, a narrower focus on one or two specific community issues is usually more appropriate. In either case, this application of community power measurement techniques is presented in a step-by-step process that allows considerable modification for different needs and issues.

STEP ONE: COMMUNITY OVERVIEW

One important similarity between *Community Power Structure* and *Who Governs?* is that both include substantial amounts of background material on the community. In fact, the first step in most reputational and decisional techniques is a thorough background analysis of the entire community.

A major lesson learned from holistic studies was that the separate structures and institutions within the community do not exist in a vacuum. This means that community power is interrelated with the class structure, economic structure, and religious and educational institutions; in short, a community's power structure is interrelated with all the other parts of the community. It is impossible to reach an understanding of a community's power structure without first possessing a considerable amount of general knowledge about that community.

How does one gather such information? Assuming that a temporal investment in several years or at least several months (as is common in holistic community studies) is impractical, a few weeks in the local library can suffice. Past issues of local newspapers and local magazines or newsletters are valuable data sources, as are published histories of the community. More sophisticated research might include analysis of census data (growth patterns, race and age composition, residential segregation, work force participation and composition), results of previous elections, financial contributors to the campaigns, and master plans for the city. The list of data sources is virtually endless, but the amount of time is not. Sometimes, shortcuts are available. If the community has a college or university, there may be a local urban or community research center that has produced community overviews with much of the needed background information. Urban planning and community development departments in the city government often have statistical profiles of the community. Planners within the school district, county, or other community-wide entities are other possible resources.

There is a temptation to devote relatively little time to this initial step or perhaps even to skip it entirely and move on to the real study of community power.[1] However, the subsequent steps of interviewing and drawing up lists of potential leaders depend upon a thorough understanding of the whole community. So, how does one know when enough background information has been gathered? There is no precise rule, but before proceeding to the second step, the following questions should be answered:

1. What are the important environmental factors affecting the community (e.g., regional characteristics, transportation arteries, nearby communities)?
2. What is the demographic structure of the community (e.g., population size, work force composition, age and race proportions, residential and business land-use patterns)?
3. What are the most important, or at least the most visible, issues before the community? Which groups or individuals are on which side?

---

[1] This temptation is especially strong for those who have lived in the community to be studied for a number of years. While such first-hand knowledge of the community certainly can be of value, it is not a substitute for this step. Holistic studies from *Middletown* to *Small Town in a Mass Society* have shown the subjective bias residents can have in viewing their own community.

4. What are the major values of the community? Are most concerns related to economic growth and a favorable business climate? Do moral or religious issues arise with any regularity? Is there an inherent desire to preserve the status quo, or is there progressive support for change?[2]
5. What are the dynamics of the above questions? How have the issues they represent changed over time?

When these questions are answered, it can be assumed that the community background information is sufficient to move on to the second step.

STEP TWO: CHOOSING THE POSITIONAL INFORMANTS

After an overview of the community has been developed, the next step is to select those people who can provide the initial responses necessary to learn about the structure of community power. Since these informants will supply crucial information about who will be interviewed next and why, we want individuals who are likely to possess knowledge about power in the community and how it is used in local issues. An effective and widely used technique is to select people who, because of their official positions in the community, are likely to be especially knowledgeable. For example, I was part of a community study that interviewed as the first set of community informants:

1. The editor of the largest daily newspaper.
2. The president of the largest bank.
3. The superintendent of the largest school district.
4. The director of the Chamber of Commerce.
5. The director of the local NAACP chapter.
6. The director of the local LULAC chapter.
7. The pastor of the largest predominantly Anglo church.
8. The pastor of the largest predominantly black church.
9. The pastor of the largest predominantly Hispanic church.
10. The mayor of the central city.
11. The city manager of the central city.
12. All minority (black, Hispanic, or female) members of the city council of the central city.

---

[2] Questions of community values are clearly subjective and difficult to answer. Nevertheless, we have known ever since the *Middletown* studies that unless local values are understood, the local actions they support cannot be understood. As an illustration of the influence of local values on community power, Miller (1970) found that business leaders were more dominant in Atlanta and Seattle than in Bristol, England, in part because business leaders are held in higher esteem in Atlanta and Seattle than in Bristol.

This list was designed for a broad view of a particular community (Waco, Texas); more specific focuses in other communities will necessitate different lists. However, regardless of the focus or community, the selection procedure for the initial informants considers *positions* rather than *individuals*. By selecting positions, the research can be replicated even if many of the original informants are no longer in the community. Specific individuals will come and go in a community, but the positions will remain.

The key question is, of course, which positions should be selected? The above list was constructed to represent a wide range of knowledgeable positions. Based on background analysis of the community, it was modified to include religious leaders and exclude union leaders. Other communities will require other modifications, just as some issues may provide a focus on one set of positions rather than another. The characteristics of the community as well as the characteristics of the issue(s) guide the choice of positions.

STEP THREE: INTERVIEWING THE POSITIONAL INFORMANTS

At this stage of the initial interviews, as well as at the second stage of interviews discussed in step five, we are attempting to converse with people who often consider themselves very important and very busy. The most efficient means of securing an interview with local elites depends upon the resources of the researcher. If he or she represents an important local organization or if influential people are associated with the research effort, then a third-party letter or call of introduction can ease the entree. If that is not possible, then a letter or call from the researcher asking for a confidential interview about key issues in the community may suffice. Mention that the interview will take only about thirty minutes and stress again its confidentiality.

As the interview begins, briefly explain your reason for talking to him or her (i.e., he or she occupies a key community position) and mention again that the source of the observations recorded (by hand, not machine)[3] will remain confidential. Then, ask the informant:

> 1. "In your opinion, what five individuals in this community are the most influential in _____?" (either a general issue, e.g., education, health care, economic growth; or, you might simply ask for the entire community, e.g., Waco).
> 2. "Now, would you please rank those individuals, one through five, in terms of their influence in _____?" (general issue or community). Be prepared at this point to answer questions from the informant

---

[3] From my experience, the use of a tape recorder is likely to cost more in lost respondent candor than can be gained through the more accurate recording of detailed responses.

such as "Influential in what way?" or "What do you mean by _____?" (issue) with a direct response that introduces as little bias as possible. In other words, develop a standard definition of influence (e.g., the ability to lead others or to get things done) and issues that can be used in subsequent interviews. When possible, allow the informant to use his or her own definitions; but if you are asked for a clarification, provide explanations that will move the informant's responses toward the information you desire.

After the ranking, a good follow-up is open-ended questions about the issue, the individuals named, and the ranking. The goal here is to gather additional background information about the people and processes involved in the topic of interest. After recording the responses to the open-ended questions, the interview can move to other issue areas. At this point, questions 1 and 2, and the open-ended follow-up questions are repeated for each issue.

If only a few issues are considered, the interview is likely to be relatively brief with time available to go over the lists again for revisions. If this is done for one positional informant, however, it should be done for all.

STEP FOUR: CHOOSING THE REPUTATIONAL LEADERS

There are several ways to combine the information gathered in the first interviews. One straightforward method is to list everyone mentioned for a particular issue and their given ranks. Then use a point system giving 5 points for a first place rank, 4 points for second, and so on. Thus, if an individual were named by three different informants for a particular issue and ranked first once ($1 \times 5 = 5$) and third twice ($2 \times 3 = 6$), the total points given to that person would be eleven ($5 + 6 = 11$). Next, prepare a frequency distribution rating the individuals mentioned by point total, and choose a cutoff point at (with luck) a natural break in the distribution.[4] For example, in Table 13–1, a numerical break occurs between Susan Silver and John April, and the ten top reputational leaders are selected for the second round of interviewing.[5]

---

[4] Another common way of establishing the cutoff point is through continuing to interview people mentioned until duplications become common and new additions rare (Bonjean 1963).

[5] If any of the top reputational leaders were interviewed as a positional informant (a common occurrence), then they may not need to be questioned in the second round of interviews since the questions to be asked are identical.

TABLE 13–1 Hypothetical ranking of reputational leaders from responses of positional informants in issue one

Aggregate rank	Name	Total points
1.	Charles Tolbert*	38
2.	Preston Dyer*	36
3.	Paulette Edwards*	30
4.	Lawrence Felice*	28
5.	Mike Mansfield*	27
6.	Nancy Evans*	24
7.	Cynthia Burns*	23
8.	Tom Meyers*	18
8.	Troy Abell*	18
10.	Susan Silver*	16
11.	John April	4
11.	Ross Staton	4
13.	Harold Osborne	3
14.	Jean Frank	2
15.	Tillman Rodabough	1
15.	John Fox	1
15.	Kjell Enge	1
15.	Larry Lyon	1

* Selected for second round of interviews.

STEP FIVE: INTERVIEWING THE REPUTATIONAL LEADERS

If these reputational leaders are issue specific (i.e., if you asked about specific issues in the interviews with the positional informants rather than about the entire community), they are only asked about those issues that resulted in their being added to the list. Thus, for many reputational leaders, there will be only one issue covered in the questioning. For some, two or more issues will be covered if they were mentioned as influential in more than one area. As was the case with the interviews with the positional informants, ask questions one and two to produce a ranking of leaders. And again, they are followed with open-ended questions designed to learn more about the issue and the leaders.

STEP SIX: CHOOSING THE "TOP" LEADERS

After this second series of interviews, issue specific leadership lists are again prepared in the same way as they were for the responses from the positional informants, i.e., establish cutoff points and choose top-ranking reputational leaders for each issue. Table 13–2 is an example of responses from the same issue as in Table 13–1. Because this second list is based on the responses of individuals who are perceived as leaders by knowledgeable informants in key local positions, it is assumed that it is more valid than the list of leaders produced by the first set of interviews. Thus, the top-ranked individuals from the second set of interviews are seen as the most powerful individuals for that particular area.

TABLE 13–2 Hypothetical ranking of top reputational leaders from responses of reputational leaders in issue one

Aggregate rank	Name	Total points
1.	Troy Abell*	43
2.	Charles Tolbert*	36
3.	Mike Mansfield*	27
3.	Robert Miller*	27
5.	Susan Silver*	21
6.	Harold Osborne*	18
7.	Nancy Evans	5
8.	Ross Staton	4
9.	John April	3
10.	Paulette Edwards	2
10.	Cynthia Burns	2
10.	Lawrence Felice	2
13.	Jean Frank	1
13.	Kjell Enge	1
13.	Tom Myers	1

* Selected as top-ranked reputational leaders.

STEP SEVEN: ANALYZING THE TOP LEADERSHIP

At this point, any individual or group who has gathered all the background material and conducted the forty or so interviews associated with steps three and five should possess considerable insight into the power structure of a community. However, much more information about local leadership can be gained from a systematic comparison of the questionnaire responses.

Decentralization

Table 13–3 illustrates some of the comparisons that can be made. If a total of four separate issues were examined, we can see, for example, that power in issue three (with twelve top-ranked leaders) is considerably more decentralized than the other areas examined. Additionally, comparing the top leadership lists of issue areas one and three shows substantial overlap between the leaders since four of the six top-ranked leaders named for issue area one are also named for issue three. In effect, we can trace two patterns of decentralization: intraissue (the number of leaders per issue) and interissue (the number of leaders with influence in more than one issue).

TABLE 13–3 Examples of comparisons between leadership lists to determine decentralization

	Issue 1	Issue 2	Issue 3	Issue 4	
Total number of individuals named	18	12	23	21	(10 positional informants interviewed)
Reputational leaders	10	8	10	12	(30 reputational leaders interviewed)
Total number of individuals named	15	10	20	15	
Top-ranked leaders	6	4	12	8	
Overlap of leader between issue areas (decentralization)		1	2	1	
		4		0	
		0			

Visibility and Legitimacy

Visibility. Further comparisons of the leadership lists can provide information on additional dimensions of community power. Comparing the lists in Tables 13–1 and 13–2 reveals three types of leaders. Notice that in Table 13–1, six persons were named as powerful in the first round of reputational interviews but were not listed among the top leadership in Table 13–2 (Preston Dyer, Paulette Edwards, Law-rence Felice, Nancy Evans, Cynthia Burns, and Tom Myers). These six individuals may be conceived of as *symbolic* leaders—leaders whose power is more apparent than real. Four persons are listed as powerful in both lists (Charles Tolbert, Mike Mansfield, Troy Abell, and Susan Silver). These four individuals may be conceived of as *visible* leaders—leaders whose power is both apparent and real. Finally, two leaders who were not in the first group were named as powerful in the second series of interviews (Harold Osborne, Robert Miller). The influence of these two leaders is *concealed* from the view of many in the community. Thus, it is possible to distinguish three types of leaders by comparing the two sets of interviews: *symbolic, visible,* and *concealed* leaders (Bon-jean 1963).

Legitimacy. Still another dimension of community power may be discerned from this technique. The *legitimacy* of the leadership struc-ture is determined by examining the elite's organizational positions in the community. For example, if the four top leaders in the issue area of education are the school superintendent, a college dean, the PTA pres-ident, and a school board member, they would all be classified as legitimate leaders for this issue area. On the other hand, if they did not hold such positions but rather had no more official authority in the area than anyone else in the community, the leadership structure would rank low in legitimacy.

Organizational Structure

Knowledge of the organizational affiliations of local elites is necessary to determine the legitimacy of their power. However, once these affili-ations are determined, it becomes possible to learn about the organiza-tional structure of community power. Through the use of sociometric or network analysis, you can trace the patterns of interconnections among key local organizations. The techniques for constructing these organizational maps of community influence were pioneered by Hunter (1953) and continue to be found in the most sophisticated of current community power research efforts (Galaskiewicz 1979).

By charting the organizational affiliations of local elites, one may find, for example, one or two organizations that include in their mem-bership a significant portion of the community's leaders. In such a case, that organization would be seen either as a base for power in the community or as a meeting place for the powerful—in the best chicken-or-egg tradition, the correct interpretation depends upon whether people are powerful because of the organizations to which they belong, or organizations are powerful because of the people who belong to them. In either case, knowledge of such organizational memberships remains useful. For example, in Table 13–4, we see the considerable influence of the chamber of commerce. However, it is important to consider in this type of analysis the size of the organization. If the chamber of commerce has two hundred members and the local philanthropic foundation has only ten, then its inclusion of six top leaders may be more significant than the chamber's eight.

TABLE 13–4   **Hypothetical distribution of top leaders by organizational membership**

Organizations with more than one member	Number of members named as top leaders
Chamber of Commerce	8
Rotary Club	6
Community Philanthropic Foundation	6
United Way	5
First National Bank	2
Big State University	2

Mapping the membership patterns of the community's leaders can also uncover various forms of organizational interlock. The same group of powerful people may belong to the same organizations. In such a case, one might assume that these organizations will pursue similar goals and represent similar interests in the community even though their formal structures and goals appear quite different. In Figure 13–1 we might expect the chamber of commerce, the United Way, and the Rotary Club to take similar positions on local issues because of the considerable overlap in membership by top leaders.

STEP EIGHT: APPLYING THE ANALYSIS TOWARD COMMUNITY CHANGE AND DEVELOPMENT

The ability to classify local leaders by various dimensions of power is of more than academic interest. Remember that the original goal of community power research was a pragmatic one: to understand better community power in order to work more efficiently for community change and a higher quality of life. Clearly, community change strategies should vary by the degree to which power is decentralized, or legitimate, or visible in the community. Producing community development models without an understanding of the structure and dynamics of community power is futile. However, two important

FIGURE 13–1   Organizational interlock among top local leaders

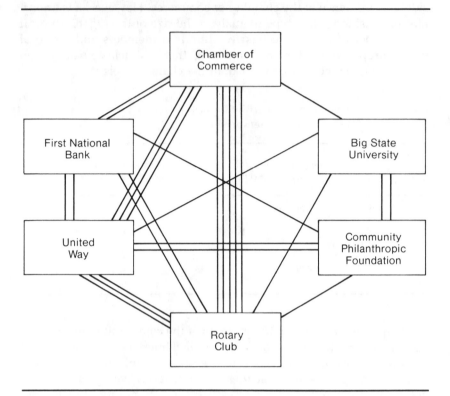

qualifiers about applying community power research should be introduced at this point.

First, it is easy to become too impressed with the findings. After hundreds of hours and dozens of interviews, it is natural for the researcher(s) to feel that something very important has been discovered. The findings are important, but the influence of the local leadership should not be overestimated. The impact of the mass society severely limits the ability of community leaders to affect community events. If the major businesses and industries are owned by organizations headquartered thousands of miles away, then the economic impact of local decisions is lessened. Similarly, if the state and national governments have more rules and money for urban development than the municipal government, then the political impact of local decision is likewise lessened. This is not to say that the community is a helpless pawn, completely manipulated by extracommunity forces, but it is necessary to acknowledge the vertical axis of the community when incorporating community power characteristics into community development strategies.

Second, while there is a long line of community power research contending that those who hold local power (especially if it is a centralized, concealed power) are exploitative, consistently making decisions that improve their own lives while lowering the quality of life for the rest of the community (Hunter 1953; Hayes 1972; Molotch 1976; Domhoff 1978), it does not follow that all communities and all leaders fit this mold. It is possible that an elite power structure is typically detrimental to a community, but to believe that this is the case without supporting empirical evidence is both simplistic and naive. The comparative research that does exist on the relationship between community power and the quality of community life is mixed, with some research indicating that power structures with certain elite characteristics may be beneficial in some instances (Hawley 1963; Crain et al. 1969; Clark 1976, 1983).

In sum, local leaders may not always be unscrupulous capitalists working behind the scenes to enrich themselves at the expense of others. Additionally, increased knowledge of the local power structure will not necessarily bring about a more just and efficacious community. Still, as we have argued in Chapter 8, it is difficult to conceive of substantial community development occurring without a systematic understanding of local decision making.

Community power research, then, is a necessary antecedent to meaningful community development, but it is not sufficient by itself. Rather, knowledge of community power should be supplemented with an understanding of other community phenomena. For example, if we discover that a hidden, centralized local elite is in opposition to increasing the number of low-cost housing units, that is an important piece of information, but without knowledge of the current number, quality, and location of low-cost housing units, the chance for a successful campaign to make low-cost housing more available is remote. Similarly, if we learn that the local leadership, as represented by the municipal government and various civic affairs groups, is strongly in favor of community growth, it is still important to discover the sentiments of the entire community as well as environmental characteristics that may inhibit or encourage growth. We are saying, then, that a holistic community research effort that considers multiple sources and types of information is best suited for guiding efforts at local change. The ways in which community power research, community polls, local indicators, and other types of community information can be combined to provide a holistic view of the community is the subject of the following chapter.

Chapter Fourteen

Field Research: Holistic Studies and Methods

In Chapter 1, holistic studies were introduced as prime examples of the community's preeminence as an object of sociological inquiry. The Lynds' description of life in Middletown, Park and his associates' analyses of Chicago, and Warner's Yankee City series all became classics that remain as widely cited examples of sociological research. In this next to last chapter, we will look back at some of the major findings from these classic studies, determine what it was about their holistic methodology that made them classics, and update our review with some recent examples. Finally, since the holistic studies' forte is describing the various characteristics of communities, we will set the stage for our final chapter—deciding which community characteristics lead to a high quality of life.

THE CLASSIC COMMUNITY STUDIES

Holistic descriptions of community life have a history that traces back at least as far as the nineteenth century and Charles Booth's (1902) monumental studies of London. No other body of community research is as widely read or cited as these attempts to describe all the interrelated parts of local life.[1] Yet, from the hundreds of holistic community

---

[1] Although holistic community studies are often difficult to distinguish from the neighborhood ethnographies that were mentioned in Chapter 3 as a descent of sociocultural ecology, among the more notable of both genre are: W. E. B. Du Bois *The Philadelphia Negro* (1899). John Dollard's *Caste and Class in a Southern Town* (1937), St. Clair Drake and Horace Cayton's *Black Metropolis*, James West's *Plainville U.S.A.* (1945), Art Gallaher's *Plainville Fifteen Years Later* (1961), John Seeley's *Crestwood Heights* (1956), Bennett Berger's *Working Class Suburb* (1960), Gerald Suttles's *The Social Order of the Slum* (1968), Elliot Liebow's *Tally's Corner* (1967), Arthur Vidich and Joseph Bensman's *Small Town in Mass Society* (1958), Ulf Hannerz' *Soulside* (1969), William Foote Whyte's *Street Corner Society* (1955), and Herbert Gans' *The Urban Villagers* (1962) and *The Levittowners* (1967).

books and articles published since Booth, the three sets of community studies mentioned in the introduction above are generally acknowledged as the most important, as the "classic" community studies. We will briefly overview each, looking at who did the research, how the community was studied, and what were some of the major findings.

THE MIDDLETOWN STUDIES

The husband and wife team of Robert and Helen Lynd did not set out to do a holistic community study in Middletown (Muncie, Indiana). Rather, their more focused initial goal was a study of religious worship[2] in a community "having many features common to a wide group of communities" (Lynd and Lynd 1929, p. 3). They soon discovered, however, that in order to study religion, they needed to study all the other local phenomena related to religion as well. Thus, during the eighteen months of 1924–25 when they lived in Middletown, their concern was with all of the "interwoven trends that are the life of a small American city" (Lynd and Lynd 1929, p. 3).

Middletown. The product of the Lynds' field research in Muncie was one of the best-written, most-interesting, best-selling books sociology has ever produced: *Middletown: A Study in Contemporary American Culture.* This book, along with the remarkably similar fictional works of Sinclair Lewis (*Main Street* and *Babbitt*), created the dominant images of small town America during the 1920s and 1930s.

The goal of the Lynds (1929, p. 3) was description: "Neither fieldwork nor report has attempted to prove any thesis: the aim has been, rather, to *record* observed phenomena." And in this regard, they succeeded almost too well. Ruth Glass (1968, p. 148) calls such works "the poor sociologists' substitute for a novel." Bell and Newby (1972, p. 13) note that "the highly descriptive nature of many community studies leads to the danger of their being dismissed as pieces of documentary social history, contributing little to our knowledge of social processes." And Stein (1960, p. 47) warns us that it is "too easy to read both *Middletown* volumes as if they were purely descriptive reports" so that the "mass of absorbing details lulls the reader into an aesthetic rather than a scientific frame of mind."

Certainly the amazingly detailed description of life in Muncie is a striking characteristic of the *Middletown* volumes. In the first book, for example, we are treated to nine pages simply describing and explaining how the residents dress:

---

[2] Robert Lynd was a Presbyterian minister in the early 1920s, but his often "radical" interpretation of the scriptures (e.g., the rich should help the poor) helped to move his orientation and vocation more toward social activist/sociologist (Lindt 1979, Lynd 1979).

Were the sole use of clothing that of protection of the body, the urgent local discussion of the "morality" of women's clothing would probably never have arisen. Today, men's clothing still covers the body decorously from chin to soles of the feet. Among women and girls, however, skirts have shortened from the ground to the knee and the lower limbs have been emphasized by sheer silk stockings; more of the arms and neck are habitually exposed; while the increasing abandonment of petticoats and corsets reveals more of the natural contours of the body . . . . All of which reveals the fact that the moral function of clothing, while it has persisted without variation among the males, has undergone marked modification among the females. As one high school boy confidently remarked, 'The most important contribution of our generation is the one-piece bathing suit for women.' . . . Even among the men, including working class men, it is apparently less common today than in the nineties to renounce any effort at appearing well-dressed by speaking scornfully of dudes. . . . The early sophistication of the young includes the custom of wearing expensive clothing; as in other social rituals, entrance to high school appears to be the dividing line. The cotton stockings and high black shoes of 1890 are no longer tolerated. The wife of a working man with a total family income of $1,638, said as a matter of course, No girl can wear cotton stockings to high school. Even in winter my children wear silk stockings with lisle or imitations underneath. . . . Only a minority of the junior and senior boys attending the big dances wear Tuxedos, but the obligatory nature of special evening dress for the girls is much more marked. . . . All of which helps to explain the observed trend in the preparation of clothing in Middletown. The providing of clothing for individual members of the family is traditionally an activity of the home, but since the nineties it has tended to be less a hand-skill activity of the wife in the home and more a part of the husband's money-earning (Lynd and Lynd 1929, p. 156–65).

The Lynds' document this movement away from home sewing with statistical data measuring how many bolts of fabric have been sold in local department stores, the amount of time Muncie women devote to sewing and mending, how the amount of time varies by class, and even whether most of the sewing is for themselves, daughters, sons, or husbands. It is, by the way, for their daughters.

In short, *Middletown* is page after page of verbal and statistical description, with largely value-neutral interpretation, in the best anthropological tradition. For example, while today's social analysts often point to the need of American women to dress in provocative styles as an example of sex-based exploitation, the Lynds (1929, p. 63) simply observe that "girls fight with clothes in competition for a mate as truly as Indians of the Northwest coast fight with potlatch for social prestige."

Middletown in Transition. Value-laden interpretations become more common in *Middletown in Transition,* however. When the Lynds returned to Muncie in 1935, they wished to learn how the residents had reacted to the Depression. Generally, they reacted surprisingly well. The business leaders saw the Depression as a temporary inconvenience and Roosevelt's New Deal as unnecessary government intrusion. The working class, even with high levels of unemployment, appeared remarkably patient, waiting for the return of prosperity. This lack of class consciousness, this "apathy" among the workers that the Lynds discovered, was so upsetting that their disappointment colored the analysis:

> the sprawled inertness of Middletown working-class opinion—as over against the more vocal and coherent opinion of the business class—may conceivably take shape slowly in a self-conscious sharpening of class lines. But neither class morale, sources of information, nor personal leadership for such a development is apparent at present among Middletown's working class. Much depends upon whether 'good times' return in as beguiling a form as they were in the 1920s. If they do, the deeper pattern of political loyalty to the old symbols, plus the willingness of these individual working-class atoms to dance to any tune that will give them an automobile and 'show them a good time,' will transform their momentary position in the political limelight under the New Deal and in the election of 1936 into only a vaguely remembered bench mark. For today, as in 1924, the Middletown voter is not a political self-starter, and Elihu Root's advice, widely heralded in Middletown at the time of the 1924 election, still applies: 'All you have got to do is to wake them up, have someone take the head of the crowd and march them. Tell them where to go, whether Democrats or Republicans, I do not care . . . and the organizers . . . will welcome them and set them to work (Lynd and Lynd 1937, p. 367).

The Lynds' values are most clearly on display, however, in their description of the X family. This powerful business family is never mentioned in *Middletown*, but in *Middletown in Transition* they dominate Muncie. While the Lynds explain that the Depression so strengthened the position of the X family that they could not be overlooked in the second book,[3] others suggest it may have been the authors' exposure to Marx's writing between the two volumes (e.g., Bell and Newby 1972, p. 90); but whatever the reason, the ability of the business class (exemplified by the X family) to define the values of Muncie is the dominating theme of *Middletown in Transition*. They quote one citizen: "the big point about this town" is that "the X's dominate the whole town, *are* the town in fact." On the same page, they conclude that "Middletown has, therefore, at present what amounts to a reigning royal family" and ominously conclude that if "one views the Middletown pattern as simply concentrating and personalizing the type of

---

[3] Ironically, while the Depression weakened most of Muncie's industries, the X's glass plant found increased demand for their canning jars.

control which control of capital gives to the business group in our culture, the Middletown situation may be viewed as epitomizing the American business-class control system. It may even foreshadow a pattern which may become increasingly prevalent in the future as the American propertied class strives to preserve its controls" (Lynd and Lynd 1937, p. 77).

The Lynds were better in their fieldwork than in their social forecasting. In terms of the X family, Muncie today has changed considerably from the Lynds' last visit. They no longer own the glass plant. Though the jars that made the X's immune to the Depression still say "Ball" on the side, ownership is in a Chicago-based conglomerate. Few of the X family are still in Muncie, and those that remain are not active in local affairs.

Middletown III. Still, it would be incorrect to assume that modern Muncie is totally different from the 1920s and 1930s. When Theodore Caplow and his associates returned to restudy Muncie in 1976, they found a community remarkably similar to the one described by the Lynds fifty years earlier. The Middletown III project replicated the Lynds' research and has thus far produced two books, *Middletown Families* (Caplow, Bahr, Chadwick, Hill, and Williamson 1982), *All Faithful People* (Caplow, Bahr, and Chadwick 1983), and numerous articles. The general theme of these publications has been the continuity of lifestyles in Muncie. They maintain that a "Middletown Rip van Winkle, awakening in the 1970s from a 50-year-long sleep, would have noticed innumerable changes but would not have had any trouble finding his way around town. . . . Robert Lynd is gone, but we, walking the same streets half a century later, feel the same continuity while noting the changes" (Caplow et al. 1982, pp. 3–4).

The changes that have occurred are almost all externally induced. Middletowners are described as grudgingly accepting the adjustments forced upon them by the larger postindustrial society. Thus, they are not surprised to find that the residents have not changed all that much since their grandparents were studied by the Lynds:

> Change, for Middletown, is something flowing irresistibly from the outside world. Continuity is furnished locally. The outside world continuously proposes new ways of living and thinking. The local community steadfastly resists most of these suggestions and modifies those it adopts into conformity with its own customs . . . .The decision to live in Middletown, a voluntary one for most of its adult residents, is a vote for custom and against innovation, and it is not surprising that a population recruited in that way should be able to resist innovation with considerable success (Caplow et al. 1982, p. 5).

One of the most intriguing findings from the Middletown III project concerns the effect of class position on lifestyles. Caplow and Bruce

Chadwick (1979) used census data to measure occupational inequality between 1920 and 1970. They found that Muncie experienced an overall increase in both occupational prestige and in inequality—a trend similar to that for the entire U.S. work force during that period. Yet, when they replicated the Lynds' community surveys and compared the responses by social class, a very different pattern emerged. By reconstructing the Lynds' detailed lifestyle descriptions, they find that the pronounced differences between the "business" and "working" classes in Muncie have virtually disappeared. For many lifestyle variations—housework (broken down by time spent washing and ironing, sewing and mending, baking), the availability of paid help, educational aspirations, desired traits for their children, time spent with children, the quality of housing, marital satisfaction, unemployment, women working outside the home, and even the time waking up— there has been a dramatic narrowing of differences between the classes. In fact, the class differences in lifestyles have narrowed to a degree that Caplow and Chadwick conclude that it is no longer the significant dividing line it was in the Lynds' day.

This Middletown III stratification research is interesting at two levels. First, it shows that the classic studies' almost obsessive reporting of detail is not altogether trivial or idiosyncratic. In this case, when replicated fifty years later, it tells us something very important about lifestyles that was missed with census data: namely, that social class differences in how we live are not nearly as pronounced as they once were. Second, this project illustrates an inherent strength in community research and an inherent flaw in much national research. When the society is the unit of analysis, as it is in most modern stratification research, it is difficult to capture the detailed description inherent in community research. National data often miss the important stuff of which lives are made. Thus, Roland Warren and Larry Lyon believe that the Middletown III replication illustrates a continuing importance for holistic community studies—an importance that extends beyond the role envisioned in Maurice Stein's *Eclipse of the Community:*

> It is interesting to note that when the objective measures of inequality commonly used in national stratification research are employed in Middletown, the local class dynamics reflect national trends. On the surface, this implies support of the 'mass society' hypothesis. But something very important has occurred in Middletown–an equalization of lifestyles between classes–that may well have also occurred throughout the United States. National data, however, do not have the intensive, descriptive quality of community studies necessary to find out. It may be, then, that we can extend Stein's conclusion about the role of holistic community studies. Communities 'do provide a meeting ground . . . which the depersonalizing forces of mass society can diminish but never destroy.' But beyond that, communities may provide a research site that allows the discovery of

mass society characteristics that are not readily observable at the national level (Warren and Lyon 1983, p. 84).

THE CHICAGO STUDIES

The studies of Chicago by Robert Park and his associates were discussed in Chapter 3. Here, rather than focusing on the ecological approach developed through these studies, we will look more generally at the views of Chicago they provided.

Disorder versus order. For Park and many of his colleagues who grew up in small communities, Chicago must have presented an extreme contrast. Chicago was huge (approximately three million), diverse (extreme wealth and poverty, ethnic neighborhoods), disorganized (youth gangs, crime) and growing (adding about one-half million per decade). Thus, it is not surprising that the Chicago studies emphasize change (urban growth models, invasion-succession processes) while all three Middletown studies emphasize the continuity in Muncie. Also, since Chicago was so large and diverse, most of their analysis is not holistic in the strictest sense (i.e., focusing on *all* of Chicago). The primary unit of analysis was the natural areas of Chicago—studies of subcommunities such as Clifford Shaw's *Delinquency Areas* (1929), Frederick Thrasher's *The Gang* (1927), Harvey Zorbaugh's *The Gold Coast and Slum* (1929), and Louis Wirth's *The Ghetto* (1928). Still, the studies are holistic in that they seek to describe everything within the natural area and to explain how the natural areas were related to the rest of the city.

In many of these studies, the overriding theme (besides the ecological emphasis on spatial patterning) was social control. Much like Durkheim's questions about how organization and integration might be maintained in a modern industrial society, Park and his associates were concerned with how order could be maintained in the face of the disorganization brought by rapid urbanization. And for the Chicago sociologists, the key to learning how social control is maintained was to be found in the natural areas. Maurice Stein (1960, p. 20), in his review of Park's work, concludes that his "starting point was existing social disorganization in the city of Chicago and his main structural units the various subcommunities in which this disorganization appeared as well as the agencies of 'secondary control' which tried to keep it from getting out of hand."

Natural areas. Zorbaugh's *Gold Coast and Slum* may be used as an example. Here we find intensive description of two contrasting natural areas: (1) the Gold Coast along Lake Michigan, where many of the wealthiest residents live "in imposing stone mansions, with their green lawns and wrought-iron-grilled doorways" (p. 7); and (2) the slums of "Little Sicily," "Little Italy," and "Little Hell," where "the criminal, the radical, the bohemian, the migratory worker, the immigrant, the unsuccessful, the queer, and the unadjusted" live (p. 11).

The physical setting of the Gold Coast is described in detail, as well as the lifestyles of the rich who live there. The various cliques of wealthy families are mapped, and the informal rules for being added to The Social Register are described in terms of a "social game." Moving away from the lake, the transient "world of furnished rooms" is described next. Then comes the radical bohemia of "Towertown," and finally the slums where "one alien group after another has claimed this area. The Irish, the Germans, the Swedish, the Sicilians have occupied it in turn. Now, it is being invaded by a migration of the Negro from the south" (p. 127). Each invasion, of course, leads to disorganization and the need to reestablish some modicum of social control.

The commonality between these contrasting natural areas was the attempts to deal with social disorganization. The "social game" and the Social Register helped establish order among the rich, just as "old world" norms and values maintained control in ethnic neighborhoods. Thus, the Chicago studies, Zorbaugh's *Gold Coast and Slum* in particular, can be seen as an attempt to document the process that concerned both Durkheim and Park—how the solidarity and control that are inherently maintained during *Gemeinschaft*-like times might be maintained during the current *Gesellschaft*-like times. The descriptive studies of natural areas in Chicago document the precarious, fragile state of a *Gemeinschaft*-based organic solidarity.

THE YANKEE CITY STUDIES

The five volumes[4] comprising W. Lloyd Warner's analysis of the New England town of Newburyport are the third of the classic community studies considered here. It is the most widely criticized of the classic studies, and most of the criticisms are well-founded. But in spite of its faults, Warner's Yankee City series has had a substantial impact on American sociology. In this section, we will look at both the shortcomings and significance of Yankee City.

The Yankee City research was connected initially with Elton Mayo's famous productivity studies at the Western Electric Plant (e.g., the

---

[4] W. Lloyd Warner and Paul S. Lunt, *The Social Life of a Modern Community* (1941), *The Status System of a Modern Community* (1942), Warner and Leo Srole, *The Social Systems of American Ethnic Groups* (1945), Warner and J. O. Low, *The Social System of a Modern Factory* (1947), Warner, *The Living and the Dead* (1959). Sometimes the Yankee City series is referred to as a six-volume set including Warner's abridged summary (Warner 1963).

Hawthorne effect). Warner's role was to study the home environment of the Western Electric workers, but he rejected all the cities (subcommunities of Chicago) where the workers lived as being too diverse and disorganized, and hence not well-suited for the anthropological field methods he had practiced with the Australian aborigines. So, after what he claims was an exhaustive search for a community that represents all of America, Warner chose Newburyport—small, organized, and "near enough to Cambridge so that [we] could go back and forth without difficulty or loss of time" (Warner and Lunt 1941, p. 43). Of course, in deliberately selecting a small, organized community, he was also selecting a community not at all representative of much of America, and by choosing a community conveniently located near Cambridge, one must doubt how thorough the selection process actually was. But in any event, Newburyport was Warner's representative for all U. S. communities.

The first volume of the Yankee City series presents Warner's most important find: the stratification system of Newburyport.[5] In a sense, when social class was discovered in America, it was discovered in Yankee City by W. Lloyd Warner. Warner empirically demonstrated that the residents of Yankee City: (1) can readily rank other members of the community even though they may disavow the existence of any local class system; (2) separate themselves into six distinct classes (in Warner's terms, upper-upper, lower-upper, upper-middle, lower-middle, upper-lower, and lower-lower; (3) do not view economic considerations as the sole indicator of class position; and (4) have much of their life determined (where they live, whom they may marry, organizations they belong to, the type job, the amount of education) by their class position. Such findings may seem obvious today, but in the 1940s these were new and rather radical discoveries in a discipline that had conspicuously ignored stratification research.

The second major contribution from the Yankee City series appears in the fourth volume, *The Social System of the Modern Factory*. While much of the volume traces ethnic mobility patterns, Warner's methodology was flawed here and his conclusions probably incorrect. However, this volume also includes insightful analysis of a strike in Newburyport that Stein uses to illustrate the bureaucratization trend in *The Eclipse of Community*.

---

[5] Warner's use (or misuse) of the terms class and status added considerably to the continuing confusion and controversy over when to use which. C. Wright Mills' (1942) review of the first Yankee City volume was one of the first (but hardly the last) critics of Warner's analysis. Mills was especially concerned with Warner's use of class in a noneconomic (and therefore in a non-Marxist) way. For other notable criticisms of Warner's treatment of local stratification, see Pfautz and Duncan (1950), Lipset and Bendix (1951), Kornhauser (1951).

Warner answers four questions about the strike:

1. In a community where there had been very few strikes and no successful ones, why did the workers in all of the factories of the largest industry of the community strike, win all their demands and, after a severe struggle, soundly defeat management?
2. In a community where unions had previously tried and failed to gain more than a weak foothold and where there had never been a strong union, why was a union successful in separating the workers from management?
3. Why was the union successful in maintaining the organization despite the intense and prolonged efforts of management to prevent unionization and to halt the continuation of the shoe union?
4. Why did Yankee City change from a non-union to a union town? (Warner and Low 1947 pp. 6–7).

At first glance, the answers to all four of these would seem to hinge on the Depression, but Warner shows that the economic problems of the 1930s are not sufficient to explain the changes in Newburyport:

> Plainly, labor had won its first strike in Yankee City, and, even more plainly, an industrial union had invaded the city for the first time and had become the recognized champion of the workers. When searching for the answers to why such significant, new changes could occur in Yankee City, the evidence is clear that economic factors are of prime importance. But before we are content to accept them as the only answers to our problems, let us once more remind ourselves (1) that there had been severe depressions and low wages before and the union had failed to organize the workers, and (2) that the last and most powerful strike which preceded the present one occurred not in a depression but during a boom period when wages where high and economic conditions were excellent. Other factors are necessary and must be found if we are to understand the strike and have a full explanation of why it occurred and took the course that it did (Warner and Low 1947, p. 53).

A full explanation included a change in factory ownership. The local owners were replaced by "a vast, complex system owned, managed and dominated by New York City" (Warner and Low 1947, p. 64). Now, the "big-city outsiders" who made the policy decisions were beyond the influence of local workers. And in response, the local workers joined extracommunity unions, aligning themselves with workers in similar factories throughout the region. The result, then, was a situation in which events in the larger mass society began dominating the local community—thus Stein's conclusion about *The Eclipse of Community*.

The final volume, *The Living and the Dead*, considers the symbolism of Yankee City, how fictionalized history and political myths integrate the community. While the first four volumes emphasize description (one table in volume II, for example, is 86 pages long), this final volume is more an exercise in theory and interpretation. The first 100 pages are devoted to one "Biggy Muldoon":

> Our present story is concerned with the good and evil fortunes of Biggy Muldoon. It tells why all of Yankee City, where he was elected mayor, and millions of people throughout the United States became emotionally involved in his political and private life. It attempts to explain how the joy, anger, and sorrow they experienced in his spectacular triumphs and bitter defeats helped to develop and expand, yet control and limit, his career. Many of the crucial factors operating in his political life have always been powerful in the political and social life of America. If we can learn the meaning of his career we may gain deeper insight into some of the more important aspects of American politics (Warner 1959, p. 9).

And we are told later that Biggy's political career is similar to those of Al Smith, Huey Long, Fiorello La Guardia, William Jennings Bryan, Andrew Jackson, Abraham Lincoln, and Franklin Roosevelt. Such comparisons of a small-town mayor with national leaders are not surprising, however, since Warner always felt his community studies could be translated to the national scene.[6]

Warner's concern with stratification continues, but in this final volume, perhaps in response to criticisms of the earlier volumes, class is not treated statistically. Rather, he returns to the ethnographic methods he used as an anthropologist in Australia to describe how Biggy's class position made him a hero of the "common man" and an enemy to the "better class" of Yankee City:

> Biggy Muldoon, the "Yankee City Bad Boy," is a big-shouldered, two-fisted, red-haired Irishman. He was born down by the river on the wrong side of the tracks, the only child of Irish-Catholic immigrant parents. Once a street-fighter, a brawler, and an all-round tough guy, he was arrested by the police for shooting dice, profane and abusive language, fighting, and other rough behavior distasteful to the pious and respectable (Warner 1959, p. 9).

Biggy's skillful use of symbols (e.g., remodeling a mansion into a gas station) to crystallize class antagonisms were the key to his rapid rise, but his antagonistic relationship with the upper class eventually led to his downfall. "Biggy's continual attacks on political authority and on the status system forced people toward either open revolt against the system—too frightening for most of them to sustain—or annoyance, embarrassment, and finally confusion and weariness" (Warner 1959, p. 95). We learn, from Biggy, how symbols may be

---

[6] In his Jonesville study, for example, Warner et al. (1949, p. XV) tells us that "Jonesville is in all Americans and all Americans are in Jonesville, for he that dwelleth in America dwelleth in Jonesville, and Jonesville in him." And, yes, Warner actually wrote such prose.

manipulated to induce change, but we also learn how the values upon which the symbols are based define limits which eventually reduce the potential for change.

Thus, Warner ends his series on Newburyport in a way not very common to his earlier volumes. Here we find less of the eclectic data collector–index builder and more of an ethnographer–novelist–political theorist–philosopher. This final volume has been ignored by most social scientists, which is probably a worse fate than being attacked (as the earlier volumes were). Still, Warner's flawed efforts continue to be cited in books on community, social change, and stratification. His works remain influential, as do the efforts in Muncie and Chicago. Our question now is, Why? Why are these studies classics? What makes them special?

WHY ARE THE CLASSICS CLASSIC?

The qualities that make one study, one book, one play, one painting, one anything more important and enduring than another are continually debated. And while it is impossible to state precisely why the studies of Muncie, Chicago, and Newburyport have become community sociology's best-known products, examining some of their common characteristics should provide clues as to why these studies have achieved such an influential status.

The Writing Style

Perhaps the most obvious trait shared by the classics is a remarkably lively, lucid writing style. They are so well written, in fact, that they sometimes seem more like classic works of fiction rather than fact. Bell and Newby (1972) compare Lloyd Warner's writings on Yankee City and Jonesville to Sinclair Lewis's Gopher Prairie and Zenith City in *Babbit* and *Martin Arrowsmith*. Warner himself felt obligated to disclaim a purported connection with his description of Biggy Muldoon and O'Connor's fictional mayor in *The Last Hurrah* (1956). Stein (1960) compares the Lynds' Middletown books with Lewis's *Babbit* and *Main Street* and compares many of the Chicago classics to the novels of Theodore Dreiser. Other near-classics, like Davis and Gardner's *Deep South* and especially John Dollard's *Class and Caste in a Southern Town*, can be seen as the sociological counterpart of William Faulkner's novels.

The ability of these classic works to describe communities without a preponderance of the jargon common in most sociological reports is unusual and no doubt accounts for much of their popularity in sales with the general public. It may also explain why so many noncommunity social scientists have read these works, and why, since their absence of jargon places them out of the main stream, they are no longer cited in most of the major community research efforts.

One reason these classics are so well written, so free of technical jargon, is that they were often written by nonsociologists. Warner, of course, was trained as an anthropologist, and Robert Lynd did not receive a sociology degree until after his Middletown research. That cannot be the whole explanation, however, since many community studies, for example the Chicago studies, were authored by sociologists.

Another possible reason for the ease with which they are read is the subject matter—the whole community. When the focus is as broad as the holistic studies, it is easier to be interesting. There is seldom extended, intensive, and often tedious attention to one phenomenon. Rather, the authors move from one local phenomenon to another and, in so doing, seldom reach the readers' boredom threshold as often as other, more tightly focused works. In any event, these classics are well-written, and that would seem to have something to do with their achieving classic status.

Holistic Approach

Another important common feature of these classics is the attempt to describe all of the community. The community is not just the place where the object of inquiry (a family, or school, or business) happens to be: *it is the object of inquiry*. The Lynds may have been interested initially in religion, and stratification may have been especially important to Warner, but both the Middletown and Yankee City books show how the various local phenomena relate to one another and to the greater whole. The Chicago studies, because of the physical enormity of the subject, focus on subcommunities ("natural areas"), but even here there is an explicit concern with the different parts of the natural area and how they relate to other parts of the city.

The Chicago studies' concern with how each subcommunity relates to the larger community makes them perhaps less vulnerable to a common charge leveled against holistic community studies: that by being so concerned with describing all the different characteristics that influence local events, important extralocal influences are ignored. Even the Chicago studies, however, paid little attention to national events affecting their community, and while Warner and, especially, the Lynds are less guilty of the omission than many holistic researchers, it is impossible to study everything. Thus, even the best holistic studies, in their attempts to describe broadly community life, often give little attention to life outside the community.

The holistic studies are deliberately, necessarily broad. The goal is to understand the community as a totality, and such a goal generally leads to extensive description. It is not surprising, then, that another commonality in these classic community studies is their abundance of descriptive detail.

Emphasis on Description

Description is often placed above analysis in the holistic community studies. The Lynds (1929, p. 3), remember, claimed that "neither field-work nor report has attempted to prove any thesis: the aim has been, rather to *record* observed data, thereby raising questions and suggesting fresh points of departure in the study of group behavior." Such a "let the facts speak for themselves" approach is the rule for most of these studies. In fact, one might argue that when the Lynds strayed too far from this rule, predicting a national centralization of capital and power à la the X family, for example, they were at their weakest. The same can be said for Warner when he ventured into the building of scales to measure social class, or the Chicago sociologists with their organic analogies. What these classic community studies do best is describe. Analysis was seldom their forte.[7]

Now it is often argued that such raw empiricism is atheoretical and hence ultimately sterile. Note, however, in the Lynds' quotation above, they imply that their descriptions can provide the basis for future analysis, and it has. As examples, Stein's *Eclipse of the Community* is an important theoretical work built upon the descriptions of local life provided by the classics, and the Lynds' seemingly trivial descriptions of how much time was devoted to household chores provided the basis for Middletown III's provocative analysis about changes in inequality.

Eclectic Methodology

For the holistic community studies, almost anything goes. That is, any method that can provide information is fair game. Bell and Newby (1972, p. 54) believe that "community study as a method has been so varied and eclectic, and so determined by the object of study, that some doubt must be cast on whether there is a single community study method." In the classic studies examined here, that is certainly the case. Surveys, analysis of available data, and, especially, field studies are part of the community methodology. In fact, all of the methods discussed in Part III of this text can be found in holistic studies. In this

---

[7] Notable exceptions include Wirth's *The Ghetto*, Dollards' *Caste and Class in a Southern Town*, and Seeley, Sim, and Loosley's *Crestwood Heights*. Each provides sophisticated insight and analysis that is, I believe, superior *to the analysis* of the classics discussed in this chapter.

section we will look briefly at how the methods discussed in the previous chapters—community surveys, measures of power, local indicators—are employed in holistic research and then consider in some detail the method most commonly associated with holistic community studies, field research.

Community surveys. Not all community sociologists believe surveys belong in holistic studies. In fact, some very influential ones have argued against surveys. Bell and Newby (1972, p. 61) maintain that "the survey is arguably of marginal relevance for studying the community." Vidich, Bensman, and Stein (1964, p. x) go even further in expressing their distaste for surveys, arguing that such "abstract" methods remove us so far from reality, that "the analyst who uses the instruments is unable to present an image of social behavior as it appears in a 'natural setting' ":

> The point may be emphasized by postulating what would result if all research were conducted by questionnaires, surveys, checklists, and the other modern technologies. These devices, which essentially allow the investigator to accumulate a relatively narrow dimension of experience from a large number of persons, produce a collective portrait of responses to an item. Theoretically a sufficient accumulation of such responses, when "recombined," should add up to a total portrait of reality. In actual fact, however, the reality evoked is in response to the research instrument (Vidich, Bensman, and Stein 1964, p. xi).

Such criticisms are indeed applicable to the *exclusive* reliance on surveys for local information, but when they are used in conjunction with other methods (as is always the case in a holistic approach), then the survey's weak points are offset by the strengths of the other methods. Certainly Warner's research was strengthened by surveys, and the Lynds' surveys provided the benchmarks necessary for the Middletown III project. In short, the local survey is an important tool for holistic study, but it is only one of many tools in the chest of community researchers.

Local indicators. Since the term *local indicators* is a recent one, it is not used by the authors of the classic community studies. However, the use of available statistics to learn about community phenomena goes back far beyond the current local indicator movement. Warner's research team, for example, may well hold the all-time record for gathering social indicators. Warner claims to have gathered and used in his study of Yankee City "lists, directories, the records, rules, and histories of institutions, the regulations governing the community . . . membership lists of the several hundred associations . . . lists of pupils, voters, customers of stores, and city officials, . . . names of persons buried in the several cemeteries . . . lists of subscribers to all the

Boston newspapers and the local newspaper . . . the city directory or the poll-tax book . . . census of the Federal Government . . . annual reports of the city government . . . records of school attendance . . . records of the books and reading club . . . records for individual attendance at the movies . . . plots of the plays . . . records of the parades" (Warner and Lunt 1941, p. 61–64) and more, much more. To a lesser extent, the use of available data is present in all the classic community studies. The rule for holistic studies is "if it's available, use it."

Field Research

Although holistic studies are eclectic in their methods, there is one method that is almost always employed—one method associated so closely with community research that it is the sine qua non for these studies:

> Community study as a method has been so varied and eclectic, and so determined by the object of study, that some doubt must be cast on whether there is a single community study method. There seem to be as many community study methods as there have been community studies. Nevertheless it is possible to make some generalizations and to underline both the strengths and weaknesses of such eclecticism.
>
> The first and most important generalization, from which much else follows, is that community sociologists have usually gone, sometimes for only a short while, to *live* in *their* community. Community sociologists are fieldworkers: they have shared *some* of the experience of *some* of the inhabitants of the locality in which they are interested (Bell and Newby 1972, p. 54–55).

Unlike the other methods in these chapters, exactly what one does in the field is difficult to specify. William F. Whyte, who was an exceptional field researcher for his *Street Corner Society* (1955), bemoaned the lack of instructional material for community field methods. Yet when he tried to explain his own field methodologies, he decided "so much of analysis proceeds on the unconscious level, I am sure that we can never present a full account of it" (Whyte 1964, p. 4).

Field work is an individualistic research method that requires unique adaptations by person and community. Training helps make a good field researcher, but insight and personality probably matter more. Whyte, for example, was studying to be a writer as an undergraduate at Swarthmore (being a good writer is a necessity for a field researcher who wants to be published) and had little instruction in field methods while he was a participant-observer in the *Street Corner Society*. Robert Lynd was trained for the ministry. Still, not everyone just stumbles into field research. Warner, an anthropologist, was trained formally in field methods. And while it may not be possible to develop a set of specific rules for effective field research, some general guidelines are available.

Definitions. So, to begin, what *exactly* is field research? The "exactly" makes this question a particularly difficult one. For example, John and Lyn Lofland (1984, p. 3), in their primer on qualitative methods, argue that field research is only *slightly* different from other techniques such as "qualitative methods, field work interactionism, grounded theory, the Chicago school of ethnography, naturalism, and West Coast interactionism." And none of these slightly different terms appear able to lead us out of what they call a "terminological jungle where many labels compete." That is, no one can say precisely where naturalism becomes ethnography or where qualitative methods differ from field methods. And yet no label has been able to stand for all the variations. For qualitative analysis generally, such confusion over the appropriate term will probably continue, but for holistic community studies, with their anthropological emphasis on living and participating in the community, it would seem that *field* research, or *field* work, or *field* methods, is the preferred term. Thus, community field research is the direct descendant of anthropological field methods and implies the same types of participation and observation as anthropologists use to describe small, isolated, primitive villages.

Research roles. Since living in the community is a necessary part of field research, it is important to analyze the role played by community researchers. Do the researchers cover up the real role of researcher and pretend to be someone else, or should they simply announce to community residents that they are there to study them? There are, naturally, advantages and disadvantages with either strategy; but whether it is because of anthropological tradition (anthropologists could not easily pretend to be natives) or because of ethical considerations involved with deceiving the town's residents, the most commonly played role in community studies is that of researcher.

How researchers announce to the community that they are there to study is called an "entry" problem. Entry problems revolve around how access is gained into the community. In the typical anthropological tradition of the lone researchers, entry is gained through the sponsorship of a key informant. For example, until Whyte was adopted by "Doc," he could not make any progress towards acceptance in the *Street Corner Society* (1955). Liebow never could have written *Tally's Corner* (1967) without Tally's sponsorship. The informants who sponsored Whyte and Liebow provided the entree that allowed them to produce books of considerable insight, but they also introduce a certain bias in that the researchers are "captured" by the informant. If Whyte or Liebow had had different informants, they would have produced different books with different views of the neighborhood. This is not to say that their view is wrong, only that it is influenced strongly by the views of their informants.[8]

When the community is studied by a team of researchers, entry is usually not dependent upon the sponsorship of a key informant. And in most cases, when the researcher moves beyond the neighborhood to an entire community, the lone researcher gives way to the team approach. Robert and Helen Lynd were assisted by two additional researchers and a secretary. Caplow's team was considerably larger for the restudy, and Warner's project engaged a research staff of thirty, eighteen of whom were field workers. For a truly holistic community study, teams are preferable because there is simply too much for one person to observe. A team can have observers in several places and can have informants from several strata. Of course, simply having a team of researchers will not, by itself, guarantee a less biased report. For example, although Warner was aware of six classes in Yankee City, his interviews were predominately from the lower-upper class, a level with which he and his team members (mostly undergraduates from Harvard and Radcliffe) could identify.

Hypothesis testing. The question of whether the field researchers should have a theoretically based hypothesis to guide their descriptive efforts has usually been answered in the negative. Remember the Lynds' goal was description rather than analysis, and most guides to field research agree that using hypotheses to guide the description is too inhibiting. Still, one often suspects hidden hypotheses may be guiding the research. For example, the Middletown III project has been criticized for describing only those events that emphasize continuity and stability while ignoring other data that suggest radical change and discord (Cherlin 1982). Caplow and his associates did not explicitly set out to find a remarkably unchanged Muncie or a continuingly strong family, but such hypotheses may have developed unconsciously during the project and affected their data collection. In any event, field work differs significantly from other methodologies in that it is more often a method for hypothesis generating than for hypothesis testing.

---

[8] Whyte and Liebow's key informants were dominant members in the neighborhoods into which the researchers wanted entry. Doc and Tally's high status obviously eased Whyte and Liebow's acceptance, but the favored position of their informants may have also contributed to the sympathetic descriptions of the residents in *Street Corner Society* and *Tally's Corner*. In contrast, Vidich and Bensman (1955) argue that alienated or marginal community members are better informants because they are more detached from the community and hence more objective. Not surprisingly, Vidich and Bensman's *Small Town in Mass Society* (1958) has a more critical, almost mocking description of the small town residents.

The role of the hypothesis is but one of the ways in which field methods differ from the other research methodologies available for community studies. It requires a distinctive kind of researcher whose personality and insight are more important than the possession of trainable skills.[9] It produces qualitative data that do not lend themselves to validation or comparison. Yet it also produces descriptions of behavior that seem much closer to the reality of human existence than other methods. This is what Vidich, Bensman and Stein (1964, p. xi) refer to when they conclude that "as a consequence of the unwillingness of most community researchers to forsake direct observation and direct reporting of community life, we still have coherent images of the community and social life that are unattainable by other methodologies." Herbert Gans (1962, p. 350) draws a similar conclusion when he argues the field research's "deficiencies in producing quantitative data are more than made up for by its ability to minimize the distance between the researcher and his object of study." So the distinctive advantages of field methods mean that it can make a unique contribution to a holistic community study, but its distinctive disadvantages also account for why other methods are typically used to supplement it.

MORE RECENT HOLISTIC STUDIES

The classic research in Middletown, Chicago, and Yankee City served as exemplars for the holistic community studies in this chapter, and they performed that role admirably. That is not to imply, however, that important holistic community research is not continuing in places besides Muncie. In this final section, we will look briefly at some of the more recent holistic studies of community.

Herbert Gans: *The Urban Villagers* and *The Levittowners*

Herbert Gans lived in what most of us would call a slum—the West End of Boston—in the late 1950s. His participation with and observation of the Italian-Americans who lived there convinced him that the West End was not a slum, but rather an "urban village" in which *Gemeinschaft*-like ties enabled poor people living in a rundown area of Boston to make the best of a bad situation. In fact, Gans concludes that, all things considered, the West Enders created a community with a reasonably good quality of life. Urban planners, however, with their

---

[9] As an example, perhaps the best field researcher *ever* (or at least the most widely cited) was Erving Goffman—*The Presentation of Self in Everyday Life* (1959), *Asylums* (1961), "On Cooling the Mark Out" (1962), *Stigma* (1963), *Gender Advertisement* (1977)—but his attempt to explain the theory and methods of his field research, *Frame Analysis* (1974), has not been as widely cited.

surveys and census data, reached a different conclusion. They designated the entire neighborhood for urban renewal. By 1960, over 20,000 West-Enders had been "relocated" to make way for the highrise office and apartment complexes.[10]

Much of *The Urban Villagers* (1962) can be read as a plea by Gans to urban planners—urging them to reassess their definitions of urban blight and slums. His book was a leader in a series of anti–urban renewal books (e.g., Jane Jacobs's *The Death and Life of Great American Cities*, 1961, and Scott Greer's *Urban Renewal and American Cities*, 1964), and perhaps even more important (since urban renewal was probably on the way out by the mid-1960s regardless), *The Urban Villagers* is a powerful testament both to what "objective" data cannot show about a community and to how community can exist in a place seemingly devoid of community by middle-class standards, a point echoed a few years later by Gerald Suttles in *The Social Order of the Slum* (1968).

Gans relied again on participant-observation when he and his wife were among the first families to move into the new suburban community of Levittown in 1958. Levittown was a working-class suburb built "from scratch" by Levitt and Sons on the New Jersey side of Philadelphia. After moving away in 1960, Gans returned to Levittown two years later to complete additional field work and interviews. *The Levittowners* (1967) is remembered today for two major findings. First, Gans (1967, p. 408) discovered that a new community "is not new at all, but only a new physical site on which people develop conventional institutions with traditional programs." The discussions of New Towns in Chapter 9 reached similar conclusions. Second, Gans found that moving to the suburbs does not change people into mass-produced, alienated status seekers.[11] When working class families leave the central city for Levittown, "they do not develop new life styles or ambitions for themselves and their children," and to the degree they do change, "morale goes up, boredom and loneliness are reduced, family life becomes temporarily more cohesive, and social and organizational activities multiply" (Gans 1967, p. 409). In short, suburbs do not change people much, and what few changes may occur are largely for the good.[12]

---

[10] Gans maintains that very few of the West Enders were actually relocated by the government. While urban renewal forced them to leave, only 10 percent found government housing. The rest were housed independently in the private housing market.

[11] This stereotype of the suburban lifestyle is often and incorrectly attributed to William H. Whyte's *The Organization Man* (1956). See Berger's *Working Class Suburb* (1960) for a detailed analysis of the "myth of suburbia."

[12] Both of Gans's works include methodological appendices. A comparison of the two shows interesting differences in how field techniques differ by field characteristics.

William Kornblum: *Blue Collar Community*

Long before Jim Croce's "Bad, Bad, Leroy Brown," sociologists took a special interest in the South Side of Chicago. W. I. Thomas, for example, found his famous "Polish Peasants" there, but more recently, William Kornblum's *Blue Collar Community* (1974) has become an important addition to the holistic community literature.

Kornblum and his wife lived in a tenement flat in Irondale from 1968 to 1970, and Kornblum returned to the South Side Chicago neighborhood again in 1972 to work with the steelworkers' union elections. Unions were a primary focus of Kornblum's work. He was especially interested in why there has never been a truly powerful, truly radical, working-class movement in the United States. From a Marxist perspective, this is a crucial question. And generally, Kornblum finds little of the alienation Marx predicted, finding rather a complicated pattern of "ordered segmentation" in which residential segregation, age and sex segregation, and especially ethnic identity all combine to provide support for various subcommunities that block a broader working-class consciousness. In fact, some of his most important findings come from a comparison of differences in Polish, Mexican, and black steel mill workers. Blacks, for example, are discouraged from living in mill towns, so labor solidarity must rely on the union's grievance system to provide the identification with the union that comes more easily to the Polish workers living in the more ethnically and occupationally homogeneous neighborhoods near the steel mills.[13]

Ruth Horowitz: *Honor and the American Dream*

Horowitz provides our most recent example of community field research. Her *Honor and the American Dream* (1983) describes an inner-city Chicano community in Chicago, with special emphasis on teenage gangs. She lived in the 32nd Street neighborhood from 1972 to 1974 and returned to complete her project in 1977. Horowitz employs the concept of "Chicanismo" to explain the lifestyles on 32nd Street. "Chicanismo symbolizes the Mexican-American desire to be neither black nor Anglo, nor 'deprived,' but to be themselves: to encourage the traditions that they brought from Mexico and to demand the rights guaranteed them and the respect they deserve as hard-working residents of the United States" (Horowitz 1983, p. 219). The culture she finds in the Chicago neighborhood is not totally a response to poverty and racial discrimination. Horowitz argues that because of Chi-

---

[13] Kornblum also concludes his book with a methodological appendix. Of special interest is his description of becoming a steel mill worker. Unlike Gans and most other field researchers, Kornblum worked with the people he studied.

canismo, even if full and equal opportunity were available for Chicanos, the racial and ethnic melting pot the United States is sometimes portrayed as being (Glazer and Moynihan 1963) still would not and should not melt away their ethnic differences. Much of the concept of "honor," as exemplified by the extended family, norms of reciprocity, distinct sex roles, rigid moral codes, and respect, will remain in the Chicano community. Thus Horowitz finds that Chicano youths are torn between two conflicting sets of values: the conventional, middle-class American dream of success and the Chicanismo-based defense of honor.[14]

SUMMARY

A common thread runs through these most recent examples of holistic community studies and separates them from the classic studies of Warner and the Lynds. No longer do we find the isolated, self-sufficient Middletown or Yankee City that is supposed to be America in microcosm. Instead, we find studies of special, distinct urban neighborhoods—neighborhoods studied because they are different from other urban neighborhoods. Or in Levittown's case, a suburb studied because it is a different kind (working class) of suburb.

The reasons for this change in site selection reflect a more sophisticated view of: (1) the community in a *Gesellschaft*-dominated America, (2) the increasingly powerful vertical ties of the community to society, and (3) the inaccurate stereotyping that comes from overgeneralizing about cities, communities, or neighborhoods. All communities are not alike. More specifically, urban neighborhoods differ, just as various types of suburbs do, and even isolated small cities can possess significant differences. In sum, we know now that while a community cannot be studied in order to generalize to all of America, in a sense, "all of America" does not exist. America remains sufficiently diverse to justify studying individual neighborhoods and communities.

---

[14] An interesting methodological note in this study concerns the techniques Horowitz, a young Jewish woman, uses to participate in the activities of young Chicano males, especially the activities of violent gangs. While being fluent in Spanish was a necessity, she mentions "my lack of care with appearance, which both males and females continually remarked upon," (p. 9) as one of her most important ways of mixing in.

Chapter Fifteen

The Quality of Life and the Quality of Communities

The good community, the better community, the very best possible community has been an elusive and value-laden goal for centuries. We will begin this chapter with two famous descriptions of the ideal community—one from Plato, the other from John the Evangelist. Plato, in *The Laws*, wrote rationally and extensively about what the best possible community would be like—centrally located, no more than 5,000 households, distributed among 5,040 plots, and grouped into twelve districts around an acropolis. Each household would be equal in both the quality of the land and number of children ("excess" children were to be transferred). In Plato's community a presribed optimum number of farmers, soldiers, artists, and priests would live together, all under the leadership of philosopher-kings.

Plato's prescriptions for a rationally designed city were not the only vision of the perfect living environment. The perfect environment is described much differently by John in his *Revelation* to the seven Asian churches. Here, the emphasis is less upon secular rationality and more on sacred spirituality:

> And I, John, saw the Holy City, the new Jerusalem, coming down from God out of heaven. It was a glorious sight, beautiful as a bride at her wedding. . . . It was filled with the glory of God, and flashed and glowed like a precious gem, crystal clear like jasper. Its walls were broad and high, with twelve gates guarded by twelve angels. . . . The twelve gates were made of pearls—each gate from a single pearl! And the main street was pure, transparent gold, like glass. . . . Nothing evil will be permitted in it—no one immoral or dishonest—but only those whose names are written in the Lamb's Book of Life. . . . The throne of God and of the Lamb will be there, and his servants will worship him. And they shall see his face; and his name shall be written on their foreheads. And there will be no night there—no need for lamps or sun—for the Lord God

will be their light; and they shall reign forever and ever (The Revelation, chs. 21–22, *The Living Bible*).

John's and Plato's visions have little in common because both make very different assumptions about the causes of and the solutions to problems in the communities of their day. Plato reasoned that if rational citizens follow his rational laws, a more efficient, more perfect community would necessarily result. John, however, believed that only Christ's return can bring the perfect community. Many other views of what a good living environment should be like have been voiced since Plato and John, and about all they have in common is their diversity. The search for a better community is a value-laden quest, and different people can have very different values. Thus, it is impossible to imagine a community that is right for everyone. Even John's New Jerusalem is designed only for "those whose names are written in the Lamb's Book of Life."

Still, the fact that one cannot please everyone should not dissuade us from striving for improvement. Rather, it means only that there are limits to our ability to improve our human condition. The community, however, presents an excellent focus for our attempts at improvement.

WHY FOCUS ON THE COMMUNITY?

The quality of our lives depends on the quality of several things besides the community: our society, our jobs, our families, ourselves. And while all of these factors are undeniably important, there is some reason to believe that the community contributes more to the quality of our lives than many of these other areas.[1] But more important to establishing the potential for the community as a focus for improving life quality is *the potential for meaningful change and improvement that exists at the community level.* Compare, for example, attempts to improve the quality of life at the community level with the more micro attempts based on providing psychological counseling or the more macro attempts based on implementing societal change.

The limitations of micro approaches to the quality of life. From a micro perspective, we can help people deal more efficiently with a myriad of personal problems (unemployment or job dissatisfaction,

---

[1] The literature on the relative contributions of various influences on the quality of life is complex and varies considerably by how life quality is measured. In one research effort by Lewis and Lyon (1986), the community contributed considerably less to overall life satisfaction than the person's family and a little less than the house or apartment the person lives in. However, the community was a more important contributor to overall life satisfaction than the person's neighborhood, age, occupation, income, or education.

parenting difficulties, alienation, sexual dysfunctions, marital conflict) through individual counseling. And many psychiatrists, psychologists, social workers, and other trained counselors do just that. The ratio of trained counselors to troubled people is so very small, however, that we must be pessimistic about the ability of micro-level counseling to substantially change the life quality for very many people. In most cases, counselors will assist only those who have the most overt problems or those with the time and money necessary to secure the counseling. In either case, counseling is a "band-aid" approach to general quality-of-life problems—a very important "band-aid," and, on an individual basis, a relatively effective "band-aid"—but the inability of counseling to impact on large numbers of people has led to attempts at *community* mental health in psychiatry and psychology and *community* organizing in social work.

Limitations of macro approaches. Macro approaches to the quality of life, by definition, will affect a large number of people. If we choose the society for our level of analysis and change, then we can potentially improve the life quality of *all* poor Americans, *all* American women, *all* black Americans, *all* American teenagers, *all* the working parents in the United States, or, more broadly still, simply *all Americans.* For example, most of our social welfare legislation contains attempts to improve the quality of life of various categories of Americans. And, broader still, attempts to stimulate the economy or protect the natural environment are attempts to improve the quality of life for all Americans.

Most sociologists lean toward the macro approach. From Durkheim's "social facts" to C. Wright Mills's "sociological imagination," sociology's most distinctive contribution has been expanding our understanding of social phenomena beyond the individual level. Indeed, those sociologists who are the most macro in their work are our "grand" masters who produce "grand" theories of entire societies. Yet, when it is time to put these theories to work and produce pragmatic guides for improving the quality of life in a society, the macro approach often has little to offer. When the source of the problem is in the basic structure of society (as it almost always is with a macro approach), then it is often argued that until truly fundamental social change occurs, truly fundamental improvement in the quality of life cannot occur. Marxist applications to American social problems often take this tack (see Chapter 5), but until the revolution, what can we do to make things better?

Admittedly, not all societal level approaches are so "all-or-nothing" in their attempts to improve the quality of life. Incremental approaches are common, producing limited changes in our society. For example, minimum-wage laws increase the wages of the working poor, and civil rights legislation has given minorities more opportunities for housing, education, and jobs.[2] And yet, many people who are resistant to fundamental social change are also disenchanted with these piecemeal government programs as well. They perceive limits in the government's ability to improve our lives. Jimmy Carter successfully ran for president by being against traditional government solutions to social problems, as Ronald Reagan did four years later, and even more successfully four years after that. Americans do appear to be increasingly skeptical of the government's ability to make things better. Government solutions are often seen as too complex, too costly, and too remote from the problem.

The community, then, whether it is a neighborhood, a city, or a county, can be a *mid-range alternative*. Like the individualistic micro approach, it is close to the problem and manageable in design and implementation. Like the societal macro approach, it is potentially substantial in its effects, impacting entire neighborhoods or communities. Thus, a case can be made for the community mattering very much in attempts to improve the quality of life. And if communities do matter, then what should good communities be like?

THE GOOD COMMUNITY

While it is true, as our opening selections from Plato and John illustrate, that different people can have very different views of what constitutes a good community, this should not keep us from striving to make clear what a good community would be like. The problem of different definitions of a good community must be considered, but let's back away from that dilemma until we examine what *most* people would include as necessary for a good community.

The Bare Necessities

The basis for a high quality of life would almost have to include six community components: (1) public safety, (2) a strong economy, (3) health care, (4) educational opportunities, (5) a clean, healthy natural environment, (6) and an optimum population size. These community characteristics are so basic that they are almost beyond debate. There will be disagreement over how best to supply health care, what constitutes educational opportunities, or how much should be spent to

---

[2] These examples are all from the federal government's realm, and this is not coincidental. Certainly since Franklin Roosevelt's New Deal, the government has been the primary instigator of *purposive* social change. Other contributors to social change (e.g., industrialization, urbanization) may have an even greater impact, but they invariably produce *crescive* social change (Warren 1977).

protect the environment, but few will argue that hospitals or schools or breathable air are not needed.

The basic components are not only necessary, they are measurable. A look back at Chapter 11 shows that they are included in the general groupings for local indicators of the quality of life. We can, to a degree then, assess the contributions communities make to life quality for these six components. This does not mean that we know exactly how to strengthen the local economy or precisely how many police are needed to help maintain public security, but it does mean we can determine which communities offer the greatest opportunity for achieving high levels of these necessary components, as well as how our own community compares with others.

The only objective component not included in all the local indicators research mentioned in Chapter 10 is population size,[3] so we will consider it briefly here. Ever since Louis Wirth's classic analysis (discussed in Chapter 2), we have appreciated the influence of population size on lifestyle. And, more recently, research has focused on how it affects the quality of life. Larger populations apparently do, as Wirth argued, lead to greater impersonality (Mayhew and Levinger 1976). And large cities usually have the highest per capita homicide rates (Archer, Gartner, Akert, and Lockwood 1978). Further, people living in large cities are likely to have more negative attitudes toward their city than those living in smaller ones (Verbrugge and Taylor 1980). In fact, smaller population levels apparently produce higher levels of life quality in all of the other five "bare necessities" except one—a strong local economy (Elgin, Thomas, Logothetti, and Cox 1974). *Large cities are very good places to find jobs and make money* (Alonso 1975), *but if you can afford it, smaller cities are generally better places to live.* Spates and Macionis (1982, p. 529), after reviewing most of the research on population size and the quality of life, conclude that "it would seem reasonable, on the basis of the data we have encountered, that the population of a good city might hover somewhere between the 50,000–100,000 mark." That seems like a reasonable conclusion, but it does remind us again that what is an excellent place to live for one person may not be best for someone else (in this case, for someone in need of a high-paying job).

A high quality of life is not guaranteed by these six community characteristics.[4] We could live in a community of about a hundred

---

[3] Olsen and Merwin, Table 10–2, give a positive effect on the quality of life for population size up to 500,000, and a negative effect beyond 500,000. Population size is not an indicator in the University of Texas or Liu studies.

[4] In fact, the *perception* of one's life quality depends so much on its quality relative to other people in the community, the correlation between these community characteristics and an individual's response to life quality usually varies between weak and nonexistent (Campbell 1981; Andrews 1981).

thousand that is secure, prosperous, and clean, with fine schools and hospitals and still not be satisfied. For example, according to Abraham Maslow's (1970) well-known hierarchy of needs, as soon as our basic needs for survival and security are met, they are replaced by higher-level needs for belonging and self-actualization. As we turn now to a consideration of these higher-level needs, it is important to remember that Maslow argued that when the lower-level needs are met, the need to fill the higher-level needs then becomes just as strong. These more subjective, higher-level community needs are more than just the whims of an affluent society. If Maslow is correct, they are just as important as the more basic needs we just discussed.

The Subjective Components

The good community has at least six more subjective, more debatable components. When the "bare necessities" are available, as they are to a substantial degree in most American communities, then a high quality of life becomes more dependent on: (1) individual liberty, (2) categorical equality, (3) communal fraternity, (4) representative, responsive government, (5) local identification, and (6) resident heterogeneity. Since factors such as these are more difficult to define, to measure, and to agree upon, we will consider each in some detail.

Individual liberty. Liberty is a basic American value (Williams 1970) that flourishes in our large cities. There is a German proverb— *Stadtluft macht frei*—that roughly translates "breathing city air makes one free." Large cities do allow us more freedom since we do not know one another, do not care very much about one another, and, therefore, do not try to control one another. All of the classic typologists (Tönnies, Simmel, et al.) have noted the individual liberty that comes with the impersonality of the large city.

The problem comes with deciding how much liberty is too much liberty. Certainly we do not want people to be free to exploit, to steal, or to terrorize, but how can we restrict these actions while at the same time preserving individual liberty? For example, we often praise large cities such as New York and San Francisco for their tolerance of deviant lifestyles (Becker and Horowitz 1971; Spates and Macionis 1982), yet this very tolerance, this encouragement of personal expression and freedom, can restrict a more basic need—security. Note how criminologist James Wilson (1983, pp. 78–79) argues that tolerance for deviant behavior is the first step toward community crime:

> I suggest that untended behavior also leads to the breakdown of community controls. A stable neighborhood of families who care for their homes, mind each other's children, and confidently frown on unwanted intruders can change in a few years, or even a few months, to an inhospi-

table and frightening jungle. A piece of property is abandoned, weeds grow up, a window is smashed. Adults stop scolding rowdy children; the children, emboldened, become more rowdy. Families move out, unmarried adults move in. Teenagers gather in front of the grocery; in time, an inebriate slumps to the sidewalk and is allowed to sleep it off. Pedestrians are approached by panhandlers. . . . Such an area is vulnerable to criminal invasion. Though it is not inevitable, it is more likely that here, rather than in places where people are confident they can regulate public behavior by informal controls, drugs will change hands, prostitutes will solicit, and cars will be stripped. Drunks will be robbed by boys who do it as a lark, and the prostitutes' customers will be robbed by men who do it purposefully and perhaps violently. Muggings will occur.

Similarly, Zorbaugh (see Chapter 3), in his classic *The Gold Coast and Slum* (1929) describes the "world of furnished rooms" as free from the prying eyes of neighbors. Yet this was also a world of extremely high crime, suggesting, unfortunately, that security and liberty are mutually exclusive. Since we can maximize one only at the expense of the other and since we value both security and liberty, there is often an uneasy compromise in our communities between those who would restrict liberty to increase security (e.g., more police, "tougher" laws) and those who would run the risk of less security to insure personal freedoms (e.g., civil libertarians' emphasis upon "due process" and "civil rights"). Again, as with population size above, we are faced with the dilemma of different people making different choices about what constitutes a good community.

Categorical equality. Individual equality has never had much appeal in America. The idea of equal *opportunity* is about as close as we come. However, equality between categories of people, especially between races and sexes, has much broader support. The idea that desirable housing should not be restricted to whites only or that men and women should receive equal pay for equal work has an established body of legal support and a growing base of popular support. Note, for example, that both examples of local indicator data in Chapter 10 include income ratios by race and sex—based on the assumption that racial and sexual equality are necessary for a good community.

Still, there is disagreement in this area. Should an individual be allowed to sell his or her home to whomever he or she wishes, even if it means black buyers will not be considered? When we find that blacks and women receive less income than white males, what do we do— focus on improving educational opportunities, on strengthening blacks' families, on redefining sex roles, on more vigorous affirmative action programs, or on comparable pay for sex segregated jobs. The value-laden implications of each proposal are significant, and the controversy surrounding each proposal is considerable (Lyon et al. 1982).

Again, we find a value conflict. Before it was between liberty and security, this time between liberty and equality. We can make a community more equal, but it will require reducing the liberty of the homeowner to sell the home or of the employer to determine the wages of the employee. And again we will find people with different views on how equal a community should be.

Communal fraternity. Here we have the very essence of the *Gemeinschaft*-like community. Baker Brownell in *The Human Community* (1950, p. 198) writes that "[a] community is a group of people who know each other well." In a true community, we are to know one another, like one another, help one another. Roland Warren (1970, p. 15) believes the basis for a good community is "a regard for the whole and a compassion for the individual, a way in which we can treat others as brothers, a sense of caring and being cared about." I suspect there is little disagreement over this characteristic. The question here is how is such a characteristic possible in a modern, often *Gesellschaft*-like America? Harvey Cox (1965, p. 41), in his treatise on religion in a secular society, notes the decline in our truly knowing people:

> During my boyhood, my parents never referred to "the milkman," "the insurance agent," "the junk collector." These people were respectively, Paul Weaver, Joe Villanova, and Roxy Barozano. All of our family's market transactions took place within a web of wider and more inclusive friendship and kinship ties with the same people. They were never anonymous. In fact, the occasional salesman or repairman whom we did not know was always viewed with dark suspicion until we could make sure where he came from, who his parents were, and whether his family was any good.

After moving to the *Secular City* (1965), Cox is no longer in Brownell's *Human Community* where everyone knows everyone:

> Now, as an urbanite, my transactions are of a very different sort. If I need to have the transmission on my car repaired, buy a television antenna, or cash a check, I find myself in functional relationships with mechanics, salesmen, and bank clerks whom I see in no other capacity. These contacts are in no sense "mean, nasty, or brutish," though they tend to be short . . . unifaceted and "segmental." I meet these people in no other context. To me they remain essentially just as anonymous as I do to them.

Cox's description of these segmental, functional, anonymous personal relationships is not necessarily a description of a social problem. Cox claims to be satisfied with them, and anonymity does bring a measure of freedom. Look back to our discussion of individual liberty. There is a trade-off here. How much freedom are we willing to surrender in return for more communal fraternity? Different people will, of course, be willing to make different trades.

Representative, responsive government. Most of us desire to be governed by leaders who represent the community's best interest. Further, we want our leaders to respond quickly and efficiently when our community needs action. What, exactly, would such a representative, responsive government be like? In order to be representative, our leaders need to be democratically elected, much like Robert Dahl's mayor of New Haven (see Chapter 12). Of course, Floyd Hunter's Atlanta also had a popularly elected mayor, but he had little real power. Atlanta was run by businessmen who were not elected by the citizens and who were bound together by a desire to create an Atlanta that increased the profitability of their businesses. Certainly Hunter's research as well as many of the community power studies that followed all desired to "expose" covert elites and thereby help make local government more democratic. However, it is not clear how one goes about establishing a more democratic local government, nor is it clear what happens when local governments become more democratic.

Democratic, pluralistic, representative local government is not necessarily the most responsive local government. The research of Robert Crain, Elihu Katz, and Donald Rosenthal (1969) into the fluoridation controversies and much of Terry Clark's (1971) analysis of the NORC 51 community sample suggest that leaders can become so responsive to various groups in the community as to be paralyzed into inaction. That is, leaders can become *too responsive* to conflicting demands and thereby become unable to respond effectively to local needs. And to further complicate matters, recent research is beginning to question Hunter's assumption that, in pursuing private gain, business leaders reduce public gain. Clark and Ferguson (1983) find that communities with significant input into decision making from business leaders are in better financial condition than those with most of the input coming from the mayor and labor unions. And while Lyon, Felice, Perryman, and Parker's (1981) research supports Molotch's (1976) contention that power in the hands of local business leaders leads to local growth, they did not find support for his contention that growth benefits local business at the expense of other residents. Rather, they find that when a community grows, property values increase, per capita local expenditures decline, and net revenues grow. The point here is that we are a long way from being able to say what is necessary for an efficient, responsive local government, and it may be that we will find democratic governments are not always the most efficient and responsive governments.

Identification and commitment. A good community should matter to the people who live there. Residents should define themselves in terms of the community, care about the community, and be willing to sacrifice to improve the community. The philosopher Lawrence Haworth (1963, p. 87) argues that is the difference between a community and a mere city when he writes that "If a city is to become a community, then, the inhabitants must identify the settlement itself as the focal point of their individual lives." In Chapter 7 we examined how difficult it is to maintain the physical community as the basis for psychological community. Yet, we also saw that for many people, the local community continues to be a place that matters, a place where friends live, a place where money is invested, where children are educated, and so on. Not all Americans are, in Robert Merton's terms, cosmopolitans; some are localites, and many of us are bits of both. So again, is it possible to devise a community that fits the needs of different people—in this case those people who see their local community as merely the location of their sleeping quarters as well as those who see it as the geographic focus for much of what matters in their lives?

Heterogeneity. It is time now to face up to perhaps the thorniest issue facing the concept of a good community: *How different should community residents be?* and *How different can community residents be allowed to be?* Roland Warren (1970, p. 20) notes that "it has simply been accepted as a value that it is better for people to live in communities which are more or less a cross-section of the population than to live in economically or racially or ethnically segregated communities." The quality of life indicators in Chapter 10 give a positive rating for a racially heterogeneous population. Spates and Macionis (1982, pp. 528–29) argue that small communities are simply too homogeneous to provide the rich experiences of a large, heterogeneous city:

> A small village-style community suggested by Ferdinand Tönnies' concept of *Gemeinschaft*, whatever its attributes (which some people quite legitimately prefer), is *not* a city. Not having the city's "critical mass," it does not (cannot) provide the stimulation and intensification of life that is the city's hallmark.

Yet, they recognize that cities can be too large, too heterogeneous:

> Just as surely, if a city has too many people, stimulation could quickly become overstimulation and the quality of life (in all areas but the economic) would decline.

The "overstimulation" Spates and Macionis refer to is among the least of the problems associated with heterogeneity. If we have John Birchers living near socialists or black nationalists living among Ku Klux Klan members, "overstimulation" would be a polite term for conflict. And although conflict emerged as a legitimate force for community change in the 1960s (see Chapter 8), most of us probably would prefer living in a community where things were not so bad as to require conflict, where things could be changed without conflict, at least without violent conflict. Still, we can see another dilemma here. Some people will want to live in heterogeneous communities, others will want to surround themselves with people like themselves. Some view conflict as sometimes necessary, often even invigorating and stimulating. Others will avoid conflict at all cost.

The idea that a heterogeneous community (consisting of diverse people with different ideas of what constitutes a high quality of life) will have a hard time being a good community for all of its residents brings us back to the problem we encountered at the beginning of this section on subjective characteristics, a problem that reappeared in our examination of every subjective characteristic. Since different people have different ideas about what constitutes the good life, how is the good community possible? The truth is, I believe, that the good community is *not* possible; good communit*ies*, however, are both possible and desirable.

Good Communit*ies*

While it is impossible to design *the* community that will maximize the quality of life for everyone, *a* community that will maximize life quality for certain kinds of people is possible. And since there are many kinds of people, our discussion must be directed toward good communit*ies*. Roland Warren (1970, p. 21), who has devoted more time and better thoughts to the issue of the good community than have most of us, concludes finally that "there is no such thing as *the* good community. There are *many* good communities, all according to the specific combination of preferences which may be held . . . [on issues where] . . . there is simply no way to demonstrate that one viewpoint is more valid or more moral than another." And that is, it seems, the key to insuring the highest quality of life for us all. The state, of course, will continue to influence the basic necessities of life quality mentioned earlier (safety, economic security, health care, environment, education), but for these more subjective components of life quality, the community— or more precisely, communities—is the key. Even if the state could provide us with the subjective elements, communities would still be the preferable source. Robert Nisbet's ideas on the primacy of the community are worth quoting at length at this point:

> It may well be asked: why should we seek communities at all? Is it not sufficient, in an age of the welfare state, that we should live simply and solely in terms of the great regulations, laws, and associations which this state provides? It is often said that today, for the first time in human history, the state has become a benevolent and protective association which is able to meet both the social and the physical demands of people formerly met by a plurality of smaller communities. To this we must say firmly, however, that the state which possesses the power to do things *for* people has also the power to do things to them. Freedom cannot be

maintained in a monolithic society. Pluralism and diversity of experience are the essence of true freedom. Therefore even if the state were able to meet the basic problems of stability and security through its own efforts, we should have to reject it as the solution simply because of our concern for the problem of freedom.

However it is to be noted that the state does not even serve the security need. No large-scale association can really meet the psychic demand of individuals because, by its very nature, it is too large, too complex, too bureaucratized, and altogether too aloof from the residual meanings which human beings live by. The state can enlist popular enthusiasm, can conduct crusades, can mobilize in behalf of great "causes," such as wars, but as a regular and normal means of meeting human needs for recognition, fellowship, security, and membership, it is inadequate. The tragedy is that where the state is most successful in meeting the needs for recognition and security, it is most tyrannical and despotic, as the histories of Communist Russia and Nazi Germany have made clear. The only proper alternative to large-scale, mechanical political society are communities small in scale but solid in structure. They and they alone can be the beginning of social reconstruction because they respond, at the grass roots, to fundamental human desires: living together, working together, experiencing together, being together. Such communities can grow naturally and organically from the most elementary aspirations, they remain continuously flexible, and, by their very nature, they do not insist upon imposing and rigid organizations (Nisbet 1960, pp. 82–83).

Communities are seldom viewed in this light—as guardians of individual liberty. Typically, communities are viewed in their *Gemeinschaft*-like nature of inhibiting free thought and action—requiring conformity to the dictates of local values. And this more common view is largely an accurate one. Although some communities will tolerate more individuality than others, most will discourage those actions that run counter to the community's norms. But Nisbet's point, I believe, is that if we have a multitude of communities, each reflecting different values, and if the state supports the basic needs and guarantees the right to move from one community to another, then a pluralistic society becomes possible—a heterogeneous society made of many, often more homogeneous, communities. In this way, then, communities become an important focus for improving the quality of life in urban America.

Bibliography

Abu-Lughod, Janet L. 1961. "Migrant Adjustment to City Life: the Egyptian Case." *American Journal of Sociology* 67:22–32.

Abu-Lughod, Janet L. 1971. *Cairo.* Princeton, NJ: Princeton University Press.

Agger, Robert E., Daniel Goldrich, and Bert Swanson. 1964. *The Rulers and the Ruled: Political Power and Impotence in American Communities.* New York: John Wiley & Sons.

Ahlbrandt, Roger. 1984. *Neighborhoods, People and Community.* New York: Plenum Press.

Ahmad, Qazi. 1965. "Indian Cities: Characteristics and Correlates." Department of Geography Research Paper no. 102. Chicago: The University of Chicago.

Aiken, Michael. 1970. "The Distribution of Community Power." In *The Structure of Community Power,* edited by Michael Aiken and Paul E. Mott. New York: Random House.

Alihan, Milla. 1938. *Social Ecology.* New York: Cooper Seiare.

Alinsky, Saul D. 1946. *Reveille for Radicals.* Chicago: University of Chicago Press.

Alinsky, Saul D. 1971. *Rules for Radicals.* New York: Random House.

Alonso, William. 1965. *Location and Land Use: Toward a General Theory of Land Rent.* Cambridge, MA: Harvard University Press.

Alonso, William. 1970. "What Are New Towns For?" *Urban Studies* 7:37–45.

Alonso, William. 1975. "The Economics of Urban Size." pp. 434–51 in *Regional Policy,* edited by John Friedman and William Alonso. Cambridge, MA: MIT Press.

Althusser, Louis. 1969. *For Marx.* London: Allen Lane.

Althusser, Louis. 1971. "Ideology and Ideological State Apparatuses." In *Lenin and Philosophy and Other Essays,* edited by Louis Althusser. London: New Left Books.

Altman, I. 1975. *The Environment and Social Behavior.* Monterey, CA: Brooks/ Cole.

American Public Opinion Index 1982. Louisville, KY: Opinion Research Service, 1984.

American Statistical Association Conference on Human Population. 1974. "Report on the ASA Conference on Surveys of Human Populations." *The American Statistician* 28:30–34.

Anderson, Nels. 1923. *The Hobo.* Chicago: University of Chicago Press.

Anderson, Theodore R. and J. A. Egelend. 1961. "Spatial Aspects of Social Area Analysis." *American Sociological Review* 26:392–99.

Andrews, Frank. 1981. "Subjective Social Indicators, Objective Social Indicators, and Social Accounting Systems." In *Social Accounting Systems,* edited by F. Thomas Juster and Kenneth Land. New York: Academic Press.

Archer, Dane, Rosemary Gartner, Robin Akert, and Tim Lockwood. 1978. "Cities and Homicide." *Comparative Studies in Sociology* 1:73–95.

Ardrey, Robert. 1966. *The Territorial Imperative.* New York: Atheneum.

Bachrach, Peter and Morton S. Baratz. 1970. *Power and Poverty: Theory and Practice.* New York: Oxford University Press.

Backstrom, Charles H. and Gerald Hursh-Cesar. 1981. *Survey Research* 2nd ed. New York: John Wiley & Sons.

Bailey, James, ed. 1973. *New Towns in America.* New York: John Wiley & Sons.

Bailey, Robert. 1972. *Radicals in Urban Politics.* Chicago: University of Chicago Press.

Bailey, Roy and Mike Brake. 1975. *Radical Social Work.* New York: Pantheon Books.

Baldassare, Mark and William Protash. 1982. "Growth Controls, Population Growth, and Community Satisfaction." *American Sociological Review* 47, no. 3:339–46.

Banfield, Edward C. 1970. *The Unheavenly City: The Nature and Future of Our Urban Crisis.* Boston: Little, Brown.

Barber, Bernard. 1961. "Family Status, Local-Community Status, and Social Stratification." *Pacific Sociological Review* 4, no. 1:3–10.

Bardo, John W. and John J. Hartman. 1982. *Urban Sociology.* Itasca, IL: F. E. Peacock.

Barkin, David. 1978. "Confronting the Separation of Town and Country in Cuba." In *Marxism and the Metropolis,* edited by William K. Tabb and Larry Sawers. New York: Oxford University Press.

Beauregard, Robert A. 1981. "The Redevelopment of Capitalist Cities: The Case of the United States." Paper presented at Conference on New Perspectives on the Urban Political Economy, Washington DC.

Becker, Howard P. 1940. "Constructive Typology in the Social Sciences." *American Journal of Sociology* 5:40–55.

Becker, Howard P. 1956. *Man in Reciprocity*. New York: Praeger Publishers.

Becker, Howard P. 1957. "Current Sacred-Secular Theory and Its Development." In *Modern Sociological Theory in Continuity and Change*, edited by Howard Becker and Alvin Boskoff. New York: Dryden Press.

Becker, Howard S. and Irving Louis Horowitz. 1971. "The Culture of Civility." pp. 4–19 in *Culture and Civility in San Francisco*, edited by Howard S. Becker. New Brunswick, NJ: *Trans-Action*.

Bell, Colin and Howard Newby. 1972. *Community Studies: An Introduction to the Sociology of Local Community*. New York: Praeger Publishers.

Bell, Colin and Howard Newby. 1983. "The American Community Studies." In *New Perspectives on the American Community*, edited by Roland Warren and Larry Lyon. Homewood, IL: Dorsey Press.

Bell, Daniel. 1969. "The Idea of a Social Report." *The Public Interest* 15.

Bell, Daniel. 1973. *The Coming of Post-Industrial Society*. New York: Basic Books.

Bell, Wendell. 1953. "The Social Areas of the San Francisco Bay Region." *American Sociological Review* 18:29–47.

Bell, Wendell. 1955. *Social Area Analysis*. Stanford, CA: Stanford University Press.

Bell, Wendell. 1958. "Social Choice, Life Styles, and Suburban Residence." In *The Suburban Community*, edited by R. Dobriaer. New York: G. P. Putnam's Sons.

Bell, Wendell. 1959. "Social Areas: Typology of Urban Neighborhoods." In *Community Structure and Analysis*, edited by M. Sussman. New York: Thomas Crowell.

Berger, Bennett M. 1960. *Working Class Suburb*. Berkeley: University of California Press.

Berger, Bennett M. 1981. *The Survival of a Counterculture*. Berkeley: University of California Press.

Bernard, Jessie. 1973. *The Sociology of Community*. Glenview, IL: Scott, Foresman.

Berry, Brian and John Kasarda. 1977. *Contemporary Urban Ecology*. New York: Macmillan.

Berry, Brian J. L. and Allen Pred. 1961. *Central Place Studies: A Bibliography of Theory and Applications*. Philadelphia: Regional Science Research Institute.

Berry, B. and P. H. Rees. 1969. "The Factorial Ecology of Calcutta." *American Journal of Sociology* 74:447–91.

Block, Fred. 1981. "The Fiscal Crisis of the Capitalist State." In *Annual Review of Sociology*, edited by Ralph Turner and James Short. Palo Alto, CA: Annual Reviews Incorporated.

Bloomquist, Leonard E. and Gene F. Summers. 1982. "Organization of Production and Community Income Distributions." *American Sociological Review* 47:325–38.

Bogue, Donald J. and Elizabeth J. Bogue. 1976. *Essays in Human Ecology I*. Chicago: Community and Family Study Center, University of Chicago.

Bonjean, Charles. 1963. "Community Leadership: A Case Study and Conceptual Refinement." *American Journal of Sociology* 68:672–81.

Bonjean, Charles. 1966. "Mass, Class, and the Industrial Community." *American Journal of Sociology* 72:149–62.

Bonjean, Charles. 1971. "The Community as Research Site and Object of Inquiry." In *Community Politics*, edited by Charles Bonjean, Terry Clark, and Robert Lineberry. New York: The Free Press.

Bonjean, Charles and Lewis Carter. 1965. "Legitimacy and Visibility: Leadership Structures Related to Four Community Systems." *Pacific Sociological Review* 8:16–20.

Bonjean, Charles and David Olson. 1964. "Community Leadership: Directions of Research." *Administrative Science Quarterly* 9:278–300.

Bonjean, Charles., and Michael D. Grimes. 1974. "Community Power: Issues and Findings." In *Social Stratification: A Reader*, edited by Joseph Lopreato and Lionel Lewis. New York: Harper & Row.

Booth, Charles. 1902. *Life and Labour of the People in London* (Vols. 1–8). London: Macmillan.

Boskoff, Alvin. 1970. *The Sociology of Urban Regions*. New York: Appleton-Century-Crofts.

Boyer, Richard and David Savageau. 1985. *Rand McNally Places Rated Almanac: Your Guide to Finding the Best Places to Live in America*. New York: Rand McNally & Company.

Bradburn, Norman M. and Seymour Sudman. 1979. *Improving Interview Methods and Questionnaire Design*. San Francisco: Jossey-Bass.

Brooks, Richard O. 1974. *New Towns and Communal Values: A Case Study of Columbia, Maryland*. New York: Praeger Publishing.

Brooks, Richard O. 1983. "New Towns and Communal Values: A New Approach to the Search for Communal Ideals." In *Perspectives on the American Community*, edited by Roland Warren and Larry Lyon. Homewood, IL: Dorsey Press.

Brownell, Baker. 1950. *The Human Community: Its Philosophy and Practice for a Time of Crisis*. New York: Harper and Brothers.

Bryant, Barbara E. 1975. "Respondent Selection in a Time of Changing Household Composition." *Journal of Marketing Research* 12:129–35.

Burby, Raymond J., III, and Shirley F. Weiss et al. 1975. *New Communities, U.S.A.* Washington, D.C.: Subcommittee on Housing of the Committee on Banking, Currency and Housing, House of Representatives.

Burgess, Ernest W. 1916. *The Function of Socialization in Social Evolution*. Chicago: University of Chicago Press.

Burgess, Ernest. 1925. "The Growth of the City." In *The City*, edited by Robert Park, Ernest Burgess, and R. D. McKenzie. Chicago: University of Chicago Press.

Burgess, M. Elaine. 1962. *Negro Leadership in a Southern City*. Chapel Hill: University of North Carolina Press.

Calhoun, J. B. 1961. "Phenomena Associated with Population Density." *Proceedings of the National Academy of Sciences* 47:429–49.

Calhoun, J. B. 1962. "Population Density and Social Pathology." *Scientific American* 206:139–48.

Campbell, Angus. 1981. *The Sense of Well-Being in America*. New York: McGraw-Hill.

Caplow, Theodore, Howard Bahr, Bruce Chadwick, Reuben Hill, and Margaret Williamson. 1982. *Middletown Families: Fifty Years of Change and Continuity*. Minneapolis: University of Minnesota Press.

Caplow, Theodore, Howard Bahr, and Bruce Chadwick. 1983. *All Faithful People: Change and Continuity in Middletown's Religion*. Minneapolis: University of Minnesota Press.

Caplow, Theodore, and Bruce Chadwick. 1979. "Inequality and LifeStyles in Middletown, 1920–1978." *Social Science Quarterly* 60:367–386.

Castells, Manuel. 1977. *The Urban Question*. Translated by Alan Sheridan. London: Edward Arnold Publishers.

Castells, Manuel. 1983. *The City and the Grassroots: A Cross-Cultural Theory of Urban Social Movements*. Berkeley: University of California Press.

Cherlin, Andrew. 1982. "Middletown III: The Story Continues." *Contemporary Sociology* II, no. 6:617–19.

Christaller, Walter. 1933. *Die Zentralen Orte in Suddeutschland*. Jena, Germany: Gustav Fisher Verlag.

Christenson, James. 1979. "Urbanism and Community Sentiment." *Social Science Quarterly* 60, no. 3:401–17.

Christenson, James. 1980. "Three Themes of Community Development." In *Community Development in America.*, edited by James Christenson and Jerry Robinson. Ames, IA: Iowa State University Press.

Christenson, James and Jerry Robinson, eds. 1980. *Community Development in America*. Ames, IA: Iowa State University Press.

Christenson, James, Larry Lyon, Michael Grimes, and Don Dillman. 1985. "Report of the Liaison Committee for the Community Section." *ASA Community Section Newsletter* 14:5–6.

Clark, Colin. 1951. "Urban Population Densities." *Journal of the Royal Statistical Society* Series A, 114:490–96.

Clark, Terry N. 1968. "Community Structure, Decision-Making, Budget Expenditures, and Urban Renewal in 51 American Communities." *American Sociological Review* 33:576–93.

Clark, Terry N. 1971. "Community Structure and Decision-Making, Budget Expenditures, and Urban Renewal in 51 American Communities." In *Community Politics*, edited by Charles M. Bonjean, Terry Clark, and Robert Lineberry. New York: The Free Press.

Clark, Terry N. 1976. "How Many More New Yorks?" *New York Affairs* 3, no. 4.

Clark, Terry N. 1983. "How Many More New Yorks?" Reprinted in *New Perspectives on the American Community*, edited by Roland Warren and Larry Lyon. Homewood, IL: Dorsey Press.

Clark, Terry N., Lorna C. Ferguson. 1983. *City Money: Political Processes, Fiscal Strain, and Retrenchment*. New York: Columbia University Press.

Clark, Terry N., William Kornblum, Harold Bloom, and Susan Tobias. 1968. "Discipline, Method, Community Structure and Decision Making." *The American Sociologist* 3:214–17.

Cloward, A. and Richard Elman. 1966. "Advocacy in the Ghetto." *Trans-Action* IV, no. 2:27–35.

Coit, Katharine. 1978. "Local Action, Not Citizen Participation." In *Marxism and the Metropolis*, edited by William K. Tabb and Larry Sawers. New York: Oxford University Press.

Coleman, James S. 1957. *Community Conflict*. New York: The Free Press.

Coleman, James S. 1983. "The Dynamics of Community Controversy." In *New Perspectives on the American Community*, edited by Roland Warren and Larry Lyon. Homewood, IL: Dorsey Press.

Coleman, James. 1966. *Equality of Educational Opportunity*. Washington, D.C.: U.S. Government Printing Office.

Coleman, James, James Hoffer, and Sally B. Kilgore. 1982. *High School Achievement: Public, Catholic, and Private Schools Compared*. New York: Basic Books.

Colombotos, John. 1969. "Personal Versus Telephone Interviews: Effect on Responses." *Public Health Reports* 84:773–82.

Coser, Lewis. 1956. *The Functions of Social Conflict*. New York: The Free Press.

Cottrell, W. F. 1951. "Death by Dieselization: A Case Study in the Reaction to Technological Change." *American Sociological Review* 16:358–65.

Cox, Harvey. 1965. *The Secular City*. Toronto: Macmillan.

Crain, Robert L., Elihu Katz, and Donald B. Rosenthal. 1969. *The Politics of Community Conflict*. New York: Bobbs-Merrill.

Cressey, Paul Goalby. 1932. *The Taxi Dance Hall*. Chicago: University of Chicago Press.

Curtis, James E. and John W. Petras. 1970. "Community Power, Power Studies and the Sociology of Knowledge." *Human Organization* 29:204–18.

Curtis, Richard F. and Elton F. Jackson. 1977. *Inequality in American Communities*. New York: Academic Press.

Curtis, Richard F. and Elton F. Jackson. 1983. "Inequality in American Communities." In *New Perspectives on the American Community*, edited by Roland Warren and Larry Lyon. Homewood, IL: Dorsey Press.

Dahl, Robert. 1961. *Who Governs?* New Haven: Yale University Press.

Dahl, Robert. 1972. *Democracy in the United States: Promises and Performance*. Chicago: Rand McNally & Company.

D'Antonio, William V., Howard J. Ehrlich, and Eugene C. Erickson. 1962. "Further Notes on the Study of Community Power." *American Sociological Review* 27:848–53.

Dewey, Richard. 1960. "The Rural-Urban Continuum." *American Journal of Sociology* 66:60–66.

Dillman, Don A., Jean Gallegos, and James Frey. 1976. "Reducing Refusal Rates for Telephone Interviews." *Public Opinion Quarterly* 40:66–78.

Dollard, John. 1937. *Caste and Class in a Southern Town*. New Haven: Yale University Press.

Domhoff, G. William. 1978. *Who Really Rules*. Santa Monica, CA: Goodyear.

Drake, St. Clair and Horace Clayton. 1945. *Black Metropolis: A Study of Negro Life in a Northern City*. New York: Harcourt Brace Jovanovich.

DuBois, W. E. B. 1899. *The Philadelphia Negro*. Philadelphia: The University of Pennsylvania.

Duncan, Beverly and Stanley Lieberson. 1970. *Metropolis and Region in Transition*. New York: Sage Publications.

Duncan, Otis Dudley. 1959. "Human Ecology and Population Studies." In *The Study of Population*, edited by Philip M. Hauser and Otis Dudley Duncan. Chicago: The University of Chicago Press.

Duncan, Otis Dudley. 1969. *Towards Social Reporting: Next Steps*. New York: Russell Sage.

Duncan, Otis Dudley. 1975. "Measuring Social Change via Replication of Surveys." In *Social Indicator Models*, edited by K. Land and S. Spilerman. New York: Russell Sage.

Duncan, Otis Dudley and Beverly Duncan. 1955. "Residential Distribution and Occupational Stratification." *The American Journal of Sociology* 60:493–503.

Duncan, Otis Dudley and Beverly Duncan. 1957. *The Negro Population of Chicago*. Chicago: University of Chicago Press.

Duncan, Otis Dudley, W. R. Scott, Stanley Lieberson, Beverly Duncan, and Halliman H. Winsborough. 1960. *Metropolis and Region*. Baltimore: Johns-Hopkins University Press.

Durkheim, Emile. 1893, 1964. *The Division of Labor in Society*. New York: The Free Press.

Durkheim, Emile. 1897, 1952. *Suicide*. London: Routledge & Kegan Paul.

Dye, Thomas R. 1970. "Community Power Studies." In *Political Science Annual*, Vol. 2, edited by James A. Robinson. New York: Bobbs-Merrill.

Edwards, Allan and Dorothy Jones. 1976. *Community and Community Development*. The Hague: Mouton and Co.

Effrat, Andrew. 1972. "Power to the Paradigms." *Sociological Inquiry* 42:3–33.

Ehrlich, Howard J. 1961. "The Reputational Approach to the Study of Community Power." *American Sociological Review* 26:926–27.

Elgin, Dane, Tom Thomas, Tom Logothetti, and Sue Cox. 1974. *City Size and Quality of Life*. Washington, DC: National Science Foundation.

Engels, Friedrich. 1958. *The Condition of the Working Class*. Translated by W. O. Henderson and W. H. Chaloner. New York: Macmillan.

Engels, Friedrich. 1969. *The Condition of the Working Class in England*. St. Albans: Panther Books.

England, Paula. 1979. "Women and Occupational Prestige: A Case for Vacuous Sex Equality." *Journal of Women in Culture and Society* 5:252–65.

Epstein, David G. 1974 *Brasilia, Plan and Reality*. Berkeley: University of California Press.

Farley, R. 1976. "Components of Suburban Population Growth." In *The Changing Face of the Suburbs*, edited by B. Schwartz. Chicago: University of Chicago Press.

Fava, Sylvia F., ed. 1968. *Urbanism in World Perspective*. New York: Thomas Crowell.

Feldman, Arnold and Charles Tilly. 1960. "The Interaction of Social and Physical Space." *American Sociological Review* 25:877–84.

Feuer, Lewis S., ed. 1959. *Marx and Engels: Basic Writing on Politics and Philosophy.* Garden City, NY: Doubleday Anchor Books.

Firey, Walter. 1945. "Sentiment and Symbolism as Ecological Variables." *American Sociological Review* 10:295–302.

Firey, Walter. 1947. *Land Use in Central Boston.* Cambridge: Harvard University Press.

Firey, Walter and Gideon Sjoberg. 1982. "Issues in Sociocultural Ecology." In *Urban Patterns*, edited by George A. Theodorson. University Park: Pennsylvania State University Press.

Fischer, Claude. 1973. "On Urban Alienation and Anomie: Powerlessness and Social Isolation." *American Sociological Review* 38:311–26.

Fischer, Claude. 1975. "Toward a Subcultural Theory of Urbanism." *American Journal of Sociology* 80:1319–41.

Fischer, Claude. 1982. *To Dwell Among Friends.* Chicago: University of Chicago Press.

Fisher, J. C. 1966. *Yugoslavia: A Multinational State.* San Francisco: Chandler Publishing.

Flax, Michael. 1978. *Survey of Urban Indicator Data 1970–1977.* Washington, DC: The Urban Institute.

Foot, David H. S. 1981. *Operational Urban Models.* New York: Methuen.

Form, William. 1978. Review of *Inequality in American Communities*, by Richard F. Curtis and Elton F. Jackson. *American Journal of Sociology* 84, no. 2:509–10.

Freedman, Jonathan. 1978. *Happy People.* New York: Ballantine.

Freedman, J. L. 1975. *Crowding and Behavior.* San Francisco: W. H. Freeman.

Freeman, Linton and Robert Winch. 1957. "Societal Complexity: An Empirical Test of a Typology of Societies." *American Journal of Sociology* 62, no. 5.

Freilich, Morris. 1963. "Toward an Operational Definition of Community." *Rural Sociology* 28:117–27.

French, Robert and Michael Aiken. 1968. "Community Power in Cornucopia: A Replication in a Small Community of the Bonjean Technique of Identifying Community Leaders." *Sociological Quarterly* 9:261–70.

French, R. A. and F. E. Ian Hamilton. 1979. *The Socialist City: Spatial Structure and Urban Policy.* Chichester: John Wiley & Sons.

Frey, James H. 1983. *Survey Research by Telephone.* Beverly Hills, CA: Sage Publications.

Friedland, Roger, Frances Fox Piven, and Robert Alford. 1978 "Political Conflict, Urban Structure, and the Fiscal Crises." In *Comparing Public Policies*, edited by Douglas E. Ashford. Beverly Hills, CA: Sage Publications.

Friedland, Roger, Frances Fox Piven, and Robert Alford. 1983. "Political Conflict, Urban Structure, and the Fiscal Crisis." Reprinted in *New Perspectives on the American Community*, edited by Roland Warren and Larry Lyon. Homewood, IL: Dorsey Press.

Friedrichs, Robert. 1970. *A Sociology of Sociology.* New York: The Free Press.

Frolic, B. Michael. 1970. "The Soviet Study of Soviet Cities." *Journal of Politics* 32:675–95.

Frolic, B. Michael. 1976. "Noncomparative Communism: Chinese and Soviet Urbanization." In *Social Consequences of Modernization in Communist Societies*, edited by M. G. Field. Baltimore: Johns Hopkins University Press.

Fromm, Erich. 1941. *Escape from Freedom*. New York: Rinehart.

Galaskiewicz, Joseph. 1979. *Exchange Networks and Community Politics*. Beverly Hills, CA: Sage Publications.

Galaskiewicz, Joseph. 1983. "Exchange Networks and Community Politics." In *New Perspectives on American Community*, edited by Roland Warren and Larry Lyon. Homewood, IL: Dorsey Press.

Gallaher, Art. Jr. 1961. *Plainville Fifteen Years Later*. New York: Columbia University Press.

Galle, Omer R., Walter R. Gove, and J. Miller McPherson. 1972. "Population Density and Pathology." *Science* 176:23–30.

Gallup, Alec. 1985. "The Gallup Poll of Teacher's Attitudes Toward the Public Schools, Part 2." *Kappan* 66:323–30.

Gallup, George H. 1972. *The Gallup Poll: Public Opinion 1935–1971*. New York: Random House.

Gallup, George H. 1978. *The Gallup Poll: Public Opinion 1972–1977*. New York: Random House.

Gamm, Larry and Frederick Fisher. 1980. "The Technical Assistance Approach." In *Community Development in America*, edited by James Christenson and Terry Robinson. Ames, IA: Iowa State University Press.

Gamson, William A. 1966. "Rancorous Conflict in Community Politics." *American Sociological Review* 31:71–81.

Gans, Herbert J. 1962. *The Urban Villagers*. New York: The Free Press.

Gans, Herbert J. 1967. *The Levittowners*. New York: Columbia University Press.

Garkovich, Lorraine and Jerome M. Stam. 1980. "Research on Selected Issues in Community Development." In *Community Development in America*, edited by James Christenson and Terry Robinson. Ames, IA: Iowa State University Press.

Glasgow, Douglas. 1972. "Black Power Through Community Control." *Social Work* 17, no. 3:59–65.

Glass, Ruth. 1966. *Conflict in Society*. London: Churchill.

Glazer, Nathan., and Daniel Moynihan. 1963. *Beyond the Melting Pot*. Cambridge: MIT Press.

Glenn, Norval D. 1967. "Massification Versus Differentiation." *Social Forces* 46:172–80.

Goffman, Erving. 1959. *The Presentation of Self in Everyday Life*. Garden City, N.Y.: Doubleday.

Goffman, Erving. 1961. *Asylums*. Garden City, N.Y.: Doubleday.

Goffman, Erving. 1962. "On the Cooling the Mark Out." In *Human Behavior and Social Processes*, edited by Arnold M. Rose. Boston: Houghton Mifflin.

Goffman, Erving. 1963. *Stigma*. Englewood Cliffs, N.J.: Prentice-Hall.

Goffman, Erving. 1974. *Frame Analysis: An Essay on the Organization of Experience*. Cambridge: Harvard University Press.

Goffman, Erving. 1977. *Gender Advertising*. New York: Harper & Row.

Goldsmith, Harold F., David J. Jackson, and J. Philip Shambaugh. 1982. "A Social Area Analysis Approach." In *Population Estimates: Methods for Small Area Analysis*, edited by Everett S. Lee and Harold F. Goldsmith. Beverly Hills, CA: Sage Publications.

Gordon, L. 1978. "Social Issues in the Arid City." In *Urban Planning for Arid Zones*, edited by Gideon Golany. New York: John Wiley & Sons.

Gove, Walter R., M. Hughes, and O. R. Galle. 1979. "Overcrowding in the Home: An Empirical Investigation of Its Possible Pathological Consequences." *American Sociological Review* 44:59–80.

Green, H. W. 1931. *Characteristics of Cleveland's Social Planning Areas*. Cleveland, OH: Welfare Federation of Cleveland.

Greenwood, Michael J. 1975. "A Simultaneous-Equations Model of Urban Growth and Migration." *Journal of the American Statistical Association* 70:797–810.

Greer, Scott. 1962. *The Emerging City*. New York: The Free Press.

Grimes, Michael D., Charles M. Bonjean, J. Larry Lyon, and Robert Lineberry. 1976. "Community Structure and Leadership Arrangements." *American Sociological Review* 14, no. 4:706–25.

Gross, B. M. 1966. "The State of the Nation: Social Systems Accounting." In *Social Indicators*, edited by R. Bauer. Cambridge and London: MIT Press.

Groves, Robert L. and Robert M. Kahn. 1979. *Surveys by Telephone: A National Comparison with Personal Interviews*. New York: Academic Press.

Guest, Avery M., Barrett A. Lee, and Lynn Staeheli. 1982. "Changing Locality Identification in the Metropolis." *American Sociological Review* 47, no. 4:543–49.

Gurin, Arnold. 1966. "Current Issues in Community Organization Practice and Education." Brandeis University Reprint Series, no. 21. Florence Heller Graduate School for Advanced Studies in Social Welfare.

Guterman, Stanley S. 1969. "In Defense of Wirth's 'Urbanism as a Way of Life'." *American Journal of Sociology* 74:492–99.

Hagen, Dan E. and Charlotte M. Collier. 1982. "Respondent Selection Procedures for Telephone Surveys: Must They Be Intrusive?" Presented at the Conference of the American Association for Public Opinion Research, Baltimore, MD.

Hall, Edward Twitchell. 1966. *The Hidden Dimension*. Garden City, NY: Doubleday.

Hamm, Bernd. 1982. "Social Area Analysis and Factorial Ecology." In *Urban Patterns*, edited by George Theodorson. University Park: Pennsylvania State University Press.

Hannerz, Ulf. 1969. *Soulside*. New York: Columbia University Press.

Hanson, Royce. 1978. "New Towns: Utopian Prospects—Hard Realities." In *Psychology of the Planned Community*, edited by Donald C. Klein. New York: Human Sciences Press.

Harris, Chauncey D. and Edward L. Ullman. 1945. "The Nature of Cities." *The Annals of the American Academy of Political Science* 242:7–17.

Harvey, David. 1973. *Social Justice and the City*. Baltimore: Johns Hopkins University Press.

Harvey, David. 1978. "The Urban Process Under Capitalism." *International Journal of Urban and Regional Research* 2:101–31.

Hastings, E. H. and P. K. Hastings, eds., 1980. *Index to International Public Opinion, 1978–1979.* Westport, CT: Greenwood Press.

Havighurst, Robert J. 1975. "The College and Youth." *New Directions for Higher Education* 3, no. 1:1–22.

Hawley, Amos. 1950. *Human Ecology.* New York: Ronald Press.

Hawley, Amos. 1963. "Community Power and Urban Renewal Success." *American Journal of Sociology* 68:422–31.

Hawley, Amos. 1968. "Human Ecology." *International Encyclopedia of the Social Sciences.* New York: The Macmillan Company and the Free Press.

Hawley, Amos. 1971. *Urban Society: An Ecological Approach.* New York: Ronald Press.

Hawley, Amos and Otis Dudley Duncan. 1957. "Social Area Analysis: A Critical Appraisal." *Land Economics* 33:337–44.

Haworth, Lawrence. 1963. *The Good City.* Bloomington: Indiana University Press.

Hayes, Edward C. 1972. *Power Structure and Urban Policy: Who Rules in Oakland.* New York: McGraw-Hill.

Heckscher, August with Phyllis Robinson. 1977. *Open Spaces: The Life of American Cities.* New York: Harper & Row.

Herman, Leon M. 1971. "Urbanization and New Housing Construction in the Soviet Union." *American Journal of Economics and Sociology* 30, no. 2:203–19.

Hill, Richard Child. 1978. "Fiscal Collapse and Political Struggle in Decaying Central Cities in the United States." In *Marxism and the Metropolis,* edited by William K. Tabb and Larry Sawers. New York: Oxford University Press.

Hillery, George A., Jr. 1955. "Definitions of Community: Areas of Agreement." *Rural Sociology* 20:779–91.

Hillery, George A., Jr. 1963. "Villages, Cities, and Total Institutions." *American Sociological Review* 28:779–91.

Hillery, George A., Jr. 1968. *Communal Organizations: A Study of Local Societies.* Chicago: University of Chicago Press.

Homans, George C. 1950. *The Human Group.* New York: Harcourt Brace Jovanovich.

Horowitz, Ruth. 1983. *Honor and the American Dream.* New Brunswick, N.J.: Rutgers University Press.

Howard, Ebenezer. 1898, 1965. *Garden Cities of To-Morrow.* Edited by F. J. Osborn. Cambridge: MIT Press.

Howard, John R. 1974. *The Cutting Edge.* Philadelphia: J. B. Lippincott.

Hoyt, Homer. 1939. *The Structure and Growth of Residential Neighborhoods in American Cities.* Washington, DC: Federal Housing Administration.

Hunter, Albert. 1974. *Symbolic Communities: The Persistence and Change of Chicago's Local Communities.* Chicago: University of Chicago Press.

Hunter, Albert. 1975. "The Loss of Community." *American Sociological Review* 40:537–52.

Hunter, Albert. 1978. "Persistence of Local Sentiments in Mass Society." In *Handbook of Contemporary Urban Life*, edited by D. Street. San Francisco: Jossey-Bass.

Hunter, Floyd. 1953. *Community Power Structure*. Chapel Hill: University of North Carolina Press.

Inkeles, Alex and David Smith. 1974. *Becoming Modern*. Cambridge: Harvard University Press.

Jacobs, Jane. 1961. *The Death and Life of Great American Cities*. New York: Random House.

Jencks, Christopher. 1972. *Inequality*. New York: Basic Books.

Kanter, Rosabeth. 1972. *Commitment and Community*. Cambridge: Harvard University Press.

Kasarda, John D. and Morris Janowitz. 1974. "Community Attachment in Mass Society." *American Sociological Review* 39:328–39.

Kaufman, Harold. 1959. "Toward and Interactional Conception of Community." *Social Forces* 38:17.

Kaufman, Herbert and Victor Jones. 1954. "The Mystery of Power." *Public Administration Review* 14:205–12.

Kennedy, Michael D. 1983. "Urban Fiscal Crisis and Forms of Expenditure." *Comparative Urban Research* no. 2:34–40.

Key, W. H. 1968. "Rural-Urban Social Participation." In *Urbanism in World Perspective*, edited by Sylvia Fava. New York: Thomas Crowell.

Kim, Kyong-Dong. 1973. "Toward a Sociological Theory of Development." *Rural Sociology* 38, no. 4:462–76.

King, Leslie J. 1966. "Cross-Sectional Analysis of Canadian Urban Dimensions, 1951 and 1961." *Canadian Geographer* 10:205–24.

Kish, Leslie. 1949. "A Procedure for Objective Respondent Selection within the Household." *Journal of the American Statistical Association* 44:380–87.

Kish, Leslie. 1965. *Survey Sampling*. New York: John Wiley & Sons.

Kohlberg, Lawrence. 1980. *The Development of Socio-moral Knowledge*. New York: Cambridge University Press.

Kornblum, William. 1974. *Blue Collar Community*. Chicago: University of Chicago Press.

Kornhauser, William. 1959. "Power and Participation in the Local Community." *Health Education Monographs*, no. 6. Oakland, CA: Society of Public Health Educators.

Kuhn, Thomas S. 1962. *The Structure of Scientific Revolutions*. Chicago: University of Chicago Press.

Lancourt, Joan. 1979. *Confront or Concede: The Alinsky Citizen-Action Organizations*. Lexington, MA: D.C. Heath.

Landon, E. Laird and Sharon K. Banks. 1977. "Relative Efficiency and Bias of Plus-one Telephone Sampling." *Journal of Marketing Research* 14:294–99.

Laue, James and Gerald Cormick. 1978. "The Ethics of Intervention in Community Disputes." In *The Ethics of Social Intervention*, edited by Gordon Bermant, Herbert C. Kehman, and Donald Warwick. New York: John Wiley & Sons.

Laumann, Edward. 1973. *Bonds of Pluralism: The Form and Substance of Urban Social Networks*. New York: John Wiley & Sons.

Lefebvre, Henri. 1976. *The Survival of Capitalism*. London: Allison & Busby.

Lenski, Gerhard. 1963. *The Religious Factor*. Garden City, NY: Anchor.

Lewis, Oscar. 1951. *Life in a Mexican Village: Tepoztlan Restudied*. Urbana: University of Illinois Press.

Lewis, Sinclair. 1922. *Babbitt*. New York: Harcourt, Brace.

Lewis, Sinclair. 1920. *Main Street*. New York: Harcourt, Brace.

Lewis, Susan and Larry Lyon. 1986. "The Quality of Community and the Quality of Life." *Sociological Spectrum*. Forthcoming.

Liebert, Roland J. 1976. *Disintegration and Political Action: the Changing Function of City Government in America*. New York: Academic Press.

Liebow, Elliot. 1967. *Tally's Corner*. Boston: Little Brown.

Lincoln, James R. 1976. "Power Mobilization in the Urban Community." *American Sociological Review* 41:1–15.

Lineberry, Robert L. 1971. "Approaches to the Study of Community Politics." In *Community Politics*, edited by Charles Bonjean, Terry Clark, and Robert Lineberry. New York: The Free Press.

Lineberry, Robert L. and Edmund P. Fowler. 1967. "Reformism and Public Policies in American Cities." *American Political Science Review* 61:701–16.

Lineberry, Robert L. and Ira Sharkansky. 1978. *Urban Politics and Public Policy*. New York: Harper & Row.

Lindt, Gillian. 1979. "Robert S. Lynd: American Scholar-Activist." *Journal of the History of Sociology* 2:1–13.

Lipset, Seymour Martin and Philip G. Altbach. 1967. "Student Politics and Higher Education in the United States." In *Student Politics*, edited by Seymour Martin Lipset. New York: Basic Books.

Lipset, Seymour Martin and Reinhard Bendix. 1951. "Social Status and Social Structure." *British Journal of Sociology* Vol. 1.

Littrell, Donald W. 1980. "The Self-Help Approach." In *Community Development in America*, edited by James Christenson and Jerry Robinson. Ames, IA: Iowa State University Press.

Littrell, Donald W. 1971. "Theory and Practice of Community Development." MP184. Columbia: University of Missouri, Extension Division Publication.

Liu, Ben-Chieh. 1976. *Quality of Life Indicators in U.S. Metropolitan Areas: A Statistical Analysis*. New York: Praeger Publishers.

Lofland, John and Lyn Lofland. 1984. *Analyzing Social Settings*. Belmont, CA: Wadsworth.

Logan, John and Mark Schneider. 1981. "Stratification of Metropolitan Suburbs, 1960–1970." *American Sociological Review* 46:175–86.

Logan, John and Mark Schneider. 1984. "Racial Segregation and Racial Change in American Suburbs, 1970–1980." *American Journal of Sociology* 89:874–88.

Long, L. H. and Paul C. Glick. 1976. "Family Patterns in Suburban Areas." In *The Changing Face of the Suburbs*, edited by Barry Schwartz. Chicago: University of Chicago Press.

Long, Norton E. 1958. "The Local Community as an Ecology of Games." *American Journal of Sociology* 64:251–61.

Long, Norton E. 1983. "The Local Community as an Ecology of Games." Reprinted in *New Perspectives on the American Community*, edited by Roland Warren and Larry Lyon. Homewood, IL: Dorsey Press.

Loomis, Charles. 1960. *Social Systems*. Princeton, NJ: D. Van Nostrand.

Lynd, Robert S. and Helen M. Lynd. 1929. *Middletown*. New York: Harcourt Brace Jovanovich.

Lynd, Robert S. and Helen M. Lynd. 1937. *Middletown in Transition: A Study in Cultural Conflicts*. New York: Harcourt Brace Jovanovich.

Lynd, Staughton. 1979. "Robert S. Lynd: The Elk Basin Experience." *Journal of the History of Sociology* 2:14–22.

Lyon, Larry. 1977a. "Community Power and Policy Outputs." In *New Perspectives on the American Community*, edited by Roland Warren. Chicago: Rand McNally and Company.

Lyon, Larry. 1977b. "A Re-Examination of the Reform Index and Community Power." *Journal of the Community Development Society* 8:86–97.

Lyon, Larry, Troy Abell, Elizabeth Jones, and Holly Rector-Owen. 1982. "The National Longitudinal Surveys Data for Labor Market Entry: Evaluating the Small Effects of Racial Discrimination and the Large Effects of Sexual Discrimination." *Social Problems* 29:524–39.

Lyon, Larry and Charles M. Bonjean. 1981. "Community Power and Policy Output: the Routines of Local Politics." *Urban Affairs Quarterly* 17, no. 1:3–21.

Lyon, Larry, Lawrence G. Felice, M. Ray Perryman, and E. Stephen Parker. 1981. "Community Power and Population Increase." *American Journal of Sociology* 86, no 6:1387–99. Reprinted in *New Perspectives on the American Community*, edited by Roland Warren and Larry Lyon. Homewood, IL: Dorsey Press.

Lystad, M. H. 1969. *Social Aspects of Alienation*. Washington DC: U.S. Government Printing Office.

Mabogunge, Akin. 1965. "Urbanization in Nigeria." *Economic Development and Cultural Change* 13:413–38.

MacDonald, A. P., Jr., and W. F. Throop. 1971. "Internal Locus of Control." *Psychological Reports*, Supplement I-V28.

Martin, Elizabeth. 1983. "Surveys as Social Indicators: Problems in Monitoring Trends." In *Handbook of Survey Research*, edited by Peter H. Rossi, James D. Wright, and Andy B. Anderson. New York: Academic Press.

Martindale, Don Albert. 1981. *The Nature and Types of Social Theory*. Boston: Houghton Mifflin.

Marx, Karl. 1867, 1967. *Capital*. New York: International Publishers Edition.

Marx, Karl and Friedrich Engels. 1846, 1970. *The German Ideology*. New York: International Publishers Edition.

Marx, Karl and Friedrich Engels. 1848, 1959. *Manifesto of the Communist Party*. In *Marx and Engels: Basic Writings on Politics and Philosophy*, edited by Lewis S. Feuer. Garden City NY: Doubleday Anchor Books.

Maslow, A. H. 1970. *Motivation and Personality*, 2nd ed. New York: Harper & Row.

Masterman, Margaret. 1970. "The Nature of a Paradigm." In *Criticism and the Growth of Knowledge*, edited by Imre Lakatos and Alan Musgrave. Cambridge: Cambridge University Press.

Mayhew, Bruce H. and Roger L. Levinger. 1976. "Size and Density of Interaction in Human Aggregates." *American Journal of Sociology*, 82, no. 1:86–110.

McKenzie, Roderick. 1923. *The Neighborhood*. Chicago: University of Chicago Press.

McKinney, John C. 1966. *Constructive Typology and Social Theory*. New York: Appleton-Century-Crofts.

McKinney, John C. and Charles P. Loomis. 1958. "The Typological Tradition." In *Contemporary Sociology*, edited by Joseph S. Roucek. New York: The Philosophical Library.

McLuhan, Marshall. 1965. *Understanding Media: The Extensions of Man*. New York: McGraw-Hill.

McNulty, Michael. 1969. "Urban Structure and Development: The Urban System of Ghana." *Journal of Developing Areas* 3:159–76.

Michelson, William. 1977. *Environmental Choice, Human Behavior, and Residential Satisfaction*. New York: Oxford University Press.

Michelson, William. 1977. "Planning and Amelioration of Urban Problems." In *Contemporary Topics in Urban Sociology*, edited by Kent P. Schwirian et al. Morristown, NJ: General Learning Press.

Milgram, Stanley. 1970. "The Experiences of Living in Cities." *Science* 167:1461–70.

Miller, Delbert C. 1958. "Decision-Making Cliques in Community Power Structures." *American Journal of Sociology* 64:299–310.

Miller, Delbert C. 1970. *International Community Power Structures*. Bloomington: Indiana University Press.

Miller, Delbert C. 1977. *Handbook of Research Design and Social Measurement*, 3rd ed. New York: McKay.

Miller, Delbert C., and James L. Dirksen. 1965. "The Identification of Visible, Concealed and Symbolic Leaders in a Small Indiana City: A Replication of the Bonjean-Noland Study of Burlington, North Carolina," *Social Forces* 43:548–55.

Mills, C. Wright. 1942. "Review of the Social Life of a Modern Community." *American Sociological Review* Vol. 7. Reprinted in Irving Horowitz, *People, Politics and Power* 1965. London: Oxford University Press.

Minar, David W., and Scott Greer, eds. 1969. *The Concept of Community*. Chicago: Aldine Publishing.

Miner, Horace. 1952. "The Folk-Urban Continuum." *American Sociological Review* 17:537–49.

Mitchell, R. E. 1971. "Some Implications of High Density Housing." *American Sociological Review* 36:18–29.

Mollenkopf, John H. 1978. "The Postwar Politics of Urban Development." In

Marxism and the Metropolis, edited by William K. Tabb and Larry Sawers. New York: Oxford University Press.

Molotch, Harvey 1976. "The City as a Growth Machine." *American Journal of Sociology* 82:309–32.

Morgan, William and Terry Clark. 1973. "The Causes of Racial Disorders." *American Sociological Review* 38, no. 5:611–24.

Moser, Charles A. and Wolf Scott. 1961. *British Towns: A Statistical Study of Their Social and Economic Differences.* Edinburgh: Oliver and Boyd.

Naisbitt, John. 1982. *Megatrends.* New York: Warner Books.

National Opinion Research Center. 1980. *General Social Surveys, 1972–1980: Cumulative Codebook.* Chicago: National Opinion Research Center, University of Chicago.

Nelson, Michael D. 1974. "The Validity of Secondary Analyses of Community Power Studies." *Social Forces* 52:531–37.

Newton, Kenneth. 1975. "American Urban Politics: Social Class, Political Structure and Public Goods." *Urban Affairs Quarterly* 2:243–64.

Newton, Kenneth. 1983. "American Urban Politics." Reprinted in *New Perspectives on the American Community,* edited by Roland Warren and Larry Lyon. Homewood, IL: Dorsey Press.

Nisbet, Robert. 1953, 1976. *The Quest for Community.* New York: Oxford University Press.

Nisbet, Robert. 1960. "Moral Values and Community." *International Review of Community Development* 5:77–85.

Nisbet, Robert. 1966. *The Sociological Tradition.* New York: Basic Books.

O'Brien, David J. 1975. *Neighborhood Organization and Interest-Group Process.* Princeton, NJ: Princeton University Press.

O'Brien, David J. 1983. "Neighborhood Organization and Interest-Group Process." In *New Perspectives on the American Community,* edited by Roland Warren and Larry Lyon. Homewood, IL: Dorsey Press.

O'Connor, Edwin. 1956. *The Last Hurrah.* Boston, MA: Little, Brown.

Ogburn, W. F. 1937. *Social Characteristics of Cities.* Chicago: International City Managers Association.

Olsen, Marvin E. and Donna J. Merwin. 1977. "Toward a Methodology for Conducting Social Impact Assessments Using Quality of Social Life Indicators." In *Methodology of Social Impact Assessment,* edited by Kurt Finsterbusch and C. P. Wolf. New York: McGraw-Hill.

Osborn, Frederich J. 1969. *Green Belt Cities.* New York: Schocken.

Osborn, Robert J. 1970. *Soviet Social Policies: Welfare, Equality, and Community.* Homewood, IL: Dorsey Press.

Pahl, R. 1968. "The Rural-Urban Continuum." In *Readings in Urban Sociology,* edited by R. Pahl, London: Pergamon.

Palen, John J. 1981. "A Note on Density." In *The Urban World,* edited by John J. Palen. New York: McGraw-Hill.

Palen, John J. 1981. *The Urban World.* New York: McGraw-Hill.

Park, Robert E. 1936. "Human Ecology." *American Journal of Sociology* 17, no. 1:1–15.

Park, Robert E. 1952. *Human Communities.* New York: The Free Press.

Park, Robert E. 1983. "Human Ecology." Reprinted in *New Perspectives on the American Community,* edited by Roland Warren and Larry Lyon. Homewood, IL: Dorsey Press.

Parsons, Talcott. 1959. "General Theory in Sociology." In *Sociology Today: Problems and Prospects,* edited by Robert K. Merton, Leonard Broom, and Leonard S. Cottrell, Jr. New York: Basic Books.

Parsons, Talcott. 1951. *The Social System.* Glencoe, IL: Free Press.

Parsons, Talcott and Robert F. Bales. 1955. *Family, Socialization and Interaction Process.* Glencoe, IL: Free Press.

Parsons, Talcott and Edward Shils, eds. 1951. *Toward a General Theory of Action.* Cambridge, MA: Harvard University Press.

Parsons, Talcott and Neil J. Smelser. 1956. *Economy and Society.* Glencoe, IL: Free Press.

Payne, Geoffrey K. 1977. *Urban Housing in the Third World.* Boston: Routledge and Kegan Paul.

Payne, Stanley L. 1951. *The Art of Asking Questions.* Princeton, NJ: Princeton University Press.

Pederson, Paul O. 1967. *Modeller for Befolkmingsstruktur og Befalkingssudvikling: Storbymorader Specielt med Henblik pa Storkobenhaun.* Copenhagen, Denmark: Stat Urban Planning Institute.

Pfautz, Harold and O. D. Duncan. 1950. "Critical Evaluation of Warner's Work in Community Stratification." *American Sociological Review,* Vol. 15.

Polsby, Nelson W. 1963. *Community Power and Political Theory.* New Haven CT: Yale University Press.

Poplin, Dennis E. 1979. *Communities: A Survey of Theories and Methods of Research.* New York: Macmillan.

Presthus, Robert. 1964. *Men at the Top: A Study in Community Power.* New York: Oxford University Press.

Preston, James D. 1969. "The Search for Community Leaders: A Reexamination of the Reputational Technique." *Sociological Inquiry* 39:37–47.

Reckless, Walter. 1929. *Six Boys in Trouble.* Ann Arbor, MI: Edwards Bros.

Redekop, Calvin. 1975. "Communal Groups: Inside or Outside the Community." In *The American Community: Creation and Revival,* edited by Jack F. Kinton. Aurora, IL: Social Science and Sociological Resources.

Redfield, Robert. 1941. *The Folk Culture of Yucatan.* Chicago: University of Chicago Press.

Redfield, Robert. 1947. "The Folk Society." *American Journal of Sociology* 52:293–308.

Rees, P. H. 1971. "Factorial Ecology: An Extended Definition, Survey, and Critique." *Economic Geography* 47:220–33.

Reich, Wilhelm. 1970. *The Mass Psychology of Fascism.* New York: Farrar, Straus and Giroux.

Reitzes, Donald C. and Dietrich C. Reitzes. 1982. "Alinsky Reconsidered: A Reluctant Community Theorist." *Social Science Quarterly* 63, no. 2:256–79.

Reitzes, Donald C. and Dietrich C. Reitzes. 1983. "Alinsky Reconsidered: A Reluctant Community Theorist." Reprinted in *New Perspectives on the American Community*, edited by Roland Warren and Larry Lyon. Homewood, IL: Dorsey Press.

Richmond, Anthony. 1969. "Migration in Industrial Societies." In *Migration*, edited by J. A. Jackson. London: Cambridge University Press.

Riesman, David. 1953. *The Lonely Crowd*. New Haven CT: Yale University Press.

Ritzer, George. 1972. *Man and His Work: Conflict and Change*. New York: Appleton-Century-Crofts.

Ritzer, George. 1975. *Sociology: A Multiple Paradigm Science*. Boston: Allyn and Bacon.

Robinson, J. P., J. G. Rusk, and K. B. Head. 1969. *Measures of Political Attitudes*. Ann Arbor: Survey Research Center, University of Michigan.

Robinson, J. P. and P. R. Shaver. 1973. *Measures of Social Psychological Attitudes*. Ann Arbor MI: Institute for Social Research.

Robinson, Jerry W. 1980. "The Conflict Approach." In *Community Development in America*, edited by James Christenson and Jerry Robinson. Ames, IA: Iowa State University Press.

Robinson, W. S. 1950. "Ecological Correlations and the Behaviour of Individuals." *American Sociological Review* 15:351–57.

Rogers, Theresa F. 1976. "Interviews by Telephone and in Person: Quality of Responses and Field Performance." *Public Opinion Quarterly* 40:51–65.

Roper Public Opinion Research Center. 1975. *Survey Data for Trend Analysis: An Index to Repeated Questions in U.S. National Surveys Held by the Roper Public Opinion Research Center*. Williamstown, MA: The Roper Center, Williams College.

Roscow, I. 1961. "The Social Effects of the Physical Environment." *Journal of the American Institute of Planners* 27:321–32.

Rossi, Peter H. 1955. *Why Families Move: A Study in the Social Psychology of Urban Residential Mobility*. New York: Free Press.

Rossi, Peter H. 1972. "Community Social Indicators." In *The Human Meaning of Social Change*, edited by Angus Campbell and Philip E. Converse. New York: Russell Sage Foundation.

Rossi, Peter H. and Robert L. Crain. 1968. "The NORC Permanent Community Sample." *Public Opinion Quarterly* 32:261–72.

Roszak, Theodore. 1969. *The Making of a Counterculture*. New York: Anchor Books.

Rothman, Jack. 1979. "Three Models of Community Organization Practice, Their Mixing and Phasing." In *Strategies of Community Organization*, edited by Fred M. Cox, et al. Itasca, IL: F. E. Peacock.

Rothman, Jack. 1968. "Three Models of Community Organization Practice." In National Conference on Social Welfare, *Social Work Practice 1968*. New York: Columbia University Press.

Rouse, James W. 1978. "Building a Sense of Place." In *Psychology of the Planned Community*, edited by Donald C. Klein. New York: Human Sciences Press.

Ruben, Julius. 1961. "Canal or Railroad?: Imitation and Innovation in the Response to the Erie Canal in Philadelphia, Baltimore, and Boston." *Transactions of the American Philosophical Society* 51, part 7.

Rubin, Israel. 1969. "Function and Structure of Community: Conceptual and Theoretical Analysis." *International Review of Community Development*, 21–22:111–19.

Rubin, Israel. 1983. "Function and Structure of Community: Conceptual and Theoretical Analysis." Reprinted in *New Perspectives on the American Community*, edited by Roland Warren and Larry Lyon. Homewood, IL: Dorsey Press.

Ryan, William. 1971. *Blaming the Victim*. New York: Pantheon Books.

Saegert, S. 1978. "High Density Environments: Their Personal and Social Consequences." In *Human Response to Crowding*, edited by A. Baum and Y. Epstein. Hillsdale, NJ: Lawrence Erlbaum Associates.

Salins, P. D. 1971. "Household Local Patterns in American Metropolitan Areas." *Economic Geography* 47:234–48.

Sallnow, John. 1983. "The USSR: New Directions for the 1980s." *Cities* 1:39–45.

Sanders, Irwin T. 1975. *The Community*. New York: Ronald Press.

Saunders, Peter. 1981. *Social Theory and the Urban Question*. New York: Holmes and Meier Publishers.

Sawers, Larry. 1978. "Cities and Countryside in the Soviet Union and China." In *Marxism and the Metropolis*, edited by William K. Tabb and Larry Sawers. New York: Oxford University Press.

Schmitt, Robert C. 1963. "Implications of Density in Hong Kong." *Journal of the American Institute of Planners* 29:210–17.

Schmitt, Robert C. 1966. "Density, Health and Social Organization." *Journal of the American Institute of Planners* 32:38–40.

Schneider, Mark and John Logan. 1985. "Suburban Municipalities: The Changing System of Intergovernmental Relations in the Mid-1970s." *Urban Affairs Quarterly* 21:87–105.

Schnore, L. F. 1957. "Satellites and Suburbs." *Social Forces* 36:121–27.

Schnore, L. F. 1965. *The Urban Scene*. New York: Free Press.

Schuman, Howard and Stanley Presser. 1981. *Questions and Answers: Experiments on Question Form, Wording, and Context*. New York: Academic Press.

Schwab, William. 1982. *Urban Sociology*. Reading, MA: Addison-Wesley.

Schwirian, Kent P., ed. 1977. *Contemporary Topics in Urban Sociology*. Morristown, NJ: General Learning Press.

Seeley, John, R. A. Sim and E. W. Loosley. 1956. *Crestwood Heights*. New York: Basic Books.

Seeman, Albert. 1938. "Communities in the Salt Lake Basin." *Economic Geography* 14:306.

Seeman, Melvin, J. M. Bishop and J. E. Grigsby. 1971. "Community and Control in a Metropolitan Setting." In *Race, Change, and Urban Society, Urban*

Affairs Annual Review, edited by P. Orleans and R. Ellis. Vol. 5. Los Angeles: Russell Sage Foundation.

Shanks, J. Merrill. 1983. "The Current Status of Computer-Assisted Telephone Interviewing." *Sociological Methods and Research* 12:119–42.

Shaw, Clifford. 1929. *Delinquency Areas.* Chicago: The University of Chicago Press.

Shaw, Clifford. 1930. *The Jack-roller, a Delinquent Boy's Own Story.* Chicago: University of Chicago Press.

Sheatsley, Paul B. 1983. "Questionnaire Construction and Item Writing." In *Handbook of Survey Research,* edited by Peter Rossi, James Wright and Andy Anderson. New York: Academic Press.

Sheldon, E. and H. E. Freeman. 1970. "Notes on Social Indicators: Promises and Potential." *Policy Sciences* 1:97–111.

Shevky, Eshref and Wendell Bell. 1955. *Social Area Analysis.* Stanford CA: Stanford University Press.

Shevky, Eshref and Marilyn Williams. 1949. *The Social Areas of Los Angeles.* Berkeley: University of California Press.

Shils, Edward Albert. 1972. *The Intellectuals and the Powers and Other Essays.* Chicago: University of Chicago Press.

Shlay, Anne and Peter Rossi. 1981. "Keeping Up the Neighborhood: Estimating Net Effects of Zoning." *American Sociological Review* 46:703–19.

Sills, David. 1957. *The Volunteers: Means and Ends in a National Organization.* Glencoe, IL: Free Press.

Simmel, Georg. 1983. "The Metropolis in Mental Life." In *New Perspectives on the American Community,* edited by Roland Warren and Larry Lyon. Homewood, IL: Dorsey Press.

Sjoberg, Gideon. 1965. *The Preindustrial City.* New York: Free Press.

Skogan, Wesley G. and Michael G. Maxfield. 1981. *Coping with Crime: Individual and Neighborhood Differences.* Beverly Hills CA: Sage.

Slater, P. E. 1970. *The Pursuit of Loneliness.* Boston: Beacon Press.

Slovak, Jeffrey. 1985. "City Spending, Suburban Demands, and Fiscal Exploitation: A Replication and Extension." *Social Forces* 64:168–90.

Small, Albion W. and George E. Vincent. 1894. *An Introduction to the Study of Society.* New York: American Book Co.

Sommer, Robert. 1969. *Personal Space.* Englewood Cliffs, NJ: Prentice-Hall.

Sorenson, Aage B. 1979. "A Model and a Metric for the Analysis of the Intergenerational Status Attainment Process." *American Journal of Sociology* 85:361–85.

Sorokin, Pitirim A. 1963. "Foreward." In Ferdinand Tönnies, *Community and Society,* edited by Charles F. Loomis. New York: Harper Torchbook Edition.

Sower, Christopher et al. 1957. *Community Involvement: The Webs of Formal and Informal Ties That Make for Action.* Glencoe, IL: Free Press.

Spates, James L. and John J. Macionis. 1982. *The Sociology of Cities.* New York: St. Martin's Press.

Spiegel, Hans B. C. 1980. "New Directions." In *Community Development in America*, edited by James Christenson and Jerry Robinson, Jr. Ames, IA: Iowa State University Press.

Spiekerman, Ruth. 1968. "Identification of Community Power Structures Using the Reputational Approach." M.S. Thesis, Texas A & M University.

Spilerman, Seymour. 1970. "The Causes of Racial Disturbances." *American Sociological Review* 35, no. 4:627–49.

Spilerman, Seymour. 1976. "Structural Characteristics of Cities and the Severity of Racial Disorders." *American Sociological Review* 41, no. 5:771–92.

Spradley, James G. 1970. *You Owe Yourself a Drunk: An Ethnography of Urban Nomads*. Boston: Little, Brown.

Srole, Leo. 1972. "Urbanization and Mental Health." *American Scientist* 60:576–83.

Stack, Carol B. 1974. *All Our Kin: Strategies for Survival in a Black Community*. New York: Harper & Row.

Stein, C. S. 1957. *Towards New Towns for America*. Cambridge, Mass.: MIT Press.

Stein, Maurice R. 1960. *The Eclipse of Community*. Princeton, NJ: Princeton University Press.

Straits, Bruce C. 1965. "Community Adoption and Implementation of Urban Renewal." *American Journal of Sociology* 71:77–82.

Strauss, Anselm. 1961. *Images of the American City*. New York: Free Press.

Sudman, Seymour and Norman Bradburn. 1982. *Asking Questions*. San Francisco: Jossey-Bass.

Suttles, Gerald D. 1968. *The Social Order of the Slum*. Chicago: University of Chicago Press.

Suttles, Gerald D. 1972. *The Social Construction of Communities*. Chicago: University of Chicago Press.

Sutton, Willis, Jr. 1970. "Visible Symbolic and Concealed Leaders in a Kentucky County." Unpublished Manuscript.

Sutton, Willis, Jr., and Jiri Kolaja. 1960. "Elements of Community Action." *Social Force* 38:325–31.

Sutton, Willis, Jr., and Thomas Munson. 1976. "Definitions of Community: 1954 Through 1973." Paper presented to the American Sociological Association. New York, August 30.

Tabb, William K. 1978. "The New York City Fiscal Crisis." In *Marxism and the Metropolis*, edited by William Tabb and Larry Sawers. New York: Oxford University Press.

Tabb, William K. and Larry Sawers, eds. 1978. *Marxism and the Metropolis*. New York: Oxford University Press.

Tabb, William K. and Larry Sawers. 1983. "Marxism and the Metropolis." In *New Perspectives on the American Community*, edited by Roland Warren and Larry Lyon. Homewood, IL: Dorsey Press.

Taylor, Brian. 1975. "The Absence of a Sociological and Structural Problem Focus in Community Studies." *Archives Europeens de Sociologie* 16.

Theodorson, George. 1961. *Studies in Human Ecology.* New York: Harper & Row.

Thibaut, John W. and Harold H. Kelley. 1959. *The Social Psychology of Groups.* New York: John Wiley & Sons.

Thomas, W. I. and Dorothy S. Thomas. 1928. *The Child in America.* New York: Alfred A. Knopf.

Thrasher, Frederick M. 1927. *The Gang.* Chicago: University of Chicago Press.

Tiebout, Charles M. 1972. "A Pure Theory of Local Expenditures." In *Readings in Urban Economics,* edited by M. Edel and J. Rothenberg. New York: Macmillan.

Tobin, G. A. 1976. "Suburbanization and the Development of Motor Transportation." In *The Changing Face of the Suburbs,* edited by Barry Schwartz. Chicago: University of Chicago Press.

Toffler, Alvin. 1980. *The Third Wave.* New York: Bantam Books.

Tönnies, Ferdinand. 1887, 1963. *Community and Society.* Edited by Charles P. Loomis. New York: Harper & Row.

Troldahl, Verling C. and Roy C. Carter. 1964. "Random Selection of Respondents within Households in Phone Surveys." *Journal of Marketing Research* 1:71–6.

Trounstine, Philip J. and Terry Christensen. 1982. *Movers and Shakers.* New York: St. Martin's Press.

Turk, Herman. 1970. "Interorganizational Networks in Urban Society." *American Sociological Review* 35:1–18.

Turk, Herman. 1977. *Organizations in Modern Life.* San Francisco: Jossey-Bass.

Ullman, Edward. 1941. "A Theory of Location for Cities." *American Journal of Sociology* 46:153–64.

U.S. Bureau of the Census. 1983. *County and City Data Book,* Washington DC: Government Printing Office.

U.S. Department of Commerce. 1973. *Social Indicators.* Washington DC: Government Printing Office.

U.S. Department of Commerce. 1976. *Social Indicators.* Washington DC: Government Printing Office.

U.S. Department of Commerce. 1980. *Social Indicators.* Washington DC: Government Printing Office.

Van Ardsol, Maurice D., Santa F. Camilleri, and Calvin F. Schmid. 1958. "An Application of the Shevsky Social Area Indexes to a Model of Urban Society." *Social Forces* 37:26–32.

Verbrugge, Lois M. and Ralph B. Taylor. 1980. "Consequences of Population Density and Size." *Urban Affairs Quarterly* 16, no. 2:135-60.

Vidich, Arthur. 1955. "Participant Observation and the Collection and Interpretation of Data." *American Journal of Sociology* 60: 354–60.

Vidich, Arthur and Joseph Bensman. 1958. *Small Town in Mass Society.* Princeton, NJ: Princeton University Press.

Vidich, Arthur, Joseph Bensman and Maurice Stein. 1964. *Reflections on Community Studies.* New York: John Wiley & Sons.

Walton, John. 1966. "Discipline, Method, and Community Power." *American Sociological Review* 31:684–89.

Walton, John. 1967. "Vertical Axis of Community Organization and the Structure of Power." *Social Science Quarterly* 48:355–57.

Walton, John. 1970. "A Systematic Survey of Community Power Research." In *The Structure of Community Power*, edited by Michael Aiken and Paul E. Mott. New York: Random House.

Walton, John. 1973. "The Structural Bases of Political Change in Urban Communities." *Sociological Inquiry* 43:174–206.

Walton, John. 1976. "Community Power and the Retreat from Politics." *Social Problems* 23, no 3:292–303.

Walton, John. 1983. "Community Power and the Retreat from Politics." In *New Perspectives on the American Community*, edited by Roland Warren and Larry Lyon. Homewood, IL: Dorsey Press.

Warner, W. Lloyd. 1959. *The Living and the Dead*. New Haven: Yale University Press.

Warner, William Lloyd. 1963. *Yankee City*. New Haven CT: Yale University Press.

Warner, W. Lloyd and J. O. Low. 1947. *The Social System of the Modern Factory*. New Haven CT: Yale University Press.

Warner, W. Lloyd and Paul S. Lunt. 1941. *The Social Life of a Modern Community*. New Haven: Yale University Press.

Warner, W. Lloyd and Paul S. Lunt. 1942. *The Status System of a Modern Community*. New Haven: Yale University Press.

Warner, W. Lloyd, Marchia Meekerand and Kenneth Eells. 1949. *Social Class in America*. Chicago: Science Research Associates.

Warner, W. Lloyd and Leo Srole. 1945. *The Social Systems of American Ethnic Groups*. New Haven: Yale University Press.

Warr, Mark. 1984. "Fear of Victimization: Why are Women and the Elderly More Afraid?" *Social Science Quarterly* 65 no. 3:681–702.

Warren, Roland. 1955. *Studying Your Community*. New York: Russell Sage Foundation.

Warren, Roland. 1963. "The Community in America." In *New Perspectives on the American Community*, edited by Roland Warren and Larry Lyon. Homewood, IL: Dorsey Press.

Warren, Roland L. 1970. "The Good Community—What Would It Be?" *Journal of the Community Development Society* 1, no. 1 (Spring 1970):14–23. Reprinted in *New Perspectives on the American Community* 1983, edited by Roland L. Warren and Larry Lyon. Homewood, IL: Dorsey Press.

Warren, Roland. 1971. "The Sociology of Knowledge and the Problems of the Inner Cities." *Social Science Quarterly* 52, no. 3:468–85.

Warren, Roland, ed. 1977. *New Perspectives on the American Community*. 3rd ed. Chicago: Rand McNally and Company.

Warren, Roland. 1978. *The Community in America*. Chicago: Rand McNally and Company.

Warren, Roland. 1983. "Observations on the State of Community Theory." In *New Perspectives on the American Community*, edited by Roland Warren and Larry Lyon. Homewood, IL: Dorsey Press.

Warren, Roland and Larry Lyon, eds. 1983. *New Perspectives on the American Community*. Homewood, IL: Dorsey Press.

Warwick, Donald P. and Charles A. Lininger. 1975. *The Sample Survey: Theory and Practice*. New York: McGraw-Hill.

Webber, M. 1963. "Order in Diversity: Community without Propinquity." In *Cities and Space: The Future Use of Urban Land*, edited by L. Wingo, Jr. Baltimore: John Hopkins University Press.

Weber, Max. 1958. *The Protestant Ethic and the Spirit of Capitalism*. New York: Charles Scribner's Sons.

Weber, Max. 1959. *Sociology of Religion*. Translated by Curt Rosenthal. New York: The Philosophical Library.

Weber, Max. 1968. *Economy and Society*. New York: Bedminister Press.

Weicher, J. C. 1972. "The Effect of Metropolitan Political Fragmentation on Central City Budgets." In *Models of Urban Structure*, edited by David Sweet. Lexington, MA: D. C. Heath.

Wellman, Barry and Barry Leighton. 1979. "Networks, Neighborhoods, and Communities: Approaches to the Study of the Community Question." *Urban Affairs Quarterly* 14, no. 3:363–90.

Wellman, Barry and Barry Leighton. 1983. "Networks, Neighborhoods, and Communities: Approaches to the Study of the Community Question." In *New Perspectives on the American Community*, edited by Roland Warren and Larry Lyon. Homewood, IL: Dorsey Press.

West, James. 1945. *Plainville, U.S.A.* New York: Columbia University Press.

White, C. B., N. Bushnell, and J. L. Regnemer. 1978. "Moral Development in Bahamian School Children." *Developmental Psychology* 14:58–65.

Whyte, Martin King. 1983. "Town and Country in Contemporary China" *Comparative Urban Research* 10, no. 1.

Whyte, William Foote. 1955. *Street Corner Society*. Chicago: University of Chicago Press.

Whyte, William Foote. 1964. "The Slum: On the Evolution of Street Corner Society." In *Reflections on Community Studies*, edited by Arthur Vidich et al. New York: John Wiley & Sons.

Whyte, William H. 1956. *The Organization Man*. New York: Simon and Schuster.

Wilensky, Harold L. and Charles N. Lebeaux. 1965. *Industrial Society and Social Welfare*. New York: Free Press.

Wilkinson, Kenneth P. 1972. "A Field-Theory Perspective for Community Development Research." *Rural Sociology* 37, no. 1:43–52.

Wilkinson, Kenneth P. 1983. "A Field-Theory Perspective for Community Development Research." In *New Perspectives on the American Community*, edited by Roland Warren and Larry Lyon. Homewood, IL: Dorsey Press.

Williams, James M. 1973. "The Ecological Approach in Measuring Community Power Concentration." *American Sociological Review* 38:230–42.

Williams, Oliver P., Harold Herman, Charles S. Liebman, and Thomas R. Dye. 1965. *Surburban Differences and Metropolitan Policies.* Philadelphia: University of Pennsylvania Press.

Williams, Oliver P., Harold Herman, Charles S. Liebman, and Thomas R. Dye. 1983. "Suburban Differences and Metropolitan Policies." In *New Perspectives on the American Community,* edited by Roland Warren and Larry Lyon. Homewood, IL: Dorsey Press.

Williams, Raymond. 1973. *The Country and the City.* New York: Oxford University Press.

Williams, Robin M., Jr. 1970. *American Society: A Sociological Interpretation.* New York: Alfred A. Knopf.

Wilson, James Q. 1983. *Thinking about Crime.* New York: Basic Books.

Wirth, Louis. 1928. *The Ghetto.* Chicago: University of Chicago Press.

Wirth, Louis. 1938. "Urbanism as a Way of Life." *American Journal of Sociology* 44:8–20.

Wirth, Louis. 1983. "Urbanism as a Way of Life." Reprinted in *New Perspectives on the American Community,* edited by Roland Warren and Larry Lyon. Homewood, IL: Dorsey Press.

Wolff, Kurt H. (ed.). 1978. *The Sociology of Georg Simmel.* Toronto: Free Press.

Wolfinger, Raymond E. 1962. "A Plea for Decent Burial." *American Sociological Review* 25:636–44.

Wolpert, J. 1965. "Behavioral Aspects of the Decision to Migrate." *Papers of the Regional Science Association* 15:159–69.

Woodbury, Robert M. 1934. "Statistical Practice." In *Encyclopedia of the Social Sciences* Vol. XIV, edited by Edward Seligman. New York: MacMillan.

Young, M., and P. Willmott. 1957. *Family and Kinship in East London.* London: Routledge & Kegan Paul.

Zablocki, Benjamin. 1971. *The Joyful Community.* Baltimore: Pelican Books.

Zablocki, Benjamin. 1979. "Communes, Encounter Groups, and the Search for Community." In *In Search for Community,* edited by Kurt Black. Boulder, CO: Westview Press.

Zablocki, Benjamin. 1980. *Alienation and Charisma.* New York: Free Press.

Zorbaugh, Harvey. 1926. "The Natural Areas of the City." *Publications of the American Sociological Society* 20.

Zorbaugh, Harvey. 1929. *Gold Coast and Slum.* Chicago: University of Chicago Press.

Name Index

Subject Index

ABOUT THE AUTHOR

Larry Lyon is a Professor of Sociology and Director of the Center for Community Research and Development at Baylor University. His community research appears in many academic journals such as the *American Sociological Review* and the *American Journal of Sociology*. Lyon has directed applied community research projects on topics including juvenile delinquency, teenage pregnancy, downtown revitalization, population and employment projections, quality of life studies, economic development, community power, local education, and job training and placement programs. He has co-edited, with Roland Warren, an anthology of community theory and research entitled *New Perspectives on the American Community*.